W O M E N
in the
LITERARY LANDSCAPE

W O M E N
in the
LITERARY LANDSCAPE

A Centennial Publication of the
Women's National Book Association

Edited by
Rosalind Reisner and Valerie Tomaselli

Contributors
Doris Weatherford, Rosalind Reisner,
Nancy Rubin Stuart, and Joyce Meskis

Foreword
Blanche Wiesen Cook

C&R Press
Conscious & Responsible

Cover photo: WNBA founder Madge Jenison in her bookstore, the Sunwise Turn.
Cover and interior design: Isolde Maher / 4eyesdesign.com
Editorial and project management services: MTM Publishing, Inc.

Library of Congress Cataloging-in-Publication Data

ISBN: 978-1-936196-82-1
LCCN: 2017954261

C&R Press
Conscious & Responsible
www.crpress.org
Winston-Salem, North Carolina

For special discounted bulk purchases, please contact:
C&R Press sales@crpress.org
Contact lharms@crpress.org to book events, readings and author signings.

*Dedicated to the founders of the Women's National Book Association,
with gratitude for their activism, foresight, wisdom, and creativity,
and all who have followed in their footsteps.*

CONTENTS

FOREWORD
Blanche Wiesen Cook

This stirring, important, galvanizing volume is much more than a celebration of one hundred years of the Women's National Book Association (WNBA). It is a history of women and words—creativity, imagination, writers and readers, editors and publishers, journalists and agents, booksellers, librarians, and activists from colonial times to the twenty-first century. Despite—and because of—all the ongoing discrimination of sexism and ageism, from the beginning women shaped our literary community and the book world. Indeed, the WNBA was founded in 1917 by a group of New York-based booksellers—when women were barred from membership in the American Booksellers Association.

Brilliantly written and researched by Doris Weatherford, Rosalind Reisner, and Nancy Rubin Stuart, among others, and edited by Rosalind Reisner and Valerie Tomaselli, every page is filled with surprises, enchantments, and exciting new information of significance. IMAGINE all the new biographies this book will engender! There are the women we knew nothing about—like the librarians, bookstore owners, and children's book editors—who transformed and enlarged our culture. There are women we thought we knew, for example, Margaret Fuller—but now we know much more. And there are life-enhancing surprises—like *Washington Post* publisher Katharine Graham, who encouraged women to become syndicated columnists, appointed Meg Greenfield the first woman editor of the *Post*'s editorial page—and who, in 1972, gifted Gloria Steinem with start-up funds to launch *Ms.* magazine. From *Godey's Lady's Book* edited by Sarah Josepha Hale to *Ms.* and beyond, our heritage as vividly described here is thrilling.

Additionally thrilling are the many movements launched by women librarians we knew—until now—so little about. The stunning contributions of the American Library Association's Office of Intellectual Freedom, launched by Judith Krug in 1967, include Banned Books Week and the Freedom to Read Foundation to counter censorship and protect librarians who have insisted on civil rights and the right to read across all state borders, and literary and segregationist barriers.

The sections on club women and bookstore pioneers are among the most informative in this splendid book. From the founding of Sorosis in 1868, to the Association for the Advancement of Women (AAW) in 1873, partly to raise funds for astronomer Maria Mitchell, to Pen + Brush in 1894, to the National League of American Pen Women—every detail is delightful. Exciting information regarding bookstore pioneers is boundless. Just one example: Transcendentalist Elizabeth Peabody (1804–1894) ran a bookstore that was also a lending library and educational center. She also published Henry David Thoreau, Nathaniel Hawthorne, and Margaret Fuller's German translations.

Since 1917, the WNBA has existed to connect, educate, advocate, and lead in the book world and literary community. Since 1959, when Pearl S. Buck urged that the WNBA become a non-governmental organization (NGO) member of the United Nations, affiliated with the Department of Public Information, the WNBA has performed its leadership role globally. WNBA Award winners Eleanor Roosevelt, Pearl S. Buck, and Rachel Carson, and all the women central to our literary and human rights legacy would be pleased—relieved to know that with the WNBA we face the unknown shoulder to shoulder, hearts open, fists high! And we will, as Eleanor Roosevelt instructed, "NEVER STOP READING!"

LETTER FROM THE WNBA PRESIDENT

A Century of Progress for Women in the World of Books

Dear Readers,

This is an exciting time for the Women's National Book Association as we celebrate and reflect on one hundred years of our remarkable history. The WNBA was formed by a group of activist women booksellers in response to the exclusion of women from the all-male American Booksellers Association and the Booksellers' League. Many of our founding members marched for women's right to vote in the historic October 27, 1917, parade in New York City. They gathered two days later, on October 29, at Sherwood's Book Store in lower Manhattan, and, since that first meeting, three years before women had the right to vote, we have grown into a national, all-volunteer organization with twelve chapters and members across the United States.

We look back on a history filled with activities that celebrate the literary world. For the past seventy-seven years, we have presented the prestigious WNBA Award to accomplished women in the book world. The Pannell Award, established in 1981, honors bookstores that provide exceptional service to their communities, especially to children. Our successful literacy initiative, National Reading Group Month, recently celebrated ten years of promoting the joy of shared reading, and we have been an NGO/DPI member of the United Nations since 1959. In addition, we are celebrating the fifth successful year of our National Writing Contest. Our Centennial year includes such new initiatives as the awarding of the Second Century Prize to a group that supports literacy initiatives; Bookwomen Speak: The WNBA Centennial Lecture

Series, and this publication, *Women in the Literary Landscape*.. As we have done for past anniversaries, we have also created two booklists of notable works to showcase the accomplishments of women writers in fiction, poetry, memoir, and nonfiction, titled Celebrating Women's Voices. Thirty books were selected from these lists to send to the new president during Women's History Month in March of this year.

The Women's National Book Association is committed to the goals of our founders to promote and support women in all aspects of the book world where, though much has changed, challenges for women still remain. Our members work in all aspects of the book community, including as authors, editors, publishers, booksellers, librarians, agents, and professors. Our programs provide networking and professional opportunities, career development, and insight into the rapidly changing publishing and marketing worlds.

The WNBA was founded in the Progressive Era, a time of social upheaval, much like today. Immigrants in large numbers were arriving in the U.S., transforming and enriching the cultural scene, and the overwhelming topic of debate was whether we should participate in the war overseas. Jeanette Rankin of Montana became the first woman in the House of Representatives that year, even before women nationally had the right to vote. On July 28, African-Americans held the Silent Protest in New York City to protest lynching and anti-black violence.

The WNBA founding members were inspired by those events and issues and the role that they could play in that national conversation. As founding member Madge Jenison stated: "It seemed to us that books are power—that if we could create a working body of all those who have to do with the circulation of ideas in books...if we could start up such an organization, we would have a mechanism, through which we could throw our weight en masse behind anything in which we believed; that we could even stop war if our organization became complete and vigorous enough."

Today, one hundred years after our founding, our world is addressing many of those same issues and we are still inspired by the message of our founders as we move confidently into our second century of connecting, educating, advocating, and leading.

—Jane Kinney-Denning
WNBA National President

PREFACE

A milestone such as one hundred—what a perfect time to celebrate our accomplishments and look forward to the next century. But also an apt occasion to assess and examine where we have been and where we've come from, to arrive at a stronger commitment to our founding ideals.

As early as 2013, when Centennial planning began, we knew that a book celebrating the organization and its history was important. But soon after we first met, we began to expand our vision. What is really interesting, we thought, is not just the WNBA's history but the significant role women as a group have played in the shaping of the literary community and the book world.

As a student of women's history, Valerie knew that women had active roles in the literary community even when their roles were limited in the public sphere. Writing and editing, after all, can be done in private settings in the confines of one's home or under the cloak of a male pen name. This tactic was practiced by many, including the inimitable Margaret Fuller, who would become one of the most public of public intellectuals and literary personages in the 1830s and 1840s and only then freely used her own name. It was also not unusual in the all-important money-making women's magazine industry of the mid- to late 1800s, when Sarah Josepha Hale edited *Godey's Lady Book*, owned by Louis A. Godey, and Miriam Folline Peacock Squier edited *Frank Leslie's Lady's Magazine*, owned by the magazine mogul Frank Leslie. Squier married

Frank Leslie soon after she divorced her husband E.G. Squier and legally changed her name to Frank Leslie after he died, a move that gave her more power over the empire she inherited.

As the nineteenth century moved forward, women built on the achievements of, and were emboldened by, those who came before. Women's suffrage groups took very public stands and agitated in the public square; the women's club movement that began in the late 1800s advocated for women's education; and in the Progressive Era women came together to address poverty in settlement houses and became involved in other areas of social activism. As part of this trend, our partner Pen + Brush, which celebrates women writers and artists, was founded in 1894, a full two decades before the WNBA. And the WNBA founders claimed a very public spot in history in 1917, when they gathered with zeal during women's suffrage marches in New York City and the WNBA was born.

When Rosalind Reisner, the chief editor of this volume, discovered, in her research into the organization's archives, how intimately the history of the WNBA was tied to the women's suffrage movement, we became even more convinced that the story we wanted to tell should be wider than the WNBA itself. It should extend outward to women's history as a whole, focus on women's leadership in the book world and literary community, and then shine a light on the WNBA's role in that history.

So the structure we developed does just that. In "Chapter 1: Women, Literary Pursuits, and the Book World: Milestones and Trends," you will find a history of women in the book world and literary community written by women's history expert Doris Weatherford, along with Rosalind, who added material specifically on book publishing, the library world, and bookselling. Composing over half of this volume, this was a history, we found, that had not been previously written. Our synthesis of historical material—how women were intimately involved in some of the literary world's most important achievements and how they led the way in some of that world's most significant innovations—is by necessity highly selective. But it is our hope that it will offer cultural historians, book professionals, and the educated public a first-stop resource that helps to fill a gap and offers a springboard for further research.

In "Chapter 2: Bookselling Then and Now," the talents and expertise of our founders guided us. They were, after all, booksellers. Again, an archival document—an article by the second WNBA president, Madge Jenison, entitled "Bookselling as a Profession for Women"—shaped our plans. We are reprinting that article, replete with surprising similarities and striking differences, between then and now. To accompany that article, we asked the legendary Joyce Meskis of the Tattered Cover Book Store in Denver to respond to Jenison's century-old reflections. Added to that are two 1930s articles from issues of the WNBA newsletter *The Bookwoman*: a bookselling quiz and reflections on the state of bookselling by women booksellers.

In "Chapter 3: From the Archives," author and WNBA member Nancy Rubin Stuart wrote five articles based on archival documents. These were selected from material Rosalind found in the archives—material that we thought was engaging from both a general historical point of view as well as from a WNBA perspective. Nancy's articles cover the founding of the WNBA and its roots in the women's suffrage movement and male-dominated bookselling community; the organization's early fund-raising dinners, reflecting the struggles and achievements of the new organization as well as the times in which it developed; the professional training of women in the publishing industry and how the WNBA helped lead the way in this regard; the unequal treatment of women in the book industry and how the WNBA addressed that issue; and second wave feminism and the WNBA's engagement with its ideals.

"Chapter 4: Supporting Literacy and Literature" focuses on the WNBA as it connects, educates, advocates, and leads in the literary world today. All the WNBA's existing programs are described in this section, including the WNBA Award, Pannell Award, and Eastman Grant, as well as the ways it supports reading, authors, and book publishing through National Reading Group Month and Great Group Reads. Its NGO status with the United Nations Department of Public Information—as an advocate for the UN's ideals and mission—is also explored.

"Chapter 5: Chapter Histories" showcases the varied and innovative ways that our chapters reflect the mission of the WNBA. Every chapter is unique in character and vision but they all share attributes common to the WNBA's ideals and goals.

Appendices provide additional details of our history, including a list of WNBA Award winners and Pannell Award winners, and a list of all national presidents. This book has been a group effort. And all deserve huge thanks: In addition to the signed contributors, the WNBA board of directors, chapter presidents, committee chairs, and members have added their own perspectives, helped compile detailed information, and fact-checked our early drafts.

Acknowledgments and a list of contributors can also be found in the back matter. Though we fact-checked all the material in this book, some oversight may have occurred. We take responsibility for all errors of fact or omission. In several places we have modernized the spelling in some of the early WNBA archival materials to reflect contemporary practice.

It is our hope that in reading this book, you will be engaged and enlightened—as much as we were when we researched, wrote, and edited it.

—Valerie Tomaselli and Rosalind Reisner

CHAPTER 1

WOMEN, LITERARY PURSUITS, AND THE BOOK WORLD
Milestones and Trends

Since the earliest times in U.S. history, women shaped the literary community and the book world. It was in the realm of the home, to which most women were confined in our country's infancy, that their talents as authors, readers, and teachers were bred. And it will come as no surprise that some of women's first forays into the professional book world were connected to education and literacy: Women found outlets and, in many cases, led the way in the development of libraries and children's literature in the nineteenth and early twentieth centuries. They also found fertile ground as editors in the world of such periodicals as *Godey's Lady's Book*, tailored to women and the home, and as taste-makers in their coverage of books and other cultural trends of the day.

Along with the growing women's rights movement during the Progressive Era, there were other advances in the early decades of the twentieth century, including Women's National Book Association cofounder Madge Jenison's Sunwise Turn Bookshop and Blanche Knopf's leading role in the 1915 establishment of Alfred A. Knopf, Inc. Throughout the twentieth century, many women broke through the confines of the male-dominated business of book publishing as publishers, editors, and marketing and sales professionals. In today's book world, it's safe to say that, while women's roles—and yes, incomes—are not fully commensurate with that of men, they now lead the way in many areas. This first section of *Women in the*

17

Literary Landscape tells the story of women's hard work, leadership, and innovation in shaping the literary community and adding to the vital cultural landscape that defines the United States.

COLONIAL AND REVOLUTIONARY AMERICA

A woman wrote America's first secular book: Without telling Anne Bradstreet, her brother-in-law took her poems from Massachusetts to London and returned with copies of *The Tenth Muse Lately Sprung Up in America* (1650). Bradstreet was the busy mother of eight, yet made time to write poetry that still stands up well today. No matter the field, women always have been there—and without women, history ends in a generation.

Moreover, until very recently, they did this without access to formal education. Harvard College had been established when Anne Bradstreet wrote, but more than three centuries would pass before women were allowed to study there. In fact, almost two centuries would pass between Harvard's 1636 founding and the admission of women to any college in the United States. The first was Oberlin College in frontier Ohio in 1833, and even there, women had to follow a "Ladies Course." Yet despite this and other routine discrimination, women were active participants in the literary community in America from the beginning.

They wrote of their own experiences, such as Mary Rowlandson's *A Narrative of the Captivity and Restoration of Mrs. Mary Rowlandson*, which told of her life when she was taken by Rhode Island's Wampanoag tribe. Published in 1682, it was reissued in at least thirty editions. Women wrote travelogues, such as Sarah Kemble Knight's account of her business trip from Boston to New York City in 1704, *The Journal of Madam Knight*, published in 1825. Her cheerful story of overcoming obstacles on the horseback journey also contained many economic and cultural observations.

Women were among the country's first publishers as they took the helm at several newspapers. Sarah Updike Goddard began Rhode Island's *Providence Gazette* in 1762 and moved on to Philadelphia, where she published the *Pennsylvania Chronicle*. Her daughter, Mary

Katherine Goddard, used the *Maryland Journal* to issue the first copy of the Declaration of Independence that included the signers' names. Other women published newspapers from Boston down to Richmond, and the governments of several colonies appointed women as official printers.

Colonial women arguably had a higher status than would later be the case. Anne Catherine Hoof Green, for example, was named the official printer of the Maryland colony in 1767, and even as she was caring for her fourteen children, she also published the *Maryland Gazette*. Clementina Rind, a widow like Green, published the *Virginia Gazette*, and that colony's House of Burgesses made her the official printer in 1774. Nor did these women hesitate to express their political opinions. Most supported the revolution, but Margaret Green Draper advocated for the established government in her *Boston News-Letter*. Her conservative views were popular enough that she drove six competitors out of business before the British evacuated and she had to flee.

Mercy Otis Warren, who lived south of Boston, anonymously wrote plays that satirized the British enemy; she later published a three-volume military record of the war that is much esteemed by historians. In 1780 in Philadelphia, Esther DeBerdt Reed argued in *Sentiments of an American Woman* for both the revolution and for women's right to participate in it. Other Philadelphia women joined her in raising substantial money to support the rebel army. Her political leadership is particularly striking in view of the fact that she was a British native who hadn't lived in America for very long.

George Washington appreciated the activism of these natural democrats and wrote thank-you notes to many women. He also took time to formally accept poetry from Phillis Wheatley, a young black woman born in Gambia, who was sold into slavery at a very young age. Her first book, *Poems on Various Subjects*, was published in London in 1773, the same year she was emancipated by the Wheatley family of Boston.

New Ideas in a New Nation

Books sold during the nineteenth century in numbers that seem astonishing today. The reason, of course, was that people spent much more time reading than now. There were no movies, televisions, or phones to distract, and in a largely rural nation, theaters and opera houses usually were beyond traveling distance. Clergymen often frowned on card playing, and other games were rare. A few families owned pianos, and singing was treasured entertainment, but when people wanted to relax at the end of the day, most had no option but to open a book.

Even for women whose days did not end when the sun went down, it was not uncommon to enjoy a book in the evening: A woman merely picked up her darning or knitting and continued to work while her husband read aloud by the fireside. Even in the daylight, some women worked out systems whereby an older child read aloud while she did her kitchen work. Mothers, in fact, were the most likely teachers of reading, and American literacy owes more to them than is acknowledged.

Free public education was slow to develop, and the urban women who ran "dame schools" supported themselves by charging tuition. A few families, especially in the plantation South, employed governesses, but most teaching was done mother to child. When their children became teens, affluent families sent boys to prep schools or colleges to be taught exclusively by male professors. Privileged girls went to finishing schools, where the faculty could be male or female.

But mostly readers taught each other. Laws in the South made it a crime to teach an enslaved person to read, but some nonetheless learned by absorbing words and text they were sometimes exposed to—or because a master or mistress found that households ran more efficiently if a slave could recognize rudimentary words. Trusted (male) slaves even became preachers capable of reading at least parts of the Bible. Women and men in the new nation were readers, and the percentage of the middle-class population who bought books puts today's publishing market to shame.

The Beginnings of Libraries

The idea of free public libraries did not evolve until well after the nation's birth. The largest library in colonial America was that of Massachusetts governor John Winthrop and his wife, Margaret; she probably was responsible for shipping at least some of the one thousand books that went from their English manor to Boston during the 1630s. John Harvard had a sufficiently large personal library that the new college at Cambridge, Massachusetts, was named for him when he bequeathed his books, some three hundred eighty of them, on his deathbed in 1638. Across the Charles River, Bostonians made an attempt to begin a library in 1659, but after a fire destroyed its beginnings, it came to naught.

Instead of public libraries, readers obtained books from subscription libraries, paying fees to borrow them. Many were in private homes, but Benjamin Franklin ran his Philadelphia subscription library from his combined printing office and post office, beginning in 1731. Women, too, ran similar combined businesses: From Boston to Richmond, women managed lending libraries/bookstores with their newspaper/book publishing office and/or post office.

Franklin, Massachusetts, created a lending library with a donation of 116 books from Benjamin Franklin in 1785. Peterborough, New Hampshire, claims the first library supported by taxation, in 1833. Those that arose in the 1840s and 1850s were likely to be in rural areas, especially in frontier states such as Ohio and Indiana. Cities were slower. It wasn't until 1848 that the Boston Public Library was firmly established, moving repeatedly to progressively larger quarters until it settled in its present Copley Square location in 1895. Baltimore's famous Enoch Pratt Free Library dates to 1882, and the New York Public Library did not begin until 1895, when several private libraries combined their resources.

Early Novelists and Journalists

Women were best-selling novelists almost as soon as that art form developed. Although it was published in England, Susanna Haswell Rowson's *Charlotte Temple: A Tale of Truth* (1791) was America's first nonreligious best seller and has rarely been out of print. Hannah Webster Foster was similarly successful with *The Coquette* (1797), which also featured feminist themes.

Margaret Fuller, a genius who read Latin at age seven, began editing *The Dial,* the publication of the Transcendentalists, in 1840, at the invitation of philosopher Ralph Waldo Emerson. Four years later, she became America's first book reviewer when famed editor Horace Greeley recruited her for the *New York Tribune.* Using its national circulation and acclaim from

Engraved portrait of American writer and editor Margaret Fuller (1810-1850), from the frontispiece of her book *Woman in the Nineteenth Century* (1845).

progressives, she played a major role in determining what Americans wanted to read. Her book *Woman in the Nineteenth Century* (1845) set a new standard for discussion about the role of women in society.

Fuller was a book reviewer and editor, as well as an author, and some consider that her letters from Italy in the 1840s make her the first female foreign correspondent. That claim also can be made for Jane Cazneau, who covered the United States' war with Mexico in the same era. The *New York Sun* alone published thirty pieces by Cazneau from Mexico City, and she would later write from the Caribbean for newspapers in New York and Philadelphia.

Many women (and men) multitasked as editors, authors, and publishers at various points in their lives, as businesses then were much less specialized than today. Anne Newport Royall, for instance, traveled alone throughout the new United States and issued ten travelogues by 1831, when she settled in Washington, D.C., and published two newspapers that promoted Jacksonian democracy. Lydia Maria Child had a long tenure of mixed roles in publishing. She began America's first magazine for children, *Juvenile Miscellany*, in 1826. It contained nursery rhymes we consider "anonymous" today—but the bimonthly magazine went bankrupt a decade later because her fellow Bostonians did not approve of Child's books advocating the abolition of slavery. Her *History of the Condition of Women in Various Ages and Nations*

(1835) predated Margaret Fuller's book on that subject by ten years. Moreover, Child set a precedent for women by taking a job in a city other than where her husband resided. While her journalist husband lived in Washington, she spent time in New York where she edited the weekly *National Anti-Slavery Standard* and wrote a weekly column titled "Letters from New-York." She was likely one of the first women to take her work on the road, a pioneer of commuter marriage. She also saw to the publication of a true case, *Incidents in the Life of a Slave Girl* (1861) by Harriet Jacobs, and personally paid for *The Freedman's Book* (1865), a collection of short stories and poems written by former slaves and activists. Today, Child may be most remembered for the poem/song "Over the River and Through the Wood."

In an era when there were few entertainment alternatives, the public welcomed female novelists, and publishers promoted their sales. For example, Maria Susanna Cummins' first novel, *The Lamplighter* (1854), sold forty thousand copies in a few weeks. A similar achiever was Susan Bogert Warner, whose 1850 story of an orphaned girl, *The Wide, Wide World*, outsold Charles Dickens' *David Copperfield* (1850),

Harriet Jacobs

> I want to add my testimony to that of able pens to convince the people of the Free States what Slavery really is. Only by experience can anyone realize how deep, dark, and foul is that pit of abominations.
>
> —Harriet Jacobs, *Incidents in the Life of a Slave Girl*

Harriet Jacobs ran away from a lecherous slave master, hiding for seven years in a tiny garret before she was able to escape to the North in 1842. Her memoir was written pseudonymously and published with the help of the (white) Lydia Maria Child, whose name appears on the title page along with Jacobs' pseudonym, Linda Brent. For many years, it was believed that the narrative was a work of fiction, written by Child. Jean Fagan Yellin, professor at Pace University and a historian specializing in women's history and African-American history, proved, in 1981, that Harriet Jacobs, not Lydia Maria Child, was the author of the astonishing memoir.

Elizabeth Peabody

Elizabeth Peabody (1804-1894) was born in Billerica, Massachusetts, and taught at home by her mother, who believed that women should be well educated. From an early age Peabody was interested in philosophical and educational issues; over the course of her lifetime she opened several schools in the Boston area and helped Bronson Alcott start his experimental Temple School. She had a reading knowledge of ten languages. (The young Ralph Waldo Emerson had been her Greek tutor.)

In 1837, she became a charter member of the Transcendentalist Club, whose members included Ralph Waldo Emerson, Margaret Fuller, and Bronson Alcott. In 1839 she opened the West Street bookstore in the parlor of her home in Boston. The bookstore served as an outlet for Peabody's many interests; it was also a lending library and educational center. It quickly became a gathering place for Boston intellectuals. Shortly after the bookstore opened, Margaret Fuller began her famous "Conversations" there, bringing women together for study and discussion. The women who attended those evening salons were expected to discuss and debate such subjects as fine art, history, and literature.

In addition to selling books, Peabody printed—on her own printing press—three of Nathaniel Hawthorne's novels, Margaret Fuller's German translations, and Henry David Thoreau's *Civil Disobedience*. She also published and wrote for *The Dial*, the literary organ of the Transcendentalist movement. Throughout her long life she wrote, lectured, and taught; she also supported women's rights, the abolition of slavery, and the rights of Native Americans. Inspired by the work of Friedrich Froebel, the German educator, she started the first English-language kindergarten in the U.S. in 1860. Over the ensuing decades her tireless advocacy for free, universal early education helped to make kindergarten an accepted institution.

On her tombstone is inscribed:

> Every humane cause had her sympathy
> And many her active aid.

Elizabeth and her two sisters were active in the literary world: Mary was the wife of educator Horace Mann and was instrumental in the founding of Antioch College during the 1850s; Sophia, an artist and illustrator, was the wife—and muse—of Nathaniel Hawthorne.

even in England. Indeed, there were so many female novelists so early in American history that Nathaniel Hawthorne complained, "America is now wholly given over to a damned mob of scribbling women, and I should have no chance of success."

Hawthorne did not mention that his sister-in-law Elizabeth Peabody published his works and promoted them through her popular bookstore. She was another who combined roles: Although known as a pioneer educator and popular lecturer, she also wrote, published, and sold books.

Of the numerous works by male authors that Elizabeth Peabody published, probably the most important was Thoreau's *Civil Disobedience*. Yet neither Thoreau nor Hawthorne properly acknowledged that it was a woman who had brought them to prominence. They shared best-seller status with the male writers Charles Dickens and Lewis Carroll—as well as female writers, including the Brontë sisters and Harriet Beecher Stowe. Literary critics in the future would acknowledge that the public chose their best sellers well, as works by these authors have been taught in literature classes for decades. A question worth pondering, however, is why that same best-seller status did not make literary classics of the novels by such women as Susan Bogert Warner and Mrs. E.D.E.N. Southworth, whose books were similarly popular during the same years.

Women from all classes of society were hungry for education and culture. The textile mills in Lowell, Massachusetts, would seem an unlikely place for an educational movement to develop, but there was an intense desire for intellectual stimulation among the female mill workers. Thousands of young, unmarried women, most between the ages of fifteen and thirty, but some even younger, were recruited from New England farms and lived in boardinghouses, often working thirteen hours a day at their looms. But in winter, work was limited to the briefer daylight hours, and many used this leisure to learn by candlelight. Throughout the 1830s and 1840s they formed study clubs, read serious nonfiction, learned foreign languages, and attended lectures and cultural events. They even published the magazines *Factory Girl*, *Operative Magazine*, and *Voice of Industry*, allowing their ideas for better working conditions to circulate among the New England textile mills.

One of the most articulate of the mill women was Lucy Larcom, who began working in Lowell when she was eleven years old. During her ten years in the mills, she wrote poems, songs, and letters describing her life, some of which were published in the *Lowell Offering*, a monthly literary magazine. She went on to teach at the Wheaton Female Seminary in Norton, Massachusetts, and helped found the *Rushlight Literary Magazine*, a student literary magazine still in existence. From 1865 to 1873 she was an editor at *Our Young Folks*, one of the first magazines for children. Her poems were widely published in her lifetime. One of Larcom's most significant contributions was a memoir, *A New England Girlhood*, which is still an important resource for historians. The nostalgic memoir and her 1881 article in *The Atlantic Monthly*, "Among Lowell Mill Girls," are worth reading in any era.

The Power of Women's Words Mid-Century

Freedom for African-Americans and freedom for women of any color were very closely tied together, and feminists of the era almost invariably began as abolitionists. In fact, the women's movement can be said to

An illustration of the character Mungo Park encountering an African woman in Lydia Maria Child's *An Appeal in Favor of That Class of Americans Called Africans*, a pioneering anti-slavery book published in 1833, two decades before Harriet Beecher Stowe's *Uncle Tom's Cabin* appeared in print.

have begun at the World Anti-Slavery Convention in London in 1840. Lucretia Mott was there as a delegate and Elizabeth Cady Stanton, on her honeymoon, accompanied her delegate husband, but they (and three other American women) were not allowed to participate. Female presence, said the clergymen in charge, would be too distracting and the women were relegated to an area where they could hear, but not be seen.

Despite exclusion from the spoken word, women contributed immensely to the anti-slavery movement through the written word. Lydia Maria Child's *An Appeal in Favor of That Class of Americans Called Africans* (1833) pioneered such writing, while works by South Carolinians Angelina and Sarah Grimké added credibility based on their experiences growing up as part of a slave-holding family in the South, unique among authors of the era. Harriet Beecher Stowe's novel *Uncle Tom's Cabin* (1852) was wildly popular; unfortunately, so many unscrupulous publishers pirated it that Stowe spent the rest of her life writing because she needed the income.

Other women published abolitionist newspapers, including Ohio's Josephine Griffing, who proposed the idea for the postwar Freedmen's Bureau in the abolitionist newspaper the *Anti-Slavery Bugle.* Jane Grey Swisshelm first published a mainstream newspaper in Pittsburgh, and after fleeing her abusive husband, began an abolitionist newspaper in frontier Minnesota. Conservatives there destroyed her press, and her third newspaper was located in Washington, D.C. Mary Ann Shadd (later Cary), a free Maryland African-American, advocated that African-Americans should relocate to places like Canada where slavery had been abolished. She moved to Canada and took over editorship of the *Provincial Freeman* in Ontario, a weekly for other blacks in the Canadian provinces.

Among the era's newspapers devoted to feminism, *The Lily,* edited by Amelia Bloomer, became the most famous. Initially a temperance publication, Bloomer's 1849 advocacy of dress reform sent subscriptions soaring, and her name became synonymous with underwear. Two Rhode Island women of that era are not as well known, but Anna Spencer began publishing *Pioneer and Woman's Advocate* in 1852; *The Una,* by Paulina Wright Davis, began the next year. In Philadelphia, Anne McDowell headed *Woman's Advocate,* whose investors and employees were all female.

The trend quickly moved west, as Amanda Way and Sarah Underhill began the *Women's Tribune* in Indianapolis in 1859. Even further west, Milwaukee's Mathilde Anneke wrote her feminist newspaper in German, appealing to others like herself who had fled Europe's repressive revolutions in 1848. Just as colonial female publishers had a century earlier, these women often did all aspects of the work: from writing articles in longhand, to setting type with hot lead, to operating the press, to taking the bundled papers to the post office.

Other white women assisted African-American women who had not had the opportunity to become literate. Olive Gilbert was the ghostwriter for the *Narrative of Sojourner Truth* (1850), while Sarah Bradford wrote *Harriet: The Moses of Her People* (1869). This enabled both Sojourner Truth and Harriet Tubman to support themselves by selling their books.

THE CIVIL WAR AND POST–CIVIL WAR YEARS

With the possible exception of World War II, no period of American history was as important to women as the years between 1861 and 1865. For the first time, necessity made it acceptable for them to travel without male escort and to take on leading roles as founders of hospitals, refugee shelters, soldiers' homes, and even cemeteries. In the North, the women of the U.S. Sanitary Commission effectively supplied the army, raising millions of dollars for food, medicine, and more. Clara Barton, who was working in the Patent Office at the time, created the world's first system of identifying the missing and dead, and later lobbied Congress to create the American Red Cross. Countless women on both sides ran farms and businesses without male assistance. Everywhere, women were forced into new roles, whether or not they wanted them. For African-American women, of course, freedom would bring wholly new opportunities.

Women's Postwar Advances

Among those women in the writing world who benefited from new prospects was Emily Edson Briggs. Recruited by the *Washington Chronicle,* she became the first woman to report from inside the

White House. Louisa May Alcott began her writing career with *Hospital Sketches* (1863), a highly realistic account of her work with dying soldiers.

At the end of the Civil War, publishers issued a flood of memoirs that would continue on into the twentieth century. Among the first, both in 1867, were *The Story of Aunt Becky's Army Life* from Union supporter Sarah Palmer, and *Richmond During the War* by Confederate Sarah Brock Putnam. The genre's top best seller was *My Story of the War* (1887) by Mary Livermore, who was also a leader in the American Woman Suffrage Association (AWSA).

That organization competed with the National Woman Suffrage Association (NWSA) in the decades immediately after the war. New Yorkers Elizabeth Cady Stanton and Susan B. Anthony led the NWSA, while the AWSA was Boston-based and led by such literati as Louisa May Alcott, Julia Ward Howe, and Harriet Beecher Stowe. Differences between the two groups were often more personal than political, but the competing organizational styles can be seen in their publications. The NWSA published a newspaper, *The Revolution*, that went bankrupt after three years; funded by an eccentric man, it included distracting issues such as vegetarianism. The AWSA's monthly magazine, *Woman's Journal*, was printed on sleek paper, not newsprint, and focused on feminist news nationwide. With articles by stars such as Alcott, Howe, and Stowe, as well as women who were stars in their own day, particularly Mary Livermore, it lasted from 1870 to 1917. Its final publisher was Alice Stone Blackwell, daughter of Lucy Stone and niece of pioneer physicians Elizabeth and Emily Blackwell. In 1917, it would adopt the new and revealing name of *The Woman Citizen: A Weekly Chronicle of Progress*.

Women's Magazines Take Off

The most important of nineteenth-century periodicals aimed at women was *Godey's Lady's Book*, begun in the first half of the century. The magazine was named for its owner, Louis A. Godey, but it was edited by Sarah Josepha Hale. She began editing *Ladies' Magazine* in 1828, when the concept of magazines was still new; it later was purchased by Louis Godey, moved from Boston to Philadelphia, and merged with *Godey's*

Lady's Book. Hale edited the magazine for forty years; while at its helm she exerted a strong influence on fashion and domestic architecture. (She is also widely considered the founder of Thanksgiving.) Many important writers contributed to *Godey's,* including Washington Irving, Edgar Allan Poe, Oliver Wendell Holmes, and Frances Hodgson Burnett, author of the much-loved children's book *The Secret Garden* (1911). Until her death in 1879, Hale argued for employment and educational opportunity for women, but stopped short of advocating for legal rights.

Peterson's Magazine followed *Godey's* model in 1842. Its editor, Ann S. Stephens, had an unusual marriage: Her husband provided most of the care for their children, while she traveled on lecture tours to increase subscriptions. In 1867, when Harper & Brothers began *Harper's Bazar* (later *Bazaar*), it hired translator and author Mary Louise Booth as editor for the new magazine, a job she held until her death in 1889.

Home Companion began in 1873 and would clarify its audience by changing its name to *Woman's Home Companion* in 1886. Clearly there was a large audience of female readers, and publishers were astute enough

Color plate illustrating women's fashions published in the March 1864 issue of *Godey's Lady's Book.*

Mrs. Frank Leslie

Miriam Leslie had long prepared for a literary life. She was born in New Orleans on June 5, 1836. Her scholarly father tutored her in the classics as well as in French, Spanish, Italian, German, Latin, and history. When the family moved to New York City in 1850, Leslie developed a lifelong interest in journalism and a love of glamour.

In 1862 Frank Leslie named her editor of *Frank Leslie's Lady's Magazine*. To woo female readers, she declared 1863 "the year of fashion" with articles on the latest styles and advertisements from dress and bonnet makers. Before long the *Lady's Magazine* was turning an annual profit of $39,000. For all of Frank Leslie's technical ingenuity, she quickly proved to be the better marketer than he and her promotion to editor of the new magazine *Chimney Corner* turned it into another moneymaker that grossed $72,000 a year. Beneath her winsome appearance and mellow Southern voice was a hard-driving manager who worked her artists and reporters relentlessly, an editor reputedly filled with "hell and hot water."

In 1873 she divorced her second husband, E.G. Squier, and a year later she married Frank Leslie. Leslie dedicated herself to the inner workings of the Leslie Publishing House, serving as literary critic and translator for its dozen periodicals as well as editor-in-chief of *Frank Leslie's Lady's Magazine*. When Frank Leslie died in January 1880, he left his wife with crushing debts and lawsuits. But the forty-four-year-old widow immediately changed her name to his and vowed to "take up the work and redeem his reputation." Sixteen months later, she stunned Publishers Row in New York City by winning the lawsuits, repaying the creditors, and expanding circulation of the Leslie publications from thirty thousand to two hundred thousand.

The challenges facing women continued to intrigue her. A few years before her death, Leslie wrote to Carrie Chapman Catt, "When I come to die you will find that, like yourself, I am interested in woman's advancement." And when she died on September 18, 1914, she proved that statement true, leaving her entire two-million-dollar estate to the suffrage association.

Catt used the gift to create the Leslie Woman Suffrage Commission and the Leslie Bureau of Suffrage Education. The bureau served as publicity agent for the association, producing syndicated news and feature articles that reached an estimated ten to twenty million readers. A very successful weekly magazine, *The Woman Citizen*, was also published with that bequest, and acknowledged as a memorial to Mrs. Frank Leslie's generosity and faith in the cause of women's enfranchisement.

—Excerpted from "Empress of Journalism: Mrs. Frank Leslie" by Nancy Rubin Stuart, *American History Magazine*, Dec. 21, 2006 to hire women as top editors. *Ladies' Home Journal* began in 1883, after Cyrus and Louisa Curtis noticed that the women's supplement of their publication for farmers attracted more readers than the "main" magazine.

Although little known today, the most recognized name in the publishing world of the late Victorian Age probably was "Leslie." Miriam Folline Peacock Squier was the twice-divorced editor of *Frank Leslie's Lady's Magazine* when she married the publishing giant Frank Leslie. After his 1880 death she inherited his massive enterprise. To protect her rights to the Leslie holdings, Miriam legally changed her name to Frank Leslie. Discovering far more debt than anyone realized, she condensed the dozen Leslie publications with low circulation into two weeklies and four monthlies. Before long the company was turning a profit of $100,000.

Journalists and Editors, East and West

Women were also part of mainstream journalism during and after the Civil War. When the *New York Tribune* hired Jane Cunningham Croly in 1855, she may have been the first female reporter to work at a desk—as opposed to the "correspondent" style. She used the pseudonym of "Jennie June," and Sara Farrington emulated her the next year, when, as "Fanny Fern," she began writing for the *New York Ledger*—at a fabulous $100 per weekly column. This set a standard that the *Brooklyn Daily Union* emulated in 1872, when it brought on Mary Clemmer Ames as a political reporter at $5,000 a year. Kate Field also wrote on mainstream politics, beginning with the *New York Tribune* in 1870; from 1890 to 1895, she would publish her own liberal periodical, *Kate Field's Washington*.

On the opposite coast, Emily Pitts Stevens bought an interest in the *California Weekly Mercury* in 1869, then became the sole owner, and changed its name to *Pioneer*, making it the voice of the suffrage movement in the West. Stevens also organized California's movement for women's right to vote. Further north, in Portland, Oregon, Abigail Scott Duniway published *The New Northwest*, a weekly newspaper that advocated for women's rights; Duniway would lead that region's women into the twentieth century. Both Stevens and Duniway made their living by publishing mainstream papers that were read by men, but they also became organizational leaders for women's rights. By 1882, enough women were writing on politics that they formed the

Mary Mapes Dodge

Mary Mapes Dodge (1831–1905), left a widow after only seven years of marriage, turned to writing children's stories to support herself and her two young children. After her collection of short stories, *The Irvington Stories*, was a success, her publisher requested more of her work. Dodge's next book, *Hans Brinker, or the Silver Skates*, published in 1865, was an instant best seller. The book went through more than one hundred editions in her lifetime and continues in print today, in multiple formats. It remains a children's classic.

Four years after the novel's success, Dodge joined *Hearth and Home*, a weekly illustrated magazine, as the publication's associate editor, where she worked in the Juvenile and Household departments. In 1873 she was asked to become the editor of a new monthly publication: *St. Nicholas: Scribner's Illustrated Magazine for Girls and Boys*. Her goal for *St. Nicholas* was to publish literature that inspired and interested children. She wrote, "A successful children's magazine must not be a milk-and-water variety of the periodical for adults. In fact, it needs to be stronger, truer, bolder, more uncompromising than the other; its cheer must be the cheer of the bird-song; it must mean freshness and heartiness, life and joy."

Dodge solicited stories from a number of well-known writers including Mark Twain, Louisa May Alcott, Robert Louis Stevenson, and Rudyard Kipling. Her greatest hit may have been Frances Hodgson Burnett's *Little Lord Fauntleroy*, which Dodge serialized prior to the book's 1886 publication. It soon was made into a play popular enough that some four hundred theatrical troupes produced it simultaneously. In 1899, she established the St. Nicholas League, which published the work of the children subscribers, offering awards and cash prizes for the best work. Edna St. Vincent Millay, F. Scott Fitzgerald, E.B. White, and Stephen Vincent Benét were all winners.

Dodge's high literary and moral standards made *St. Nicholas* one of the most successful and widely read magazines for children during the second half of the nineteenth century, with a circulation of almost seventy thousand. She remained as editor and contributor until 1905.

—Linda Rosen

Woman's National Press Association, with Civil War reporter Emily Edson Briggs as president.

As the frontier moved west after the Civil War, women led the way in publicizing the plight of Native Americans. The most famous book on the subject was Helen Hunt Jackson's *A Century of Dishonor* (1881). Susette La Flesche, a member of the Omaha tribe, addressed both race and gender with nationwide lectures titled "The Position, Occupation, and Culture of Indian Women." Mary Mapes Dodge, an editor at *Scribner's*, publicized La Flesche. During a long career, Dodge would introduce to the public such giants as Alfred Lord Tennyson, Mark Twain, Edna St. Vincent Millay, and even a young Rachel Carson.

Mary Abigail Dodge (no relation to Mary Mapes Dodge) was a ghostwriter for the 1884 Republican presidential nominee James G. Blaine and, earlier, had used the pseudonym of "Gail Hamilton" for articles in prestigious magazines such as *The Atlantic Monthly* and *The Independent.* She showed courage in taking on the publishing world with *A Battle of the Books* (1870), a fictionalized but truthful account of how her longtime publisher had underpaid her. That did not hurt her career: A decade later, she was popular enough to insist on a minimum of $200 per magazine article.

Early Years of the Women's Club Movement

To understand American women's history, including women's role in the literary community and the world of books, it is vital to understand how little association women traditionally had with each other. Except for a few "moral reform societies" and church-related missionary auxiliaries, women's organizations simply did not exist. As an example, when the women's rights movement began in Seneca Falls, New York, in 1848, Lucretia Mott's husband presided because no woman had experience in that role. The Civil War changed attitudes on what was proper female behavior, especially in regard to traveling and public speaking.

The war ended in 1865, and in 1868, English novelist Charles Dickens toured America. It was the exclusion of the *New York Tribune's* Jane Cunningham Croly from an event at the New York Press Club honoring Dickens that led to the founding of Sorosis, the first association for professional women. Sorosis, which preceded even the 1873 founding of the Woman's Christian Temperance Union (WCTU), was very different from anything the world had ever seen and was especially unprecedented in that it consciously excluded philanthropy from its agenda. Sorosis unabashedly promoted careers, and New York had so many women eager for such networking that within a year, eighty-three members had paid the five dollar annual dues—a week's wages for an average woman.

Poet and essayist Alice Cary was its founding president; she and her sister Phoebe had moved to New York from Cincinnati, and work by both sisters regularly appeared in magazines such as *Harper's* and *The Atlantic Monthly*. Their home was a literary salon, but with its large membership, Sorosis meetings were held at the elite Delmonico's Restaurant. Female presence in restaurants without male escort was unusual, and the group was widely criticized.

Boston women formed the New England Women's Club in 1868, the same year as Sorosis' founding. Less career oriented and more political, it succeeded in 1874 in a tough election by adding four women to the city's school governance board. Its influential president was Caroline Severance, a close associate of Julia Ward Howe. Harriot Hunt, a popular if uncredentialed physician, hosted the first meeting. Dr. Hunt earlier had offered Harvard Medical School $50,000 to admit women, but the offer was refused.

The Association for the Advancement of Women (AAW), formed in 1873, was also Boston based, and among its goals was purchasing scientific equipment for astronomer Maria Mitchell. After more women became college educated, it would be replaced by today's American Association of University Women (AAUW). These organizations aimed to give their members the college education (but not the degree) that they had been denied in their youth.

Although cited less by historians, married women on the frontier also organized study clubs—and did so sooner than the more famous ones in Boston and New York. Study clubs may have existed in Connecticut and Rhode Island in the very early 1800s, but the first that left extended records was in Bloomington, Indiana, in 1841. Another frontier example is that of Catharine Beecher, half sister of Harriet Beecher Stowe. Although Beecher is remembered for her books on domesticity, she founded the American Woman's Educational Association as a self-education society in 1852 when she was living in Cincinnati.

Women and Libraries

Meanwhile, in 1876, Americans went to Philadelphia to celebrate their country's centennial—and Susan B. Anthony led a group that took over a bandstand and read aloud its declaration of women's independence. Some librarians may have cheered them on, as thirteen women and ninety men created the American Library Association (ALA) during that national gathering.

Caroline Hewins was one of the early members of the ALA. In 1876, she became the librarian at the Hartford (Connecticut) Young Men's Institute and launched a long career of providing services to children, at this time a group not generally welcomed in libraries. She began the first story hour for children, wrote up reading lists, and made sure that furniture was suitably sized and that the library was cheerful and attractive. Her many innovations would become standard practice in the years ahead. Her articles on children's literature reflected her belief that children needed better books than the formulaic literature of that time; her advocacy would provide the underpinnings for scholarly attention to children's literature in years to come.

Hewins was also a force to reckon with in the fledgling American Library Association (ALA). In 1882, she sent out a famous letter to twenty-five libraries around the country, asking, "What are you doing to encourage a love of reading in boys and girls?" When the answers were discouraging, she lobbied the ALA to establish a Children's Section so that ideas could be shared among librarians. When she died, in 1926, at the age of eighty, *Library Journal* wrote that she was "one of the beloved in the library profession. She made of herself a center from which radiated an immeasurable influence, especially in the great revolution in the library world which, instead of banning the children, made them the first thought of the librarian who could look at the future as well as the present."

THE PROGRESSIVE ERA

What historians mean by the "Progressive Era" can be elusive. For women and minorities, the early part of the era instead meant stagnation and even reversal. Lynching soared in the South, for example, as the federal government abdicated its role of protecting African-Americans. Native

Americans lost their last stand in 1892, and most did not see the new land reservation system as progressive. The "Gilded Age" and the "Age of Robber Barons" are terms that also apply to the early part of the Progressive Era—and the 1893 depression was the worst in U.S. history up to that point. Urban families starved, while farmers went bankrupt. Policies that favored plutocrats resulted in several new political parties, including the one called "Progressive."

Labor unions, which had been semi-secret societies, adopted open activism, and strikes in both urban industries and rural mining towns turned violent, with women as both participants and victims of police brutality. The Democratic Party moved to the left with populist William Jennings Bryan as its nominee in 1896, 1900, and again in 1908. After an anarchist assassinated Republican president William McKinley, Theodore Roosevelt pushed for the adoption of many planks of the Progressive platform. Some, such as state regulation of public utilities and the federal Pure Food and Drug Act (1906), were especially important to women.

Perhaps the height of progressive success was the 1913 adoption of two constitutional amendments, the first since the Civil War era. The Sixteenth Amendment authorized Congress to tax the rich at a higher rate than the poor, while the Seventeenth allowed voters to elect their U.S. senators; previously state legislators chose them. The Eighteenth Amendment was a nationwide ban on alcohol sales, which finally ended the Prohibition argument that was long entangled with women's rights. Although relatively few women could vote on these major amendments, many women advanced them and other reforms by writing.

Literary "Clubwomen"

By 1890, so many groups had grown from the 1868 examples of Sorosis and the New England Women's Club that journalist Jane Cunningham Croly united them into the General Federation of Women's Clubs (GFWC). Within two decades, the GFWC would have some two million members in thousands of clubs across the nation. Many members did not favor the vote for women, but they took their first timorous steps towards full citizenship by encouraging improvements in state and local government, especially public libraries. Working with grants from industrialist Andrew

Carnegie, the GFWC ultimately would claim a role in establishing 75 percent of the nation's libraries.

As it became respectable—perhaps even socially mandated—for women to have interests beyond church and charity, Pen and Brush formed at New York's Fifth Avenue Hotel in 1894. Its founder was Janet C. Lewis, a painter who envisioned an organization for women interested in both the arts and literature. The purpose, according to its website, would be for "mutual improvement, advancement and social intercourse." In 1912, under the presidency of writer and feminist Grace Seton, Pen and Brush became an established legal corporation. "The organization continued to flourish under the 30-year presidency of investigative journalist and writer Ida Tarbell. Members included Pulitzer Prize winning authors Marianne Moore, Margaret Widdemer, and Pearl Buck, who also received the Nobel Prize in Literature; as well as renowned visual artists Isabel Whitney, Malvina Hoffman, Clara Sipprell, and Jessie Tarbox Beals." Beals, a pioneering photojournalist, traveled widely in the early 1900s taking photographs that she sold to newspapers. Almost 125 years old, Pen and Brush (now known as Pen + Brush) maintains a Manhattan gallery, a publishing program, and an active calendar of events, pursuing its original goal of helping female artists and writers create sustainable and significant careers.

While some organizations, like Pen and Brush, were regional, the National League of American Pen Women (NLAPW), founded in 1897 in Washington, D.C., quickly became a truly national organization. Its chief organizer was Marian Longfellow O'Donoghue, niece of famed poet Henry Wadsworth Longfellow. Members were required to have publishing credentials, and according to its website, women joined from "Maine to Texas, from New York to California" within its first year. Its initial goals were strongly feminist, insisting that "pen women" be paid for their work and even calling themselves a "progressive press union." In 2017, NLAPW celebrated its 120th anniversary.

Hundreds of "pen women" and tens of thousands of "clubwomen" went to Chicago in 1892 and 1893, when the world unabashedly celebrated the four hundredth anniversary of Columbus' first voyage. Quietly led by Susan B. Anthony, women successfully lobbied for a congressional appropriation to fund their participation, and Chicago's Bertha Palmer, a brilliant businesswoman and liberal leader, chaired a Board of Lady Managers that included two women from every state. Young architect Sophia Hayden designed the Woman's Building; the sculptors and artists who decorated it were women; and even the music played was composed and performed by women.

Indiana's May Wright Sewall presided over a World's Congress of Representative Women at the expo in May of 1893. She recruited women from twenty-seven nations, and over one hundred and fifty thousand people attended a week of three hundred and thirty seminars—some of them led by librarians and addressing literary subjects. Records of the speeches and discussions filled fat volumes that were distributed to libraries nationwide. Thousands of books by women were displayed in the building's second-floor library. Indeed, a recent book has been published about them: *Right Here I See My Own Books: The Woman's Building Library at the World's Columbian Exposition* (University of Massachusetts Press, 2012).

Librarianship: A New Profession for Women

Melvil Dewey, the librarian at Columbia University (then called Columbia College), recognized a need for trained librarians for the many libraries opening in communities around the country. He convinced Columbia's Board of Trustees of the viability of such a program, and in 1887, the School of Library Economy opened with twenty students, seventeen of them women.

Dewey, who developed the Dewey Decimal System, considered women inherently suited for the vocation. In a speech in 1886, he claimed that women had a "natural housekeeping instinct"; they valued order, accuracy, and most of all, were devoted to the cause. Dewey insisted on the admission of women over objections from the college's regents—and ultimately was fired. He found a new home for the school in Albany, where it became the New York State Library School, remaining there until 1926, when it was transferred back to Columbia. The school remained in existence until 1992.

More than any other factor, it was probably the New York State Library School that created the image of the female librarian, as, during its first three decades, 94 percent of its graduates were women. For decades into the future, though, most top jobs at large libraries nonetheless went to men, even when women had objectively better credentials of education and experience. Even in small towns where a woman headed the library, the library boards that employed them frequently viewed the job as a sort of charity for widows and spinsters.

Despite this, women were often the innovators in the library world. Bookmobile service was started by Mary Titcomb for the Washington County Free Public Library in Maryland in the early 1900s from a specially designed wagon. When automobiles became more widespread, librarians put cases of books in the back seats and went on the road. In Hibbing, Minnesota, the heart of iron ore country, a truck was built that could hold a thousand books with room for six people at a time to browse. Librarians in rural areas went out on horseback with books.

At the Los Angeles City Library in the 1890s, Tessa Kelso revolutionized library service by eliminating membership fees and opening up the bookstacks to the public. Before Kelso, the first female director of the Los Angeles library was eighteen-year-old Mary Foy, who was appointed

A photograph of Ina Coolbrith printed in her book of poetry, *Songs from the Golden Gate* (1895).

by the City Council in 1880. Women had only recently—and reluctantly—been admitted to that library as patrons. In 1876 they were relegated to a "Ladies' Room," which had sofas and magazines, but no books. Even earlier, in 1874, Ina Coolbrith became the director of the Oakland (California) Library Association, a subscription library. Coolbrith, by contemporary accounts, was quite charismatic: She befriended and mentored the young Jack London and

Isadora Duncan. After eighteen years at the library she was fired and returned to writing poetry, her first love. She became the first Poet Laureate of California in 1919.

Theresa West Elmendorf became the ALA's first female president in 1911—thirty-five years after its 1876 founding. A Wisconsin native, Theresa West had worked her way up to head the Milwaukee Public Library in 1892. She resigned in 1896 to marry ALA leader Henry Elmendorf when she was forty-one, and they moved to Buffalo, where he headed its public library. Despite not having an official occupational title, she was elected president of the New York Library Association in 1903, and eight years later, moved on to the top national position. Mary Wright Plummer, a graduate of the first class at Columbia's School of Library Economy, headed the library school at Pratt Institute in Brooklyn, as well as the Pratt Institute Library. Plummer was the first to speak and write about issues of ethics in the library profession. She became the second female president of ALA, in 1915.

Nothing would be as important to the library profession as the Carnegie Foundation. Steel industrialist Andrew Carnegie was born in Scotland and came to the United States as a teenager. He endowed his first U.S. public library in Pittsburgh in 1881—and by 1920, there would be some twenty-five hundred Carnegie libraries, primarily in the United States, Canada, and Great Britain. In the United States, the General Federation of Women's Clubs worked closely with the Carnegie Foundation, which insisted on local support—as well as the use of its standard architecture, including basements, even in locations that regularly flooded, such as Tampa, where the water table can be just three feet underground. But at the same time that Carnegie executives might have been arbitrary about architecture and other things, the foundation was progressive on social issues. It insisted that libraries be open to patrons of all races, with the result that West Tampa, a separate municipality with many African-Americans and Hispanics, had a Carnegie Library three years prior to the City of Tampa, where white officials resisted the foundation's mandates. This was typical of the South, as city fathers neither wanted to expand educational opportunities for African-Americans nor add librarians to payrolls. GFWC women played a strong role in persuading men of their class to cooperate with the New York-based foundation.

Women's Rights and Women's Stories

The Progressive Era was not all that progressive for women's right to vote: Women lost nineteen statewide elections on the issue in the years between 1871 and 1910. Women in eastern states couldn't even get the question on the ballot, and so all but one of these elections were in the West—where the Wyoming Territory had been first to enfranchise women back in 1869. The Utah Territory was second in 1870, but Congress required repeal of that right for statehood. Colorado was third in 1893—and the very next year, elected three women to its legislature. Utah women re-won their vote in 1895, and Idaho followed in 1896. But no more states would join the list until 1910, when Washington granted women suffrage.

California helped lead the revived movement for the vote with a campaign that used sophisticated techniques such as electric billboards. It even hired detectives to protect ballot boxes, as referenda in many states had demonstrated conservatives' willingness to steal elections, usually with funding from the liquor industry. The next year, 1912, not only brought the first Democratic president in decades (Woodrow Wilson), but also three more Western victories: Arizona women won the franchise in the first year of transition from territory to state; Kansas, which had held the first referendum back in 1867, finally granted full rights in 1912; in the same year—and after six losing referenda beginning in 1884—Oregon feminists at last won. Alaska's territorial government granted the vote at its first meeting in 1913, and in 1914, women won referenda in Montana and Nevada, both on the first attempt. By 1916, women in every western state except New Mexico were enfranchised.

Many women in eastern states, however, focused on other issues, and some became authors as a result of their activism. Immigrants from Europe streamed into New York via Ellis Island, with rising annual numbers that reached a height of one million in 1907. American women in urban areas responded with settlement houses that helped immigrants adjust, the most famous being Jane Addams' Hull House in Chicago. Her *Twenty Years at Hull-House* (1910) proved a publishing phenomenon, as did Lillian D. Wald's *The House on Henry Street* (1915), which explained the new profession of visiting nurses in New York. Other women also wrote of their experiences with immigrants, and these books became classics in new academic fields such as sociology and economics.

Those issues drew dramatic national attention in 1909, when women in the garment industry, mostly young immigrants, went on strike. New York police brutally attacked picketers, and over seven hundred were arrested. The Women's Trade Union League, however, was an unusual combination of working-class women and their upper-class customers, and after six months of battle, the league largely won its objectives. Still, one of the companies that refused to accept the league continued its unsafe business practices—and as a result, one hundred forty-six people, most of them young female immigrants, died in the infamous 1911 Triangle Shirtwaist Factory fire.

Most newcomers to America were indifferent to politics, but a few—especially Jews escaping czarist Russia—were active leftists. The most influential may have been the anarchist Emma Goldman, who was eventually deported because of her opposition to World War I. "Red Emma" was the label that conservatives gave to her, but she was more than just a political firebrand. In addition to political writings, essays advocating free love and birth control, and an autobiography (*Living My Life*), she wrote *The Social Significance of the Modern Drama* (1914), introducing the liberated ideas of George Bernard Shaw, Henrik Ibsen, and other playwrights.

The best-selling memoir of 1912 was *The Promised Land* by Mary Antin, a Jewish immigrant from Russia. Antin's graceful account of her embrace of American culture helped interpret the immigrant experience for Americans who were suspicious of the cultural changes the newcomers brought; it has remained in print ever since. Later, in the 1920s, novelist and short story writer Anzia Yezierska would write less idealized accounts of the lives of Jewish immigrant women in her novels and short stories, notably *Hungry Hearts* and *Bread Givers*.

Perhaps no book was as influential as journalist Ida Tarbell's *The History of the Standard Oil Company* (1904). Despite its dry title, it was a huge success in drawing attention to corrupt business practices. Tarbell wrote for the popular *McClure's Magazine*, where the founder Samuel Sidney McClure followed a practice unique in that day of giving his journalists all the time they needed to write their muckraking articles. Tarbell spent years digging through documents and interviewing executives, regulators, and competitors; in short, she was an early practitioner of investigative journalism. Her exposé of John D. Rockefeller's and Standard Oil's corrupt business practices was serialized for three years in *McClure's*; it was an unqualified success and drove up circulation.

Gene Stratton-Porter's name has been mostly forgotten, but she was a tremendous publishing success, as well as a pioneer in expanding literature to film. At the suggestion of her husband, she changed her name from Geneva and wrote ecologically oriented novels from her Indiana home. *Freckles* (1904) sold 1,400,000 copies, and the total sales of her many works attracted an international audience estimated at fifty million. Eight of her novels were made into films, and in 1922, she would form her own film company.

In other forms of media, Zitkala-Sa, a member of the Lakota tribe who was also known by her missionary-given name Gertrude

Simmons Bonnin, was editor of *American Indian Magazine* in Washington, D.C. Jessie Redmon Fauset was literary editor of *Crisis*, the publication of the National Association for the Advancement of Colored People (NAACP), which began in 1910; she was a graduate of Cornell University and the first African-American woman admitted to Phi Beta Kappa. Alice Dunbar-Nelson, an African-American who specialized in short stories, wrote compellingly of mixed-race people. Kate Chopin was white, but interpreted Louisiana's unusual race

Photographic portrait of Zitkala-Sa, a member of the Lakota tribe and editor of *American Indian Magazine*, taken in 1898 by the influential American photographer Gertrude Käsebier.

culture. Neither Dunbar-Nelson nor Chopin, however, was well known in her time.

My Ántonia (1918), a poignant interpretation of life on the Nebraska prairie for a Bohemian family, would make Willa Cather a household name. She had been published in a Boston magazine while still a student at the University of Nebraska, and S.S. McClure offered her a job at his magazine in 1906 as a result of stories she wrote during summer vacations. By 1911 she had risen to managing editor, but left *McClure's* to devote all her time to writing. Cather published her first novel, *Alexander's Bridge* (1912), after serializing it in *McClure's*. *O Pioneers!* (1913) followed, but despite her novels' Midwestern settings, she continued to live mostly in New York. Ultimately, she probably did a disservice to female authors by forbidding the anthologizing of her work. Given that she had been an editor, this clause in her will is perplexing, and the unfortunate result is that fewer of today's students read her outstanding literature.

Margaret Anderson left a career as a pianist and book reviewer to start *The Little Review* in Chicago and made it a success from the first issue in 1914. With an uncanny eye for budding genius, she introduced work by such giants as T.S. Eliot, Gertrude Stein, Ernest Hemingway, and Amy Lowell. Also in 1914, Margaret Sanger was arrested under the Comstock Act for writing about birth control in her periodical, *The Woman Rebel*. She fled to Europe shortly before the war broke out in August.

World War I Brings Worldwide Change

War motivated authors Jane Addams, Charlotte Perkins Gilman, and others to sail to Europe in 1915 under the banner of the Woman's Peace Party (WPP). Addams would be the first woman to win the Nobel Peace Prize, in 1931, but these early efforts of the WPP were in vain. Some of the forty-two women went as far as Russia and met with high-ranking officials, but the United States nonetheless entered the war in April 1917—soon after the re-election of President Woodrow Wilson, who had campaigned on "keeping us out of war." The first woman, Jeannette Rankin of Montana, entered the U.S. House of Representatives that year; she joined about fifty men in voting against the declaration of war.

Harriet Monroe

Another woman who pushed the boundaries of the literary world was Harriet Monroe (1860–1936). Monroe discovered a love of literature in her father's library. She studied literature at the Visitation Convent in Washington, D.C., graduating in 1879. Frightened of posthumous anonymity, Monroe professed her determination to become "great and famous" as a poet or playwright when she said, "I cannot remember when to die without leaving some memorable record did not seem to me a calamity too terrible to be borne."

Over the next decade, her aspiration to become a dramatist and a poet was encouraged by Robert Louis Stevenson, with whom she corresponded. Success came when *Century Magazine* published her poem "With a Copy of Shelley" in 1889, but it was sadly evident to Monroe that she could never make a living from selling her poems. She never forgot that disappointment. In 1891, with a solid reputation as a freelance correspondent to the *Chicago Tribune*, Monroe was commissioned to write a commemorative ode to be read at the opening ceremonies of the World's Columbian Exhibition. The poem was well received but was later printed by the *New York World* without her consent. Incensed, she filed a lawsuit against the newspaper and was awarded $5,000 in damages. She used the money, along with subscriptions she procured from wealthy Chicago patrons, to launch *Poetry: A Magazine of Verse* on September 23, 1912. In its second

Most women supported the war, though, and Carrie Chapman Catt, president of the mainstream National American Woman Suffrage Association (NAWSA), used their participation in the war effort as a justification for the vote. Women replaced men in such occupations as streetcar drivers and postal workers. Over a thousand women contracted with the military to work in Europe, especially as translators and telephone operators. The American Women's Hospitals were in Europe, but financed and staffed by American women. Other organizations sponsored women who worked with refugees, and several Young Women's Christian Association (YWCA) employees earned France's prestigious Croix de Guerre. Although they were not allowed to go abroad, some 12,500 women joined the U.S. Navy and edition she wrote: "Open Door will be the policy of this magazine—may the great poet we are looking for never find it shut, or half-shut, against his ample genius! To this end the editors...desire to print the best English verse which is being written today, regardless of where, by whom, or under what theory of art it is written."

For the first two years as editor of *Poetry*, working simultaneously as an art critic for the *Chicago Tribune*, Monroe did not take a salary. Validation came when a contributor to the magazine, Rabindranath Tagore, won the Nobel Prize for literature in 1913. The following year, Monroe resigned from the *Tribune* and accepted a small stipend from *Poetry*, remaining its editor until her death. Her eye for enduring quality and talent allowed her to avoid being seduced by literary trends.

She nurtured a wide readership, raised the status and increased the visibility of poetry, promoting the careers of those who came to define twentieth-century modernism: Carl Sandburg, T.S. Eliot, Ezra Pound, D.H. Lawrence, Marianne Moore, Wallace Stevens, William Carlos Williams, Robert Frost, and Langston Hughes, among many others. Today, the magazine continues to uphold her promise to contributors for adequate payment and still offers the annual prize that she established. *Poetry* continues to flourish as a major cultural influence. Indefatigable until the end, Monroe died at the age of seventy-six in Arequipa, Peru, as she was preparing to climb Machu Picchu.

—Linda Rosen

the Marine Corps, where they staffed headquarters in Washington and on the coasts. Many other women went overseas under the aegis of civilian agencies such as the American Red Cross and as members of the military's nursing corps. More than two hundred members of the Army Nurse Corps died, some because of breathing the lethal mustard gas unleashed in this war.

The American Library Association also supported the war, approaching the Army and Navy about supplying books for young recruits. Officers initially were reluctant to accept the idea, but quickly came to understand the morale-building value of recreational reading. Wayne Wiegand, library historian, wrote: "The ALA established its Library War Service in 1917 to provide books and library services to U.S. soldiers and sailors both in training at home and serving in Europe. [The] second book drive in early 1918 generated 3 million books, many going overseas, others ending up on the shelves of thirty-six training-camp libraries erected through Carnegie Corporation funding and managed by ALA volunteers across the country."

Librarians in cities and small towns around the country planned creative opportunities for people to attend library programs and donate books. Overseas Army transports had space to carry one hundred thousand books a month. Books also were sent to military hospitals for convalescing soldiers. Booksellers were not unmindful of this chance to encourage people to buy books for the war effort. A note in the March 16, 1918, issue of *Publishers Weekly* stated: "Here it would seem is a perpetually alive sales appeal which can be brought home as a personal opportunity and responsibility to everybody who opens a periodical or passes a bookstore."

New York women were particularly active in the war effort, and New Yorker Daisy Harriman not only chaired the government's Committee on Women in Industry, but also went to France to supervise about five hundred ambulance drivers in the Red Cross Motor Corps. Rheta Dorr, an outspoken feminist, reported from Europe for the *New York Evening Mail*, and Gertrude Battles Lane, longtime editor of *Woman's Home Companion*, also sent female reporters abroad. A parade for the vote in October 1917 featured a petition signed by a million women working in wartime industry, and was a large factor in New York women winning the vote on their second attempt, in November 1917.

Bookselling in the Early Twentieth Century

In 1915, an influential article appeared in the March issue of *The Atlantic Monthly* with the title "A New Profession for Women." The author, Earl Barnes, decried the statistics that showed that U.S. per capita consumption of books was "ridiculously small.... Bookstores are vanishing from cities and towns as are the [male] staff who 'knew books and loved them.'" Barnes proposed that college-educated women, many of whom lacked opportunities to use their education constructively, would find bookstore ownership attractive. "About 70,000 women are now undergraduate students in American institutions of higher learning. When they graduate, many of these women will face a period of unemployment. Of 1,076 women who had graduated from Bryn Mawr...[by] 1911, 27 per cent were married, 28.5 per cent were teaching, while 25.6 per cent were unmarried and without paid occupation." Female booksellers could be recruited from the newer professions of librarianship and social work, where the fields were so overcrowded that many women were working for nominal fees.

College-educated women, Barnes noted, were widely distributed around the country, preferred to remain in their home communities, and had a keen desire for social service. Despite Barnes' reservations about women's ability to handle the finances and logistics of running a bookstore, he wrote, "Why may they not establish bookstores in their own cities and towns in all parts of the country? Such stores would meet the need for a calling, and should yield a fair income." He did acknowledge the reluctance of men to see women enter the business, citing the few women who were in attendance at the American Booksellers Association (ABA) convention in 1913, but suggested that "women would win [acceptance] if they could offer superior preparation, numbers, and consequent willingness to work for less money."

A number of women did open bookstores before and after Barnes' article was written and succeeded in creating the "personal bookshop" that welcomed customers into a cozy, well-stocked, friendly place. Madge Jenison—one of the founding members of the Women's National Book Association—and Mary Horgan Mowbray-Clarke opened a bookstore on East 31st Street in Manhattan called the Sunwise Turn, which featured author readings, art exhibits, and a mail-order book service. Priscilla Guthrie was the proprietor of a bookshop in Pittsburgh that focused on personal service and expressed the owner's personality and standards. Sally H. Burch and Maude S. Odell began the Wayfarer's Bookshop in Washington, D.C., and women all over the country became the heads of book departments in the large department stores. (See Chapter 2: "Bookselling Then and Now" for more information.)

Marian Cutter was a librarian who dreamed of opening a children's bookstore offering the best in children's literature to her customers. She found a small space in midtown Manhattan, a slice of the store vacated by the Sunwise Turn Bookshop when it moved further uptown. As she wrote in a 1920 article in *Publishers Weekly*, "Does the Librarian Make

Bertha Mahony

Earl Barnes' 1915 *Atlantic Monthly* article also inspired Bertha Mahony (later Miller) to open The Bookshop for Boys and Girls in Boston in 1916. Mahony was working for the Women's Educational and Industrial Union in Boston, which was founded in 1877 to assist immigrant women, young mothers, and their children. Mahony sought advice about the bookshop from several eminent children's librarians, including Anne Carroll Moore at the New York Public Library and Alice Jordan at the Boston Public Library. This specialized bookshop was the first of its kind and offered reading contests and a variety of children's programs. The recommended booklists that Mahony began to publish in 1916 became well known and influential. In 1921, the bookshop moved nearby to larger quarters and began to stock adult titles as well.

Mahony's many creative efforts to bring children's books to a wider audience led her to start the Book Caravan, a truck stocked with books that traveled around New England in the summers. Mahony wrote, "It does not seem possible that there can be any profession with greater satisfaction, a higher daily excitement or a more vital sense of the surging tides of life than that of a bookman in a bookshop." The Bookshop for Boys and Girls was a part of the unique collaboration among booksellers, librarians, and editors that flowered in the 1920s and 1930s, forever changing the world of children's literature.

a Good Bookseller?" she learned several lessons very quickly. When her very first customer asked if she had children's series books—anathema to a good children's librarian of that day—"there was a dawning consciousness that the Public's desires had to be considered to a broader degree in a book-shop than in a library." She also learned that it was helpful to have a small, carefully chosen stock of books, one that she could, in modern terms, hand-sell. Her customers "enjoyed the small stock, it was not bewildering, decisions were simplified and appreciation lent zest to the selling."

Women's Enfranchisement and the Founding of the Women's National Book Association

Not only was New York the first eastern state to fully enfranchise women, but it was also home to the world's first formal demand for it, which happened on July 20, 1848, in the upstate town of Seneca Falls. Elizabeth Cady Stanton lived there; she organized a meeting on women's rights when Philadelphia's Lucretia Mott visited her sister, who lived in nearby Auburn. Stanton and Mott had vowed to organize such a meeting when they met in London in 1840 at the World Anti-Slavery Convention— but both were busy mothers, and eight years passed before they could fulfill this promise to themselves. The meeting was a huge success, as was another in Rochester two weeks later.

Rochester's Susan B. Anthony attended her first women's rights meeting in 1852, and New York women won their first political victory in 1860, when the legislature granted married women the right to their own earnings. Women's rights advocates temporarily suspended their conventions during the Civil War, but Anthony and Stanton (who moved to Brooklyn during the war) formed the Woman's National Loyal League. It supported women's rights, as well as loyalty to the union, and collected some four hundred thousand signatures on a petition to abolish slavery. They astutely charged a penny for each signature, and Anthony paid herself a salary to run their New York City headquarters.

Women in Nyack and Fayetteville (home to Matilda Joslyn Gage, an author and perhaps the movement's best theorist) tested the Fifteenth Amendment by trying to vote in an 1871 election. In 1872, Manhattan stockbroker Victoria Woodhull grabbed headlines by running for president of the United States. With her sister, Tennessee Claflin, she published *Woodhull & Claflin's Weekly*, which revealed the underside of New York society, especially in regard to popular preacher Henry Ward Beecher's adulterous behavior.

It was Harriot Stanton Blatch, the daughter of Elizabeth Cady Stanton, who was most responsible for reviving the movement in the twentieth century. Blatch reached out to the working class more than her predecessors, forming the Equality League of Self-Supporting Women in 1902. Beginning in 1910, feminists staged giant parades in Manhattan, something that was new for women and controversial—but many New Yorkers soon came to look forward to the annual marches. In 1912, feminists walked the one hundred seventy miles from New York City to the state capital at Albany, preaching the vote in every village along the way.

A women's suffrage parade in New York City in October of 1915; two years later, women booksellers would participate in a similar march—helping to spur the launch of the Women's National Book Association.

New York had several large feminist organizations by then, and they worked together without the rivalry that characterized some states. For the 1915 referendum on the vote, the Manhattan-based Woman Suffrage Party alone canvassed almost four hundred thousand male voters and sent mail to more than eight hundred thousand. Other women greeted men at factory gates; they stood on soapboxes to speak on street corners; and they paid theaters to show advertising slides. They also held oration marathons, and on the eve of the election, spoke for twenty-six hours in Columbus Circle. Nevertheless, they lost, with 238,098 in favor but 320,853 opposed.

All of the effort would pay off, though, as the legislature again put the question on the 1917 ballot, and this time, women won by about one hundred thousand votes. New York women cast their first ballots in the congressional elections of November 1918, a few days before the end of World War I. The next June, Congress adopted the Nineteenth Amendment granting all voting rights to all American women and sent it to the states for ratification. Carrie Chapman Catt—who led the national movement from a Fifth Avenue headquarters where Alva Vanderbilt

Belmont paid the rent for an entire floor—wanted the enfranchised women of New York to set an example for the nation. She persuaded Governor Al Smith to call a special session of the legislature, and within days, lawmakers met in Albany. It was a near-unanimous vote, with one senator voting against ratification.

New York in 1917 was thus full of excitement, energy, and hope. It is not surprising that the Women's National Book Association began then, in the exhilaration of the October 27 parade in support of the referendum to obtain the right to vote. The march featured women in a variety of occupations; Madge Jenison, a bookseller and one of the WNBA's founding members, was invited to form a sixteen-member parade unit. As she recollected in *The Woman Citizen* on December 6, 1919: "But where to find them? Men had an organization…to which women were occasionally invited to appear in the capacity of an admiring audience, not as members." Through the book salesmen who came to her shop, she was able to find seven other women to march with her. Years later, at a meeting of the WNBA, Jenison spoke about the parade: "…a florist…made us up very handsome boutonnieres—corn flowers and calendulas—blue and orange. Anyone who has never swung around on Fifth Avenue…to march for something she believes in, with bands before and behind, banners fluttering everywhere, and crowds of people to cheer, has missed a very great emotion. Marching in itself is a terrible and wonderful thing. You get to be a part of some bodily thing, big and more than yourself." Newspaper accounts describe a parade of twenty-five thousand people—women and men—marching on that afternoon of October 27.

It was only two days later that a group of fifteen women met for the first time at Sherwood's Book Store, 19 John Street, in Manhattan. Pauline Sherwood and her husband owned that store, and she had sent a formal announcement to women in the business inviting them to attend a meeting on "Monday, October 29th, 1917, at 8 P.M." to discuss "ways and means toward the organizing…among women in all branches of the book trade." On November 13 they met again at the Sunwise Turn Bookshop; this time there were thirty-five women, and the Women's National Book Association was founded. (See Chapter 3: "From the Archives" for more information about the founding of the WNBA.)

An item in the WNBA archives from 1940 names Sherwood as the first president, but documents closer to the founding date indicate that parade organizer Madge Jenison was seen by the public as WNBA's founder. Jenison was able to say by December 1919: "Our little association is fast growing into a big association, so big that it is now wooed by the men's league… But we are going to maintain our separate association for a time, at least." She emphasized that the organization was open and democratic, welcoming "all trades and professions which enter into the 'circulation of thought.'"

The year 1917 was indeed significant, as the first Pulitzer Prizes were awarded then. Women swept the category for biography with *Julia Ward Howe*, written by her daughters Laura E. Richards and Maude Howe Elliott, both of whom had writing careers independent of their mother. The precedent, unfortunately, was not repeated for decades: Although a few men won for biographies of women and a few women won for biographies of men, no woman writing about a woman would win again until 1986.

In his speech to Congress on January 9, 1918, President Wilson formally endorsed an amendment to the Constitution that would grant full voting rights to women in every state—and the next day, the House passed it by 274–136, exactly the number necessary to meet the Constitution's requirement of a two-thirds majority. The Senate, however, would remain obdurate until after that fall's election. Catt and her chief lobbyist, the very astute Maud Wood Park, targeted opponents in Massachusetts and Delaware, and that made all the difference. The war ended on November 11, 1918, just days after the election. Senate President Henry Cabot Lodge of Massachusetts procrastinated as long as he could, but on June 4, 1919, the Senate narrowly adopted the Nineteenth Amendment.

The Constitution requires its amendments to be ratified by three-quarters of the state legislatures, which means both chambers in dozens of states. This high standard means that most issues are passé by the time such unanimity can be reached—and the vote for women still was controversial. With incredibly good lobbying, however, women (and men) managed to do that. Scenes in several states, especially West Virginia and Tennessee, were worthy of movies. Personal betrayals, spying, bribery, and astounding court claims all played into the complex struggle—but on August 26, 1920, the Nineteenth Amendment was added to the Constitution, granting all American women voting rights equal to those of men.

THE INTERWAR YEARS

Women won a great political victory in 1920, and leaders Carrie Chapman Catt and Maud Wood Park did an excellent job of summarizing that with highly readable memoirs. Catt's *Women Suffrage and Politics: The Inner Story of the Suffrage Movement*, cowritten with Nettie Rogers Shuler, was published in 1923, but Park's *Front-Door Lobbying* would not see print until 1960. That alone speaks volumes about the Roaring Twenties, as the decade would be one of social change, not political reform.

Instead of the Equal Rights Amendment, which would have expanded legal equality beyond merely the vote, the flapper of the Roaring Twenties celebrated social freedoms not previously known to American women: Flappers sported short hair and short skirts; they drove new cars and danced to jazz; they smoked cigarettes and drank illegal alcohol. Their mothers' civic activism might have seemed old-fashioned, and even those older women themselves failed to follow up on their gains. Only about one in ten members of the National American Woman Suffrage Association bothered to join the new League of Women Voters.

Meanwhile, Congress rejected the League of Nations that grew out of World War I. Many women supported it—at least as evidenced by a 1923 offer from *Ladies' Home Journal*: $50,000 in a contest for the best plan to promote world peace, to which twenty-two thousand readers responded. Yet as the twenties continued to roar, the nation became increasingly isolationist and self-absorbed.

In the Great Depression of the 1930s, however, the "New Woman" of the 1920s suffered a setback, as most people agreed that scarce jobs should go to men. The long-term obstructions to equality faced by women can be seen in this one statistic: In 1930, the first full year of the Depression, women in college faculty or administrative positions peaked at 32 percent; by 1960, the percentage had dropped to 19 percent. And while women would earn positions in the workforce during the next world war, they would lose them at the war's end. A whole generation grew up believing

The History of Woman Suffrage

When the first two volumes of *The History of Woman Suffrage* were published in 1881, Susan B. Anthony, Elizabeth Cady Stanton, and Matilda Joslyn Gage had worked on it for most of three decades. In 1886, the three women would add a third volume that included a much-needed index to the whole. This massive work is akin to a scrapbook, with newspaper clippings, letters, speeches, programs, and meeting minutes for dozens of gatherings from 1848 until 1880. Especially in the early days prior to the Civil War, the debates at annual conventions often were reprinted verbatim. A bequest from an anonymous supporter allowed the three authors to place more than twelve hundred copies of the three-volume work in libraries throughout the United States and Europe. Although she is the least known of the trio, Matilda Joslyn Gage of upstate New York was probably the movement's most original thinker and best writer. As the National American Woman Suffrage Association (NAWSA) grew more conservative late in the nineteenth century, however, she (and to a lesser extent, Stanton) were ostracized by the organization they founded. Members particularly objected to Gage's critique of Christianity, *Woman, Church, and State* (1893).

Anthony thus continued alone with the fourth volume, assisted only by her secretary and publicist, Ida Husted Harper. Published in 1902, it is the fattest of the six volumes, at 1,144 pages. It contains particularly valuable reports on the status of women by state and territory, including laws on inheritance, divorce, child custody, and even comparisons of male and female teachers' salaries. Of particular interest to bookwomen, some states reported on the status of librarians.

Harper was the sole editor for the last two volumes, which were published in 1922, two years after ratification of the Nineteenth Amendment that granted the vote. Volume Five recounted each NAWSA convention and other activities between 1901 and 1920. Volume Six emphasized state and international histories, usually written by leading activists in those places. Together, the six volumes provide incomparable insight into the building of a movement to liberate women.

that the only rightful place for women was in the home. At the same time, though, female authors did well during the Great Depression, winning Pulitzer Prizes at the same rate as in the Roaring Twenties—and more than they would in later decades.

Literary Women Look Abroad and to Harlem

Disillusioned with America after World War I, some idealists, especially writers, moved abroad. This "Lost Generation," a term credited to the American expatriate author Gertrude Stein, was concentrated in Paris, where Caresse Crosby was a "godmother." She and her husband Harry founded Black Sun Press, which first published the works of future literary giants, including famed diarist Anaïs Nin and Kay Boyle, a prolific writer in several genres. Americans in Paris networked at Shakespeare and Company, a bookstore founded by American Sylvia Beach in 1919. Like Elizabeth Peabody long before, Beach functioned as both a seller and a publisher. She offered hospitality and encouragement to many writers, and was the first to publish all of James Joyce's handwritten *Ulysses*. When the Nazis occupied Paris in 1940, Beach closed her store and hid its books, but nevertheless was interned for six months by the Gestapo.

A 1935 portrait of Gertrude Stein, who coined the term "Lost Generation," referring to the cohort—especially its writers, artists, and intellectuals—who came of age during and immediately after World War I.

Margaret Anderson, mentioned earlier, also had a connection to James Joyce's *Ulysses*. Anderson and her partner Jane Heap had begun to serialize the book in their *Little Review* in 1918. After the publication of the "Nausicaa" episode, in 1920, the New York Society for the Suppression of Vice filed a lawsuit alleging obscenity. A New York court convicted Anderson and Heap in 1921 under the Comstock Act, which prohibited using the U.S. mail to circulate materials judged obscene. They were fined $100 and forced to cease publication of *Ulysses*. This was not the first time that the two women had been sued for obscenity, and they considered closing the magazine. Anderson resigned as editor and they went to Paris, where *The Little Review* continued to publish irregularly until 1929. Anderson and Heap became part of the expatriate literary community, publishing the works of Stein, Ezra Pound, e.e. cummings, and other modernist authors.

Despite the liberated image of the Roaring Twenties, American bureaucratic obsession with obscenity continued, even in nonfiction. Mary Ware Dennett, a colleague of Margaret Sanger, endured a decade of legal troubles because of her educational pamphlet, "The Sex Side of Life," which she had written for her sons. Both she and Sanger fled to Europe at points to escape prosecution. Although she was not truly part of the Lost Generation, Edith Wharton, the first woman to win the Pulitzer Prize for a novel (for *The Age of Innocence*, 1921), would also make her home in France, as did Anna Julia Cooper, an African-American author. Born into slavery—probably fathered by her master—Cooper wrote her first two books of historical fiction in French and earned a doctorate in history at the Sorbonne. After returning to Washington, D.C., she would live to 104 years old—long enough to support the modern civil rights movement. Cooper's words are inscribed on pages 26 and 27 of recent U.S. passports: "The cause of freedom is not the cause of a race or sect, a party or a class—it is the cause of humankind, the very birthright of humanity."

Back home, the "Harlem Renaissance" turned one of New York's African-American neighborhoods into the literary and artistic equivalent of Paris. Many black Southerners moved North during and after World War I, and the cultural energy that swept Harlem included music and art, as well as the written word. Although mostly associated with men such as James Weldon Johnson and Langston Hughes, the movement also included women. Jessie Redmon Fauset, mentioned earlier as literary editor of the NAACP's magazine, fostered the careers of many younger writers. Among them were Nella Larsen (*Quicksand*, 1928; *Passing*, 1929), who was of both African and Danish heritage, and poet/playwright Georgia Douglas Johnson, whose multiple works remained largely unpublished, even though she sometimes disguised her gender, writing as "John Temple." For forty years Johnson held "Saturday Salons" at her Washington, D.C., home, attended by many of the Harlem Renaissance writers.

Zora Neale Hurston did not really consider herself part of the Harlem Renaissance, although she lived in the same place and time. A Floridian, she was the first African-American admitted to Barnard College. After graduate study in anthropology at Columbia University, she published what she called "Negro folklore," the most famous of which is *Their Eyes Were Watching God* (1937). Fellow Floridian Marjorie Kinnan Rawlings introduced her to the great Scribner's editor Maxwell Perkins, and Hurston was also befriended by white author Fannie Hurst, whose *Imitation of Life* (1933), a novel on racial themes, was a best seller. Unfortunately, Harlem Renaissance leaders did not support Hurston when a boy unfairly accused her of sexual abuse, and she died back in Florida in extreme poverty. Decades later, African-American author Alice Walker would successfully urge that publishers reissue Hurston's work.

Inroads into Literary Journals and Learned Societies

The New Yorker began in 1925, and cartoonist Helen Hokinson was featured in one of the first issues of the magazine. Dorothy Parker joined *The New Yorker* as an editor after publishing her first book, *Enough Rope* (1926). The very talented Parker wrote in many genres, including witty feminist screenplays for Hollywood, as the writing industry expanded to that medium. Arguably the most important woman at *The New Yorker* in those early years was Katherine Angell, who joined the magazine six months after it was founded by Harold Ross and became its first fiction editor. Angell, a Bryn Mawr graduate of sophisticated literary taste, changed *The New Yorker* from a humor magazine into an important literary presence. She published the early work of, among others, Mary McCarthy, Shirley Hazzard, Vladimir Nabokov, John Cheever, and John Updike. Her editorial skills and concern for her authors were legendary. Angell's second husband was another *New Yorker* writer, E.B. White, journalist and author of beloved children's stories. Katherine Angell White remained as fiction editor until 1957, after which she continued to write occasional pieces for the magazine.

The year 1926 indeed was exceptional, as Edith Wharton, along with Mary Wilkins Freeman and Margaret Deland, both poets, novelists, and short story writers, and essayist Agnes Repplier, became the first women admitted to the National Institute of Arts and Letters (later the American Academy of Arts and Letters). Also that year, Irita Van Doren became the book review editor of the *New York Herald Tribune*—a position first held by Margaret Fuller in the 1840s. Van Doren was a member of an old New York literary family by marriage, but had grown up poor in the South. She graduated from Florida State College for Women at age seventeen and came to New York to pursue a doctorate in English literature at Columbia University. At the *Herald Tribune*, she would have a strong voice in determining what Americans read during the next four decades; booksellers depended on her weekly columns to decide what to order. From 1938 to 1963, she was the host of the popular Book and Author Luncheons cosponsored by the American Booksellers Association (ABA) and the *Herald Tribune*. The luncheons were held eight times each year and featured a wide variety of notable literary figures, including Vladimir Nabokov, Barbara Tuchman, James A. Michener, Kay Boyle, and Herman Wouk. The programs were aired on WNYC Radio; audio of many of the programs still can be accessed on its website. Van Doren received the WNBA Award (then known as the Constance Lindsay Skinner Award) in 1942.

Pearl S. Buck's China-based novel *The Good Earth* (1932) not only won the Pulitzer Prize, but in 1938, she would be the first American woman to win a Nobel Prize in literature. The daughter of missionaries to China, she did her first work there during an unhappy marriage and kept her name after marrying her publisher, Richard Walsh, in 1935. She wrote at a furious rate for the rest of her life, publishing fiction and nonfiction in both books and magazines, while also encouraging others in the industry.

Women in the Newsroom and at the Magazine Stand

Just as bookwomen, such as those of the WNBA, were more and more influential in the literary world, women were shaping the "circulation of thought," to use the WNBA founder Madge Jenison's term, in journalism. Cissy Patterson, a member of a powerful publishing family, gave up her life

Amy Loveman

Amy Loveman (1881–1955) was a founding editor of the *Saturday Review of Literature* and a member of the Book-of-the-Month Club staff. Those titles barely describe her enormous contributions at those two organizations; she was indeed the power behind the throne. After her death, Norman Cousins described her work at the *Saturday Review*: "During the first fifteen years Amy Loveman assigned most of the books for review, wrote reviews of her own, handled a regular department in the magazine...edited copy, pinned up the dummy, read page proofs, and put the magazine to bed at the printer's." For the Book-of-the-Month Club, she was an early member of the preliminary reading committee; later she was named head of the editorial department; still later she served on the Board of Judges. She read voraciously, widely, and with great discretion and insight. In her roles at the two organizations, she exerted a tremendous influence on what Americans read in the 1920s and 1930s. Friends and colleagues valued her unfailing integrity, kindness, and hard work. Loveman received the WNBA Award (then known as the Constance Lindsay Skinner Award) in 1946. From 1962 to 1969, the Women's National Book Association joined with the *Saturday Review* and the Book-of-the-Month Club to create the Amy Loveman Award, given to the college student with the best personal library.

as a socialite in 1930 to buy the moribund *Washington Herald*. She hired female reporters, assigned them topics that women found interesting, and circulation soared. Patterson took over the competing Hearst papers, and by World War II, her *Washington Times-Herald* had the largest circulation in this most news-wise of cities. Her kinswoman Alicia Patterson had the same eye for the future and would begin *Newsday* in 1940.

Dorothy Schiff pulled off the same phenomenon of reviving a dying publication in 1939, when she became publisher and editor-in-chief of the *New York Post*. Calling herself "a crusading liberal," she championed "honest unionism, social reform and humane government." Schiff also syndicated female columnists, including economist Sylvia Porter and the inimitable Eleanor Roosevelt. In another instance of women in the journalistic vanguard, Freda Kirchwey became publisher in 1933 of *The Nation* and purchased the weekly in 1937. At its helm she would shape the opinions

Former First Lady Eleanor Roosevelt and Clare Booth Luce (right) in 1955 in Rome, when Booth Luce was the U.S. ambassador to Italy.

of opinion makers until 1955. A visionary whose thought ran about a decade ahead of political trends, she was especially influential with the Roosevelt administration's New Dealers.

Clare Booth Luce, too, had developed a life of her own prior to marrying powerful publisher Henry Luce in 1935. She held top positions at Condé Nast, including as editor of *Vogue* and *Vanity Fair;* her first book, *Stuffed Shirts*, was published in 1931. Her 1936 play, *The Women*, might have been too feminist for some Depression-era audiences, with its notably all-female cast. But it nevertheless had a long life in its initial Broadway run and revivals thereafter, as well as in transfers to film (in 1939) and television (1955). She would go on to other achievements in both the literary and political worlds.

Children's Publishing Comes of Age

The "New Woman" of the 1920s also had new ideas about children, and this manifested itself in a wide range of ways in children's literature, publishing, and bookselling. Although *St. Nicholas Magazine* would stay in business until 1940, it went through a number of editors in the 1920s and was sold several times, changing its name to *St. Nicholas for Boys and Girls*. May Lamberton Becker, the journalist and literary critic, served as its editor from 1930 to 1932.

Not content with selling books, Bertha Mahony, of The Bookshop for Boys and Girls in Boston, joined with Elinor Whitney Field to create

The Horn Book Magazine, which debuted in October 1924, the first periodical to review children's literature. *The Horn Book* was a sensation in the library and publishing worlds; it continues to be a highly respected publication, true to the goals of its founders, to "blow the horn for fine books for boys and girls," as Mahony wrote in her first editorial. The 1924 timing was fortuitous; there was a groundswell of interest from several quarters in providing quality children's literature and in nurturing the authors and illustrators who could produce it.

The result benefited women, too, as children's literature further expanded into its own separate publishing empire, with room for not only writers and illustrators, but also editors and librarians who specialized in this new field and weren't shy about expressing their opinions. From 1906 to 1941 librarian Anne Carroll Moore was in charge of the Department of Work with Children at New York Public Library (NYPL) and from that perch cowed authors, publishers, and staff with her blunt critiques. She disliked E.B. White's *Stuart Little* and wrote the author a scathing letter, telling him it would ruin his career. Margaret Wise Brown's *Goodnight Moon* was another book Moore disliked; her influence was so strong that NYPL wouldn't purchase it until 1973. Despite these harsh judgments, Moore was a force for professionalism in children's library work and a tireless advocate for children's reading. At NYPL she introduced story hours, celebrated the holidays of immigrant communities, convinced the administration that children should be able to take books out of the library, wrote up standard lists of good books, and developed a stellar training program for children's librarians. During her tenure at NYPL she wielded tremendous influence in the children's publishing world.

In 1919, George Brett, the president of Macmillan, hired the first children's book editor, Louise Seaman, to head a new department of Books for Boys and Girls. Mahony, Seaman, and Moore became friends and advocates for the best in children's literature, a triumvirate that would begin to change the world of children's literature, ushering in a golden age. The year 1919 also saw the creation of Children's Book Week, founded at the urging of Franklin K. Mathiews, the librarian of the Boy Scouts of America, who was dismayed over the poor quality of literature available for children, most notably the series novels published by the Stratemeyer syndicate such as the *Hardy Boys* and the *Bobbsey Twins.*

Mathiews, Moore, and Frederick Melcher from R.R. Bowker started this annual event that was later taken over by the Children's Book Council. The 1921 creation of the Newbery Medal, for excellence in children's literature, added significant prestige to the field. The name recognized a London bookseller who was probably the first to emphasize children as book owners. The Newbery Medal has been given annually by the Association for Library Service to Children, a division of the American Library Association. Later, in 1934, ALA created the Caldecott Medal for excellence in illustration of children's books.

Publishers saw the growing market for children's books but weren't sure about its longevity or profitability, so women—still considered unfit

Virginia Kirkus

In 1925, Virginia Kirkus (1893–1980) became the founding editor at the newly established Department of Books for Boys and Girls at Harper & Brothers, one of the first such departments in the country. She was responsible for the publication of the first of the Laura Ingalls Wilder books, *Little House in the Big Woods*, but in 1932, the children's department was eliminated to cut costs. Children would have to make do with books already published. Kirkus was offered a position in the religious books department, but declined and set off on a trip to Europe.

During the trip, she refined an idea that had been percolating in her mind for several years: the Virginia Kirkus Bookshop Service. She planned to obtain galleys of forthcoming books from publishers and review them objectively, then distribute the reviews to booksellers. At that time, booksellers had no access to reviews for forthcoming books. "It struck me the booksellers were usually in the position of buying a pig in a poke," she explained later in life. "They looked over all the publishers' lists and ordered books with nothing but the publishers' say-so to guide them in deciding which books they needed in quantity." In that year, in the depths of the Depression, no one had an encouraging word for her idea. Publishers had never supplied galleys for review. Twenty publishers signed on to her plan and the first newsletter went out to ten bookstore subscribers in January 1933. Two years later, librarians began to request subscriptions.

The early issues—all titles reviewed by Kirkus herself—primarily covered popular adult books. Her reviews were short, incisive, and unbiased.

for adult book editorships—were relegated to run these new departments. It wasn't until well into the 1930s that publishers understood the windfall that could accrue from the valuable backlists these brilliant editors created. One of these exceptional women was May Massee, who founded the children's department at Doubleday, Page & Co. in 1922, only the second such department after Macmillan's. Massee stayed at Doubleday until 1933 when she left to found the children's department at The Viking Press, remaining there until 1960. She worked with a stellar lineup of children's authors, including Robert McCloskey (*Make Way for Ducklings*), Ludwig Bemelmans (*Madeline*), Marjorie Flack (*The Story About Ping*), and Munro Leaf (*The Story of Ferdinand*). Four of the

Children's book reviews started as a quarterly supplement, then advanced to twice-monthly coverage as librarians and booksellers clamored for more reviews to make the best use of their funds. The newsletter also included tips on promoting new books, and the service grew by word of mouth. In the early years, there was some grumbling from publishers about the impartiality of her reviews, but Kirkus refused to compromise the integrity she promised her subscribers. She was often correct about a book's sales potential and uncovered many "sleepers" that went on to strong sales and library circulation.

Kirkus had a strong, contemporary philosophy regarding book selection for children: "I'd give them history and politics and social problems not prettied over for the tender-minded. These young people will inherit the world we've made. Let us give them tools for understanding that world." She was active in the business until 1964, when she retired, but remained as a consultant to the new owners, Alice E. Wolff and Ruth Bernhard. In 1969, the newsletter was renamed *Kirkus Reviews*, its current title.

Kirkus' replacement at Harper's children's department was Ida Louise Raymond, who continued to acquire books from Laura Ingalls Wilder. When Raymond left, in 1940, the mantle passed to her assistant, Ursula Nordstrom, who would become the most important editorial figure in children's literature during the thirty-three years she served as editor. There were other distinguished women who headed children's departments in trade publishing houses in those years. It was an exceptional time for children's literature because of these talented women who nurtured many outstanding writers.

books she edited received the prestigious Caldecott Award and ten were Newbery Medal winners. (The WNBA gave the Constance Lindsay Skinner Award, now known as the WNBA Award, to both Massee and Moore in recognition of their stellar contributions.) By the late 1920s children's book departments had become commonplace among trade publishers, all headed by women.

Milestones for Publishing Houses

Minneapolis had been home to DeWitt Wallace, until he married Lila Acheson and moved to New York, where they used her savings to begin *Reader's Digest*. They put advertisements in the mail on their wedding day in 1922, and upon returning from their honeymoon, found fifteen hundred checks from eager subscribers. The magazine specialized in condensed versions of books, something that was of great benefit to authors and booksellers. After World War II, *Reader's Digest* would expand to publishing books of those condensed works. It did not accept advertising until 1955, and even then limited ads to products of which it approved. Lila Wallace especially promoted the arts and the publishing industry in all its aspects.

Blanche Wolf was just twenty years old in 1915 when she persuaded her fiancé, Alfred A. Knopf, to set up a publishing firm of their own. (They were married a year later.) Knopf, vice president of the firm, became one of the most influential editors of her time. She brought Harlem Renaissance writers to the firm, including the poet Langston Hughes. She traveled frequently to Europe, where she signed important writers including André Gide, Albert Camus, and Sigmund Freud. Her list appealed to changing values and literary tastes after World War I, and in 1941 she published William Shirer's *Berlin Diary* (1941), which would earn the house $1.5 million in its first year of publication. After World War II cut off European access, she turned her attention to Latin America, bringing such authors as Jorge Amado and Gilberto Freyre to American readers. Blanche Knopf was fiercely loyal to her authors, as they were to her. Among the women she published were Elizabeth Bowen, Ivy Compton-Burnett, Muriel Spark, and Nobel Prize winner Simone de Beauvoir. She received numerous honors and awards, including the Légion d'Honneur from the French government, the Brazilian National

Order of the Southern Cross, and the WNBA Award. Yet, when she occasionally met her publishing colleagues at New York's Harvard Club, she had to use the side-door "Ladies' Entrance." She also famously rejected an invitation to speak at a women's college on the future of women in publishing, saying that there was "no future worth mentioning."

Despite her huge contribution to the industry, Blanche Knopf's name may be remembered because it was her husband's name—just as was the case for Lila Wallace of *Reader's Digest* and Ellen Knowles Eayres (later Harcourt) of Harcourt Brace Publishing. Eayres offered her New York apartment as a temporary headquarters to Alfred Harcourt in 1919. He and his partner Donald Brace had worked for Henry Holt, where Eayres, a Vassar graduate, had risen from secretary to editor and publicist. Both resigned because of disagreements with Holt, and when Sinclair Lewis encouraged them to form their own publishing house, Eayres joined them.

The second book they published, *The General Theory of Employment, Interest and Money* (1936) by John Maynard Keynes, would become a bible of macroeconomic principles and put them on a solid financial basis. Eayres became the company's first children's books editor and manager of sales promotion. She traveled to publicize their list and became a director of Harcourt Brace and Company in 1921. Eayres and Harcourt later married. John Tebbel, a historian specializing in the industry, wrote, "Harcourt Brace was probably the first publishing house that even attempted to give women equal rights."

Women Booksellers Excel at Innovation

Sylvia Beach's Paris bookstore, Shakespeare and Company, was replicated by women in the United States, as *Publishers Weekly* reported that at least thirty women owned successful bookstores in the Roaring Twenties. As had Elizabeth Peabody in her Boston bookstore in the 1840s, these women were likely to offer tea and comfortable chairs for pleasant book sampling, and the same salon atmosphere for which Paris was famous.

In 1926, Madge Jenison, second president of the WNBA and cofounder of the Sunwise Turn Bookshop, wrote that "women have overrun book selling." She added that they headed most book departments in New York's department stores, and that Marcella Burns, at Chicago's Marshall

Field's book department, was particularly influential. "America will in time have a book fair conducted by the book trade," Jenison said, "but in the meanwhile, Miss Burns is doing it."

Although the trade publications of the publishing industry emphasized New York (and to a lesser extent, Chicago), in fact women were running bookstores all over the country. A 1923 article in *Independent*, an important opinion magazine of the era, detailed one in Minneapolis: "The shop has its own label, and each purchase is enticingly wrapped in lettuce-green paper and tied with tape to match. The women booksellers give the shop a personal touch; they carry sentiment into business."

An article in *Publishers Weekly* in 1928 stated that "one of the most significant developments in the field of American bookselling has been the increased coming of women into the field, not only as salesmen, as has always been the case, but in executive positions and as the organizers of new shops. This tendency is very interestingly shown in a study recently made by Marion Humble, executive secretary of the NABP. The number of new shops studied, which does not include department stores, has grown from 32 in 1919 to 206 in 1927 and 107 in a half-year of 1928—1100 bookshops all together. Of these 396, or 36% have been started by women, the percentage rising from 3% in 1919 and 16% in 1920 to an average of 40% in the later years of the record."

The WPA Offers Opportunities

The greatest impact of the Great Depression years, however, was provided by the federal government's Works Progress Administration (WPA). Along with countless blue-collar jobs, the WPA also hired people in white-collar occupations. Starving artists painted murals in post offices and courthouses, while both women and men taught music and produced plays. Its Federal Writers Project (FWP) was vital to that field, providing paychecks to people in every state. Most state FWP directors were men, but among them were fourteen women. Ethel Schlasinger was hired for the North Dakota project at the age of twenty, the only qualified person to be found in that sparsely populated state. Carita Doggett Corse headed the project in Florida and made a point of hiring black women. Other women headed the FWP in Nebraska, Minnesota, New Jersey, Maine, and New Mexico.

Frances Steloff

Frances Steloff and the Gotham Book Mart were beloved fixtures on the New York literary scene for many years. Steloff came to the book business by accident; she was a poor girl from Saratoga Springs, New York, who came to the big city at age nineteen and found a job selling corsets at Loeser's department store. A holiday transfer to the book department settled her future. She worked in various bookstores for the next few years and, despite the fact that her education had ended at seventh grade, she developed a sense for the best in literature.

In 1920 she opened the Gotham Book Mart on West 45th Street, which quickly became a haven for authors and book lovers. George and Ira Gershwin, Theodore Dreiser, Eugene O'Neill, and Ina Claire were customers in the early days, along with a distinguished roster of other artists, dancers, and playwrights. Allen Ginsberg and LeRoi Jones worked there as clerks. Steloff was a constant presence, wrapping the books, operating the cash register, pressing books on customers, always ready to talk about literature. She was feisty and indefatigable, and spent long hours doing the daily hard work of running the store. She championed the experimental and avant-garde in literature and purchased copies of *Lady Chatterley's Lover* directly from D.H. Lawrence. When she did the same for Henry Miller's *Tropic of Cancer*, she found herself in trouble with the censors. She was one of the founders of the James Joyce Society, which met at the bookstore for many years.

She sold the store in 1967, but remained an active presence, descending to the store daily from her upstairs apartment. Steloff was awarded a prize for distinguished service by the National Institute of Arts and Letters; an honorary doctorate from Skidmore College in her home town; and was honored by the WNBA as one of the Seventy Bookwomen Who Made a Difference in 1987, the year she turned one hundred. She died in 1989. Her obituary in the *New York Times* quoted her as saying, "I used to feel bitter and cheated about not having a formal education. But why should I? How could I, no matter what my education, ever have had the wonderful chance to have Thornton Wilder and other people talk to me personally and right here in my shop! As if they were in their classrooms. I couldn't ask for anything more."

Many states used the funding for tourist guides, which eventually proved to be excellent histories. Southern states did this, too, but were particularly creative in sending writers to interview elderly people who had been enslaved. The typed interviews were bound into seventeen volumes by state and became known as the "slave narratives." These books were far from fancy and were largely ignored in their own time, but three decades later, they formed a key part of the new field of African-American history.

Libraries Weather the Depression

Library patrons still expected to see women at the reference and circulation desks in their local libraries, and women were often innovators of unusual programs throughout the 1920s—but the Depression had a significant impact on libraries and many librarians lost their jobs. Although funding was drastically reduced, library services were in greater demand because people had less income and needed to borrow, not buy. Libraries became community gathering places, hosting art exhibits, recitals, and special events.

Along these lines, the Oklahoma Library Commission reported in 1934: "Economic conditions throughout the state during the past two years caused thousands of citizens to turn to the library for inspiration, economic assistance and information…[I]n spite of the handicap caused by the great reduction in appropriations, which curtailed book collections and reduced the staffs, the large increase in circulation figures is testimony to the demand which taxed the ingenuity and strength of every library in order that all might be served." In Oklahoma, as in many other states, women's clubs had been instrumental in establishing public libraries; they were often important in maintaining the libraries during the Depression by donating books and funds and providing volunteer staff.

In the array of federally funded agencies in the 1930s, there was money for library construction and programs; one of the goals was to extend library service to previously unserved areas. WPA funds were put to use renovating older library buildings and building new ones; women were hired to repair and catalog books; and traveling libraries were created to serve rural areas. In addition to providing work for writers and artists, the WPA supported libraries in some unexpected ways. Demonstration projects brought library services to remote areas, such as the project undertaken by a WPA librarian who used a houseboat to deliver books to isolated communities along the Yazoo River in Mississippi.

The Tennessee Valley Authority (TVA) engineering project, authorized by the federal government in 1933, covered multiple states in Appalachia and was designed to harness the power of the rivers in the area for energy and economic development. There was a huge influx of workers and towns built to accommodate them; in addition to housing, the TVA wanted to provide for the intellectual needs of the workers and their families. A young librarian named Mary Utopia Rothrock was hired to coordinate library services to the towns where the TVA was active.

Rothrock devised a system whereby books could be checked out to workers when they picked up their toolboxes in the morning. She went on to work with the towns under TVA jurisdiction to provide library service in any way possible: She established deposit collections in post offices, general stores, and gas stations and sent out bookmobiles and librarians on pack horses. In 1938 Rothrock was awarded the first Joseph W. Lippincott Medal by the American Library Association for her innovative approach to library service.

"Packhorse librarians" ready to deliver books to rural readers, in a program promoted by the WPA.

Pura Belpré

Pura Belpré (circa 1899–1982), librarian, author, and storyteller, was the first Puerto Rican hired by New York Public Library. In 1929 she became the Hispanic Assistant at the branch library at 135th Street in Harlem. There, in the Children's Division, Belpré discovered her love of story-telling and children's literature. At that time, NYPL had its own library science program and Belpre began her formal studies there. In a sto-rytelling course, she wrote her first children's story, *Perez and Martina*, about the love between a cockroach and a mouse. It became one of the earliest books published in English by a Puerto Rican author. In 1929 she transferred to the branch library at 115th Street where she developed Spanish-language programs for the community, including bilingual story hours, holiday celebrations, and puppet workshops.

Belpré's advocacy made the branch a cultural center for the Latino community and enriched the lives of countless children. Belpré left NYPL in 1940 to devote her time to writing her own stories and collect-ing and translating Puerto Rican folktales. She returned to NYPL in 1960 to work part-time as the Spanish children's specialist, working wherever there were large numbers of Puerto Rican children. She began work in 1968 with the South Bronx Library Project, a community outreach pro-gram to encourage library use and services in Latino neighborhoods. In 1996, several divisions of the American Library Association established the Pura Belpré Award, "presented annually to a Latino/Latina writer and illustrator whose work best portrays, affirms, and celebrates the Latino cultural experience in an outstanding work of literature for chil-dren and youth."

The WNBA Prospers

The WNBA gathered steam through the 1920s and 1930s; membership increased and programs were varied and well attended. The American Booksellers Association quickly recognized the value of the organization and proposed a merger, but was politely turned down. The Booksellers' League, however, kept its distance for another twenty years.

Monthly meetings reflected members' interests in book production, distribution, and sales, as was the case at the February 1920 monthly meeting held at the Sunwise Turn Bookshop. According to the *Publishers Weekly* reporter in attendance, a large group heard several speakers talk about the progress of a book from author to reader. Author and illustrator Hendrik W. Van Loon—who was the first to win the Newbery Medal, in 1922—spoke about the role of the illustrator; Edmund Lester Pearson from the New York Public Library spoke about how the library reaches its public; and Frederic G. Melcher of *Publishers Weekly* spoke about the connection between bookseller and reader. Minutes in the archives for the October 1920 meeting record a discussion about the establishment of a WNBA job clearinghouse. Throughout the 1920s there was a resoundingly popular annual dinner dance, with a toastmaster, author talks, and sometimes homegrown skits.

The WNBA was successful enough by 1928 that an ad headlined "Make Way for the Ladies" in *Publishers Weekly* for the WBNA's eleventh annual dinner limited ticket sales to eight hundred. The event was at the Grand Ballroom of the Hotel Commodore, with dinner "promptly at seven" and dancing at "ten sharp." The dancing slowed when Wall Street collapsed late in 1929, and in 1930, "a despairing" WNBA leader wrote of that year, "three speakers, two reporters from *Publishers Weekly*, and eleven members attended the meeting." (See Chapter 3: "From the Archives" for more information about the WNBA dinners.)

The Women's National Book Association not only survived the Depression, but under the energetic presidency of Alice E. Klutas, began its publication, *The Bookwoman*, in November 1936. Its founding editor (and financial supporter) was Constance Lindsay Skinner, a popular author, lecturer, and

From WNBA meeting minutes, May 24, 1938:

"Advances in the growth of the Association were marked by the interest and support of the American Booksellers Association and the Booksellers' League. In view of the fact that the W.N.B.A. was originally founded in defiance of the A.B.A. because the prejudice against women booksellers was still extant, the fact that this is not only completely a thing of the past but that the A.B.A. now comes to the W.N.B.A. for suggestions, is encouraging in the extreme. This has also been the case with the Booksellers' League, its President having been a guest at the February meeting."

WNBA activist. A native of British Columbia who grew up in California, she moved to New York in 1907 and was one of the many women who wrote for the *Herald Tribune.* As an editor at Farrar & Rinehart, Skinner conceived of the book series *Rivers of America,* in which writers, rather than historians, wrote about the great rivers of the United States. When she died in 1939, the WNBA created an award in her name (now the WNBA Award), honoring women for their outstanding contributions to books and through books to society. Skinner's support in creating the WNBA newsletter in 1936 helped spread the word about the organization's activities and was critical in the formation of chapters beginning in the late 1940s.

WORLD WAR II AND THE POSTWAR WORLD

While Americans were isolating themselves during the Great Depression, Asia was deep into what became World War II, as Japan conquered China and other nations during the 1930s. Relatively few Americans were caught up in that—although Eleanor B. Roosevelt, a cousin of the First Lady, was among several hundred women and children who were evacuated in 1938 after Shanghai fell. She and others wrote of the dangers there, but almost no one read Agnes Smedley's *China Fights Back: An American Woman with the Eighth Route Army* (1938). Knopf published it, and Blanche Knopf was so aware of the fascist takeovers in Europe that were forcing intellectuals into exile that she said in 1936: "There is not a...writer left in Germany who is worth thinking about." Even earlier, in 1931, author and magazine editor Dorothy Thompson interviewed Hitler. As a result of her writing, she was expelled from Germany in 1934, and *Let the Record Speak* (1939) predicted the disaster to come.

Few Americans paid attention, though, even after Germany's invasions set the continent ablaze. By 1940, Britain stood alone against dictatorship, with every other nation conquered or neutralized. Norway was one of those conquered, and Ambassador Daisy Harriman published *Mission to the North* (1941) about her harrowing escape from German planes that shot at her and others headed to neutral Switzerland. Still, most Americans wanted to stay out of the war until December 7, 1941, when Japan bombed the U.S. naval fleet docked at Hawaii's Pearl Harbor. On Christmas Day, women in the Army Nurse Corps became prisoners of war in the Philippines, and by the following June, the military was recruiting women for hundreds of non-nursing military occupational specialties. Conservative congressmen even introduced bills to follow the British example of drafting women for jobs in defense plants.

In no time at all, everything about women's traditional roles changed. They went to work in shipyards and aircraft manufacturing; they were the prime employees in dangerous munitions plants. The Women's Land Army harvested crops in the absence of male farmers; the Women's Airforce Service Pilots tested planes and taught male pilots. Millions of women earned their first paychecks, and some factories created twenty-four-hour childcare facilities. Hundreds of thousands of women learned differing cultural values as they went to far-flung parts of the world, either as part of the military or as civilians working for agencies such as the American Red Cross. Relationships between men and women changed dramatically: Countless hurried weddings meant a subsequent baby boom, while young war widows and war brides from abroad meant new issues. State laws finally began to catch up with reality, as women needed legal empowerment for such things as opening a bank deposit box without a husband's signature. Divorce laws were revised in many states. Prior to the war, for example, South Carolina law simply had no provision for divorce. Even household management had to be relearned, as everything from shoes to meat was rationed. The longtime middle-class aim of at least one maid in every home disappeared, as poor women could find jobs that were more rewarding. African-Americans and other minorities also became aware of a wider world, and many returned from their wartime experiences ready to fight for full civil rights.

These and other societal changes happened quickly, between December 1941 and September 1945. Throughout the war, Americans assumed that they would win, and postwar plans were put in place early. For many women, the intention was to return to the kitchen, families, and traditional roles. Indeed, the war was scarcely under way before the media began subtly warning women that they should not view the jobs they were begged to take as permanent. Indicative titles include "Give Back the Jobs," published by *Woman's Home Companion* in 1943, two years before the war ended. Margaret Culkin Banning had barely issued her recruitment book, *Women for Defense* (1942), when she wrote a 1943 magazine article, "Will They Go Back Home?" Many polls on the subject boiled down to one, somewhat tentative, conclusion: Most women had gone to work thinking they would do so only "for the duration," but discovered they liked being part of the labor force. What ultimately happened was that during the next decade, Rosie the Riveter would transform herself into Patsy the Pink-Collar worker.

Other surveys revealed that women—and men—intended to have children when the war ended. Young people told pollsters that they wanted large families, although not as large as their parents often had. The wartime and postwar baby boom was a happy affirmation of the future from those who felt fortunate to be alive, but the long-term trend of the twentieth century would show a rising birth rate to be a temporary blip on an otherwise downward trend. With the introduction of the birth control pill in the mid-1960s—merely two decades after the war was over—it would soon be clear that parents opted for smaller families, and that women especially opted for space in their lives beyond motherhood. Some wanted a college education, although many more continued to work and financially support their veteran husbands, whose tuition would be paid by the GI Bill. Postwar colleges, in fact, were so overcrowded with returning veterans that many states gender-integrated their previously single-sex institutions—and a few coed schools refused to accept female applicants at all. Wives of male veterans nonetheless benefited from the GI Bill, which not only subsidized education, but also granted money for starting a business or buying a home. The latter meant an especially important economic change, as millions of families moved to newly built houses in new suburbs.

Those homes were the heart of much printed material during the war, especially advertising copy. Corporations that were building tanks and trucks instead of household appliances wanted to retain customer loyalty, and they especially filled the pages of women's magazines with dream houses. Yet, even though some male advertisers cynically said that they would have to sell women on the idea of home, just as they sold them on entering defense plants, women were capable of envisioning new homemaking conveniences for themselves. Indeed, to the extent that there was a campaign to encourage women to return to homemaking, it succeeded beyond its creators' wildest dreams and soon went full circle, negating any aim of turning women into full-time homemakers. They and their families wanted not only a dream house, but also a television, a freezer, a clothes dryer, and other new products—and wanted them enough that women went back to work to pay for them. Although the back-to-the-kitchen culture was real in the immediate postwar years, it was neither as large nor as long as often portrayed.

Women also had valuable role models beyond the ubiquitous Eleanor Roosevelt: A woman, Anna Rosenberg Hoffman, held the high Pentagon rank of assistant secretary of defense and several women held powerful positions in Congress. They included New Jersey's Mary T. Norton, who chaired the House Labor Committee when labor was a major issue, both during and after the war. Edith Nourse Rogers of Massachusetts chaired the House Veterans Affairs Committee, another of the era's important concerns. Women were also involved in the creation of the United Nations and other peace-promoting organizations. Ruth Bryan Owen, who had been ambassador to Denmark in the 1930s, was one of the architects of the UN; she had already laid out her vision for world peace, *Look Forward, Warrior*, in 1942. Appointed by President Harry Truman, Florida educator Mary McLeod Bethune was the only woman of color in the entire world with an official status at the founding UN meeting. In 1946, Emily Greene Balch, an author who worked for the League of Nations after World War I, became the second American woman to win the Nobel Peace Prize.

The postwar era began, however, with the most serious reign of intellectual terror in national history. After China went communist, the House established an Un-American Activities Committee, while Joseph McCarthy—whose name became synonymous with censorship—controlled the Senate. These right-wingers subpoenaed many thoughtful writers to testify in Washington, and nervous publishers and filmmakers blacklisted them. Playwright Lillian Hellman, for instance, ironically went from earning a high income during the Great Depression to near poverty in the booming postwar years—despite her strongly anti-fascist work *Watch on the Rhine* (1941). McCarthyism was strongest during the Truman administration, and after President Dwight D. Eisenhower replaced McCarthy in 1953, the committee calmed down—although it stayed in existence for another decade.

More than anything else, it would be the advent of television that defined the 1950s. Book readership fell from its high point just a few years earlier, and some people predicted that libraries would no longer be needed. The "boob tube" took over American living rooms, with programming that portrayed an idealized version of white traditional family life. Hollywood suffered as movie attendance plummeted. Rock-and-roll music allowed teenagers of the baby boom generation to express their rebellion against authority, much to the dismay of their parents.

African-Americans took strong steps for equality during the 1950s. When Alabama's Rosa Parks refused to give up her bus seat to a white man in 1955, sparking the Montgomery bus boycott, national attention became focused on segregation in the South. In the last half of the 1950s there were many nonviolent civil rights protests, setting the stage for the passage of federal civil rights laws of the next decade. There were literary milestones as well, notably *A Raisin in the Sun*, by Lorraine Hansberry, which was the first play by an African-American woman to be produced on Broadway. *A Raisin in the Sun* went on to win the New York Drama Critics' Circle Award for best play.

More Women Write the War

As the world geared up for its biggest war, women who begged for jobs in the 1930s found themselves being begged to take jobs in the 1940s. The war also meant a shortage of everything, including paper, but the publishing industry nonetheless thrived, churning out new kinds of books in tremendous numbers. Titles alone can capture the scene. Susan B. Anthony II, niece of the famous activist, for instance, wrote *Out of the Kitchen and into the War* (1943), while well-known leftist Elizabeth Gurley Flynn penned *Women Have a Date with Destiny* (1944). These visible feminists were honest about the sexual harassment and pay discrimination that women could expect—but they also publicized what employers could do to attract women to shipyards and airplane factories, including offering childcare and take-home meals.

Even traditional homemakers got new attention with books such as M.F.K. Fisher's *How to Cook a Wolf* (1942), which dealt creatively with the war's serious changes in domesticity. Ethel Gorham's *So Your Husband's Gone to War* (1942) contained both practical advice and emotional support, including how to deal with men who preyed on women who were alone. Other telling titles from 1942 and 1943 include *Calling All Women*; *Women for Defense*; *Mothers in Overalls*; *Wanted: Women in War Industry*; *Punch In, Susie!*; *Hit the Rivet, Sister!*; and even *Wenches with Wrenches*. These and other such books attempted to persuade middle-class, literate women that they would be comfortable making bombs or assembling gas masks. A few, such as Josephine Von Miklos' *I Took a War Job* (1943), were genuine examinations based on personal experience, but many of these books were published under pseudonyms, and almost all employed the cheerful tone that the Office of War Information (OWI) wanted. Publishers and editors became a real arm of the OWI, as they decided at regular meetings (largely attended by middle-aged men) what would appeal to the young, unmarried women they wanted to attract to the military and defense industries. From books to magazines to movies and more, writers usually used a cheerful "we're in this together" style.

Women enlisted in the new military units created for them, and, as with civilian women in defense industries, commercial publishers helped recruit them. Again, the "authors" often were actually ghostwriters, but booksellers and librarians stocked titles that portrayed military life as exciting and fun: *Helmets and Lipstick*; *By Your Leave, Sir*; *Four Jills in a Jeep*; *They're All Yours, Uncle Sam!*; and *All Out, Arlene! A Story of the Girls Behind the Boys Behind the Guns*. Among the publishers responsible for such titles were Random House; Doubleday; Dodd, Mead; and G.P. Putnam's Sons.

Photojournalist Margaret Bourke-White issued several books during the war, including depictions of the Soviet Union and Italy, and, at its end, her photos in *Life* magazine were the first evidence that many Americans had of German genocide. *Life* editors debated long and hard about this decision, but in the end, Bourke-White created a new standard of what was publishable. After that, it was no longer acceptable to keep war's realities from the public. Ruth Benedict, a pioneer anthropologist at Columbia University, had a similar longtime impact. The War Department employed her as a consultant on enemy peoples during the war, and *The Chrysanthemum and the Sword* (1946) was her resulting study of Japanese culture, which the military found very useful in occupying Japan.

The cheerleader attitude that characterized much of wartime publishing diminished with its end, and books more seriously reflective of the war's devastation began to appear. One of the first was *With Love, Jane: Letters from American Women on the War Fronts* (1945), by Alma Lutz, an active feminist and Women's National Book Association member. Perhaps the most poignant memoir was that of Mary Lee Settle, a Virginian who waited until 1966 to issue *All the Brave Promises*, her unsettling account of serving in the British military before the U.S. entered the war.

Women of the Beat Generation

While most women were encouraged to stay home and provide a domestic paradise for their husbands and children after World War II, there were some who took another route. The 1950s saw the rise of the Beat Generation, and while the men received most of the attention, women were there too, as authors in their own right. Diane di Prima, Elise Cowen, Joyce Johnson, Hettie Jones, and Denise Levertov, among others, read their stories and poems in coffeehouses along with Allen Ginsberg, Jack Kerouac, William S. Burroughs, and Gregory Corso. As Brenda Knight has written in *Women of the Beat Generation: The Writers, Artists and Muses at the Heart of a Revolution*: "Women of the fifties were supposed to conform like Jell-O to a mold.... There was only one option: to be a housewife and mother.... Beat was a countercultural phenomenon, a splash of cold water in the face of a complacent society, that radiated out from certain places in America, primarily New York City and San Francisco.... Nothing could be more romantic than joining this chorus of individuality and freedom, leaving behind boredom, safety, and conformity. In many ways, women of the Beat were cut from the same cloth as the men: fearless angry, high risk, too smart, restless, highly irregular. They took chances, made mistakes, made poetry, made love, made history.... They were compassionate, careless, charismatic, marching to a different drummer, out of step.... Such nonconformity was not easy...and social condemnation was high. Joyce Johnson and Elise Cowen fled respectable homes and parental expectations. Others married and raised families, but in an utterly unorthodox manner.... Their iconoclastic lifestyle matched their literary work."

Women's Magazines Reflect Wartime Concerns

Magazines generally did a better job than books at helping women cope—especially magazines that did not measure up to the standards of literary critics. While "liberal" ones such as *The Atlantic Monthly, Harper's,* and *Saturday Review* had almost nothing to say about women's quickly changing roles, most women's magazines, even domestic magazines such as *Redbook,* realized a global transformation was underway. Indeed, *McCall's,* which was seen as so low-class that academic libraries did not bother to preserve it, was very nearly the only periodical that addressed young widows and the trauma faced by women whose men were physically or mentally disabled. *Ladies' Home Journal* once again was published by a couple, Beatrice and Bruce Gould, and it ran important articles in every issue.

Farm magazines also paid respectful attention to the effect of war on their female readers, and other women's magazines covered it as effectively as mainstream magazines. As it had done in World War I, *Woman's Home Companion* sent female reporters to battlefields and was exceptional in investigative journalism, especially exposing businesses that cheated in the rationing of scarce goods. Jesse Vann was the era's outstanding periodical publisher for African-Americans. After obtaining sole ownership of the *Pittsburgh Courier* in 1940, she informed her fifty-five thousand subscribers nationwide of new opportunities for blacks created by the war. Vann was the publisher until her 1963 retirement, and her editorials made her a pioneer in the modern civil rights movement.

But *Independent Woman,* the monthly magazine of Business & Professional Women (BPW), far exceeded any other periodical in its range of wartime topics. BPW began in the Midwest in the 1920s, and by the 1940s, was more feminist than the League of Women Voters, which had been established at the same time. *Independent Woman* editorially supported women in the military, endlessly urged women to take jobs in defense industries, crusaded for equal pay, and regularly asked readers to use their vacations to serve with the Women's Land Army, an arm of the Agriculture Department. The magazine was unparalleled in its realistic tone: It did not engage in faux morale building or gloss over women's genuine problems. Others would have done well to emulate it, but its audience was limited to BPW members.

Women also entered advertising in greater numbers. Because many corporations could not sell their longtime products, they placed ads to retain postwar loyalty. Women were particularly good at writing ads that promised wonderful new refrigerators and washing machines when, at last, factories retooled from making guns and tanks. Again, though most advertising agencies were run by men, and despite wartime shortages, magazines continued to profit from ads featuring liquor and cigarettes.

The transition from war to postwar can be seen in the life of Oveta Culp Hobby. Head of the Women's Army Corps during the war, she returned to Texas but then went back to Washington, D.C., in the 1950s as the first head of the Department of Health, Education, and Welfare. After that, she had a third career as publisher of the *Houston Post* and as a pioneer investor in television.

Women in Publishing at Mid-Century

As John Tebbel writes in *A History of Book Publishing*, a survey done in 1918 during the last gasps of the Edwardian era showed eleven New York publishing houses that employed no women at all, while a 1950 study by the Magazine Guild showed that 80 percent of people employed in publishing were women. Of course, the study went on to show that women were chief executives at just four of the 546 respondents. Women's weekly salaries in publishing averaged around $50 in 1950, while male associate editors were paid more than twice that, about $125. Even for executives, salaries were low, but women's salaries were the lowest.

Women continued to be most likely to hold executive positions in the world of children's books. Ursula Nordstrom and Margaret McElderry were in the second generation of children's book editors, but their contributions were arguably even greater than their predecessors. Nordstrom followed Louise Raymond as head of the department of Books for Boys and Girls at Harper & Brothers in 1940 and remained in that position until 1973. Laura Ingalls Wilder and Margaret Wise Brown were among the authors she inherited and nurtured. Nordstrom believed that children needed the most creative, imaginative literature; she was a tireless crusader against the older moralizing children's books. For teenagers, she championed psychological realism against the pallid books previously available. She encouraged many writers and illustrators whose books have become well-loved classics: Maurice Sendak, E.B. White, Tomi Ungerer, Louise Fitzhugh, Shel Silverstein, and Karla Kuskin, to name only a few. Her impact and influence have earned her comparison with Maxwell Perkins, the legendary editor of Thomas Wolfe, F. Scott Fitzgerald, Marjorie Kinnan Rawlings, and Zora Neale Hurston.

Margaret McElderry worked with Anne Carroll Moore at the New York Public Library in the 1930s. During World War II she worked in the Office of War Information, and in 1945 she became the editor of children's books at Harcourt Brace, where she remained until 1971, when, amazingly, she was told her point of view was passé. She left for Atheneum, where she founded Margaret McElderry Books, the first imprint to bear an editor's name. At Atheneum she continued to nurture writers and edit until well into her nineties. Her books are staples of children's and young adult literature, including *The Borrowers* by Mary Norton and Susan Cooper's *The Dark Is Rising* series. She searched out the best in foreign literature, introducing U.S. children to the best postwar picture books and novels from Europe and Japan. In 1952, her books won both the Newbery and the Caldecott Medals, a first for any children's editor.

Inspired by the success of Nordstrom, McElderry, and their brilliant predecessors, as well as by the profits to be made, publishers hired more women to shepherd children's books into the hands of young readers. Between 1940 and 1960 the number of children's editors grew: Helen Hoke at Messner; Lillian J. Bragdon at Knopf; Alice Dalgliesh at Scribner's; Beatrice Creighton at Lothrop, Lee & Shepard; Marie Jessup at Morrow; and Virginia Fowler at Holt were among them.

Among the top women in the circulation of thought was Helen Rogers Reid. She took over sole editorship of the *New York Herald Tribune* in 1947 and hired an unprecedented number of women, many of whom held multiple roles as bookwomen. Ishbel Ross, for example, not only wrote for the newspaper, but also published some twenty biographies, many of them about women. Also in 1947, Agnes Rogers Allen became the founding editor of Reader's Digest Condensed Books, which revolutionized the industry with its abbreviated versions of books. She, too, contributed to the feminist movement, especially with *Women Are Here to Stay* (1949). That year also saw the publication of Margaret Mead's important *Male and Female*, as well as *An American Argument*, written by the famed Pearl S. Buck with a foreword by Eslanda Goode Robeson, an African-American writer.

New Markets for Booksellers

World War II brought opportunities into the bookselling arena. An article by Rosejeanne Slifer in the Spring 1944 *Bookwoman* cited the war as an opportunity to enlarge the market of book buyers: "The tire and gasoline situation and the shortage of merchandise in other fields are diverting more people with greater purchasing power into the bookshops each day. Many of them have never bought books before. Will they again? Will they after the war, or will the acquisition of books be a mere stop-gap until they have more ways to spend their money? Frankly, I believe this to be...the responsibility of the far sighted bookseller."

"Servicemen are excellent bookstore customers," she added, and recounted a story of a Navy man who was buying books for his baby "in case he wouldn't be around later." The previous Christmas had seen the greatest sales ever of children's books, partly because toy manufacturers could not get materials. Yet, Slifer wrote a few paragraphs later, "children's classics have in large part gone out of print for the duration." Presumably publishers decided to use scarce paper for new books, not classics—a decision that probably was shortsighted in terms of welcoming people who never before had bought a book.

Women booksellers found niches in the antiquarian field, like Elisabeth Woodburn, who sold agricultural and horticultural books from her farm in Hopewell, New Jersey (which she named Booknoll Farm), from the 1950s through the 1980s. Woodburn was one of the founders and a president of the Antiquarian Booksellers' Association of America. Eleanor Lowenstein opened the Corner Book Shop in 1940 along a stretch of Fourth Avenue in New York called Book Row and despite her intent to specialize in psychology, she and her shop became internationally known as a source for new, used, and rare books on food, cookery, and wine.

Leora Rostenberg and Madeleine Stern

Columbia University was the meeting place for two of the most influential women in the antiquarian book trade. Madeleine Stern and Leora Rostenberg became friends in the 1930s when they were both graduate students there. Columbia rejected Rostenberg's dissertation, and she apprenticed herself to a rare book dealer in New York. Several years later, Stern loaned her $1,000 to set up her own dealership and then joined her as a business partner. Rostenberg and Stern Rare Books, run out of their Upper East Side apartment, became an institution in the antiquarian book trade for over fifty years. The two women were known for their acuity in identifying and evaluating rare books; they had *fingerspitzengefühl*, which best describes their rare talent to sense the electricity emanating from a literary treasure. Even before their business began, they had made a remarkable discovery: that Louisa May Alcott had written racy thrillers anonymously or under the pseudonym A.M. Barnard. Alcott wrote these risqué—and very successful—stories to support herself and her family. In the 1970s, Stern oversaw the publication of the stories in several anthologies, including *Behind a Mask: The Unknown Thrillers of Louisa May Alcott*.

Stern and Rostenberg were indefatigable searchers for literary treasure, traveling through Europe as well as digging in old libraries and barns. They were at the first meeting of the Antiquarian Booksellers' Association of America in 1949 and Rostenberg was a past president of the organization. Stern founded the New York Antiquarian Book Fair, held annually since 1960. In 2006 the Grolier Society honored Stern for her efforts to have women accepted in the antiquarian book world. They received other awards and honors, especially for their Alcott scholarship. Rostenberg and Stern wrote two delightful books about their work and their friendship: *Old Books, Rare Friends: Two Literary Sleuths and Their Shared Passion* (1997) and *Bookends: Two Women, One Enduring Friendship* (2001).

Library Expansion in the War and Postwar Periods

The Victory Book Campaign during World War II brought the American Library Association, the American Red Cross, and the USO together to collect seventeen million books and periodicals for American soldiers. Volunteers collected, sorted, and packed the donated materials for shipment to military bases and hospitals in the U.S. and Europe. Libraries were facing shortages

Volunteer service members of the Red Cross, along with soldiers from Fort Myer, Virginia, at the U.S. Capitol building, helping as members of Congress donated books for the Victory Book Campaign.

and funding cuts during the war, but references to Nazi book burning gave urgency to the book drives. Posters quoted President Roosevelt: "No man and no force can take from the world the books that embody man's eternal fight against tyranny. In this war, we know, books are weapons."

In the early 1950s, when fear of communist conspiracies was at its height and censorship of literature and the arts was rampant, the American Library Association met with the American Book Publishers Council and responded with the Freedom to Read statement, which begins, "The freedom to read is essential to our democracy." The statement affirms, among other things, the right of readers to choose their own reading materials without judgements or labeling; the responsibility of librarians and publishers to make available the "widest diversity of views and expressions, including those that are unorthodox, unpopular, or considered dangerous by the majority."

In 1956 Congress authorized the Library Services Act (LSA), which provided funds to extend library service to areas with a population under ten thousand. As a result, bookmobiles became a familiar sight in the rural landscape. In Hennepin County, Minnesota, for example, two bookmobiles made stops in small towns but often traveled from farm to farm. Farm families filled washtubs with books to have enough until the next monthly visit. In the 1920s, Boston bookstore owner Bertha Mahony had experimented with the idea of a motorized vehicle. With support from the Boston Women's Educational and Industrial Union, she created a $5,500 truck designed to carry books to rural areas—but after the Great Depression and the fuel rationing of World War II, the idea had died. With the impetus of the Library Services Act, new cars, and new prosperity of the 1950s, it was revived.

The LSA also provided funds for state agencies to expand programs and create multi-type library systems, allowing shared resources among academic, public, private, and school libraries. These years also saw the development of multi-branch public library systems, another way in which the reading public benefited from pooled resources. Library services were extended to prisons, hospitals, and other nontraditional settings. All these new services provided opportunities for women, who still dominated the profession numerically; gradually they rose through the ranks into management positions. The 1970s would see women make real gains.

Some librarians found interesting careers in nontraditional jobs, but unlike men they had to demonstrate the value of their work. Margaret Herrick began working as a volunteer at the Academy of Motion Picture Arts and Sciences in the early 1930s. She saw the need for a film study collection and laid the groundwork for what has become one of the finest film libraries in the world, but it wasn't until 1936 that her position was made formal and she was given a title and a salary. In 1943, with the men off at war, she became executive director of the Academy, a position she kept until her retirement in 1971. Herrick expanded the programs and services of the Academy, including the transformation of the Academy Awards ceremony into a nationally televised event. She is also credited with naming the Oscar. The library at the Academy was renamed in her honor.

The WNBA Expands

When the WNBA held a regular meeting in January of 1943, the topic was "Book Publishing in War Times"—but the evening's hit was Mrs.

Marion Kister, a Polish exile who had been in the book business there until the war began. *The Bookwoman* reported: "She told of the type of books that people were reading in those war-ravished countries—and quite tore our heart-strings with her stories of the books (or pamphlets) that they printed on *Cooking Without Meat, Cooking Without Flour,*

Librarians of Distinction: *Clara Estelle Breed*

Clara Estelle Breed (1906–1994) was a beloved children's librarian in the San Diego Public Library from 1928 to 1945. In 1942, when one hundred and twenty thousand Japanese-Americans were forced from their homes into internment camps, Breed stood at the train station to wave goodbye to her young friends. As she saw them off, she distributed stamped self-addressed postcards, asking them to write to her and describe their life in the camps. A reliable correspondent, she became their contact with home, sending books and packages, assisting with requests for supplies, and providing emotional support. Many of the children were in the Poston War Relocation Camp in Arizona where she made several visits.

Breed's commitment to her young Japanese friends was remarkable because of the widespread fear and hatred associated with anything Japanese at that time. She was outspoken about the injustice the U.S. government had committed against the Japanese-American community and wrote to members of Congress protesting the internment. She also wrote articles that appeared in *Library Journal* and *The Horn Book Magazine*.

After the war, Breed continued to correspond with many of the children. In the early 1990s, she offered the correspondence, along with the journals, notebooks, and manuscript copies of the articles she'd written about the children in the camps, to one of her former correspondents, Elizabeth Yamada. In 1993, Yamada donated them to the Japanese American National Museum in Los Angeles.

After the war, Breed became San Diego city librarian, a position she held for twenty-five years, during which time she introduced many innovative services. In 1991 she was honored at the Poston Camp III reunion in San Diego. The story of her friendship with the interned Japanese-American children is told in the children's book *Dear Miss Breed: True Stories of the Japanese American Incarceration During World War II* and a *Librarian Who Made a Difference*, by Joanne Oppenheim. Clara Breed died in 1994, aged eighty-eight.

—Linda Rosen

Cooking Without Vegetables—particularly when she said a title should have been Cooking Without Food."

The WNBA heatedly debated whether to hold its annual festive dinner in March: "Some of our members said to go ahead and have one—we needed it. Others said, 'This is war times! We must not do it!' However, we had it!

Augusta Braxton Baker

The life of Augusta Braxton Baker (1911–1998) was driven by a love of stories and storytelling. From her childhood, spent with her beloved grandmother, who told her stories and taught her to read, she knew that books were the love of her life. In 1934 she was the first African-American to earn a master's degree in librarianship from the New York College for Teachers (now the State University of New York at Albany). Baker was initially denied a place in the program but Eleanor Roosevelt advocated for her acceptance. In 1937 she was hired by the New York Public Library at the 135th Street library (now the Countee Cullen Library) in Harlem. While there, Baker was dismayed by the stereotypical, negative portrayals of black children in much of the literature she saw and established the James Weldon Johnson Memorial Collection of Children's Books in an effort to foster the publication of quality literature for African-American children. She provided encouragement to authors and illustrators and published bibliographies of recommended books, including *Books About Negro Life for Children*, published in 1946, updated in 1971, and renamed *The Black Experience in Children's Books*, so that libraries would have a resource for purchases.

In 1953, Baker became the storytelling specialist and assistant coordinator of children's services at NYPL, the first African-American librarian in an administrative position. Later, she became the coordinator of children's services, overseeing all children's programming. During those years she was a consultant to the television program *Sesame Street* and she began to teach and lecture on storytelling and children's literature. She was also active in the American Library Association's Children's Services Division and served on the Newbery and Caldecott Medal committees. Although she retired from NYPL in 1974, she became storyteller in residence at the University of South Carolina, where she remained for ten years.

No dancing this year, just a good dinner, as inexpensively as possible, with some top-flight speakers." Among those speakers was Dorothy Thompson, who recently had added to her anti-fascist books with *Listen, Hans* (1942), a title that reflected enmity with Germany. The Soviet Union, of course, was an ally during World War II, something that was confirmed by another speaker, the wife of the ambassador from Moscow.

The end of the war meant an end to the problems of scarcities, but the Fall 1945 edition of *The Bookwoman*, which coincided with the war's September end, showed little evidence of a changed place for female authors. It recommended ten books on the postwar world—all by men. In an editorial choice that might sound odd to our ears today, it quoted an editorial from *Yank*, the military publication for soldiers overseas: "The books that are read and bought in quantity are the books that people make friends with, that they like as men like an old hat or women a comfortable girdle."

The war had been over for two years when the WNBA launched its first expansion outside of New York City. Margaret Kinzer of the Methodist Publishing House founded a Chicago chapter in 1947. A Boston chapter would develop in 1954, and one in Nashville the following year. The 1958 winner of the Constance Lindsay Skinner Award (now the WNBA Award) was author Edith Hamilton, who surprised publishers with the popularity of her scholarly books on ancient civilizations. The *Baltimore Sun* ran a feature article on the award, complete with a photograph of Hamilton at her writing desk at age ninety.

The WNBA was interested in giving women the education they needed for their careers, whether in bookselling or publishing. Courses in bookselling, which began in the 1920s, were continued in the 1940s in the New York and the Chicago chapters. The classes covered children's bookselling and general bookselling, aiming to give young women the expertise they needed for their careers. Beginning in 1950, the WNBA awarded an annual scholarship to a woman to attend the prestigious Radcliffe College Summer Course in Publishing Procedures. In May 1952, *The Bookwoman* reported: "This scholarship has just been awarded to Rose-ellen Currie. Miss Currie attended New York State College for Teachers, Albany, and graduated cum laude from Adelphi College in January 1952. For the past few months she has been employed as a

WNBA Sponsors Interview with Eleanor Roosevelt at the Festival of Books, on WNYC Radio

"On Saturday, March 27th, WNBA's contribution to the 1954 Festival of Books on WNYC was a discussion by Mrs. Eleanor Roosevelt, of 'How Books Influenced My Career,' with Margaret Scoggin of the New York Public Library as interviewer. Miss Scoggin's gifts as an interviewer are well known and on this occasion there was an added quality. The respect and affection in which the world holds Mrs. Roosevelt were in Margaret Scoggin's voice as she asked her questions. As was to be expected, it made rewarding listening.

"Mrs. Roosevelt spoke of her own early reading, an almost constant occupation, interrupted only by necessary chores, speedily dispatched, in order to return to her book. She grew up in a home where she was surrounded by books—constantly exposed to all kinds. There was no censorship, but occasionally a book on which she had commented 'disappeared from the shelf for a time.' To her own children she read the classics aloud, skipping the long-winded passages to hold their interest.

"'If children are really to read and love books,' Mrs. Roosevelt continued, 'parents must read and love them too, and make books easily available to their children. If parents fail to do this then librarians must take up the responsibility.'

"The discussion turned on leading women in America who depended a great deal on books for their education. Miss Scoggin spoke of Mary McLeod Bethune, Catherine Cornell, Constance Lindsay Skinner and asked about eminent women in other countries. Mrs. Roosevelt told of Mme. Pandit, one of the most cultivated women in the world, for whom books built the road to an understanding of the world and its people.

"'There was my husband,' said Mrs. Roosevelt. She dwelt on President Roosevelt's wonderful ability to read any kind of book at any time. She attributed to this informal reading his depth of understanding and breadth of knowledge in so many and such widely varied fields.

"Never stop reading, was the sum of Mrs. Roosevelt's advice. Education is a lifelong process and does not end with school; books carry on where formal education leaves off."

—Reported in *The Bookwoman* (vol. 16, no. 2. Spring, 1954)

secretary at Charles Scribner's Sons. There were, this year, 36 applicants for the scholarship, from 16 states including MA, NY, PA, OK, and

WA. The applicants were college students, teachers, authors, secretaries, librarians and women employed in newspapers and book and magazine publishing." (See Chapter 3: "From the Archives" for more information about courses sponsored by the WNBA.)

The relatively new chapter in Chicago hosted an extremely popular event in January 1950, when an overflow crowd appeared at the literary seminar "Writing and its Consequences" cosponsored with the University of Chicago. According to Fanny Butcher, who would receive the Constance Lindsay Skinner Award in 1955, "Nearly 75 people who hadn't been foresighted enough to get series tickets had to zip up their galoshes, put on their overcoats, and go back home." Chicago's welcoming attitude for bookwomen meant that not even standing room was available.

In this era, much of the networking among bookwomen took place at book fairs, which, of course, attracted many booksellers, as well as countless readers who otherwise might not have bought books. Schools frequently sent busloads of children chaperoned by librarians, as book fairs became an annual feature of almost every city in the 1950s. Postwar prosperity allowed families to travel to fairs and buy books, and book fairs provided an excellent venue for sellers, publishers, authors, and others at which to meet. National and even international fairs would do a great deal in the next decades to expand the circulation of thought.

At intervals throughout the 1950s, the WNBA participated in projects for the collection and distribution of books to settlement houses, libraries, and centers serving underprivileged children and adults in poor areas in the U.S. and other countries. The WNBA archives contain a photograph of a group of women packing books for shipment to India, most likely to the Indian Office of Education in New Delhi, which had been receiving books from the Cleveland chapter.

In 1959, at the urging of Pearl S. Buck, the WNBA became a non-governmental organization (NGO) member of the United Nations associated with the Department of Public Information. In this position, the WNBA has promoted UN goals and worked for the support of those goals in the wider community, in effect serving as a spokesperson for the UN, with its members attending briefings, workshops, and conferences. The WNBA has had five NGO representatives: Beatrice James, Helen Wessells Hettinger, Rose Eichelberger, Claire Friedland, and Sally Wecksler.

Book-A-Day Program for President Dwight D. Eisenhower

In the fall of 1955, President Dwight D. Eisenhower suffered a heart attack while vacationing in Colorado. In those days, cardiologists favored a long convalescence, and he spent several months at his farm in Gettysburg, Pennsylvania. WNBA members saw this enforced rest as an opportunity to supply the president with reading material that reflected his interests; thus the "Book-A-Day Plan" was born. Gathering books from friends in the book industry, the WNBA sent the president a book every day for twenty-six days. Each book had a special bookplate designed by the artist Joseph Trautwein and the daily packages each bore a stamp reading "Postmaster: Please Rush—It's A-Book-A-Day for President Eisenhower."

A letter to the president on April 5, 1956, read in part: "We are very happy to know that you are on the road to good health. To provide some restful entertainment and pleasure, the Women's National Book Association has collected from publishers new books for you which we hope you will enjoy." Everyone knew that the president was an avid fisherman, golfer, painter, and bridge player, and that he had played football at West Point. The books reflected those interests as well as American history, historical fiction, and even a book of cartoons.

At the Eisenhower Presidential Library and Museum, notations in the card catalog about each book state that it was donated by the WNBA, part of the Book-A-Day program, so the gifts will always be remembered. Jo Jasper Turner, then president of the WNBA, received a thank-you note from the president, in which he wrote: "I am grateful to you, and to the Women's National Book Association, for your kindness in sending me a book for each day of the remainder of my stay here. It is a unique and thoughtful gift and one that I am thoroughly enjoying since in Gettysburg I have more time for reading than ordinarily I can find. Won't you please accept for yourself, and convey to your membership, my warm and sincere appreciation?"

Some of the titles included in the mailing:

The Field and Stream Treasury
The Bridge Player's Bedside Companion by Albert Ostrow
Football's Greatest Coaches by Edwin Pope
Andrew Jackson: Symbol for an Age by John William Ward
Andersonville by MacKinlay Kantor
The New Yorker 1950–1955 Album

In January 2001, Jill A. Tardiff (WNBA-NYC chapter) was appointed to the position of chief representative, and is currently serving in that role.

An unsigned article in *Publishers Weekly* for February 23, 1952, had the following to say about the WNBA:

> *There is no necessity of separating women's contributions to the book trade from that of men—we are not usually in favor of segregation in any form—but it must be admitted that the WNBA, in the 35 years since Madge Jenison of Sunwise Turn started it on its way, has done much to make clear that women have very special contributions to make to the affairs of the American book trade.*

THE ERA OF SECOND WAVE FEMINISM

Because millions of potential fathers were overseas during World War II, a baby boom followed during the 1950s—but within a decade, in the 1960s, women would have access to convenient and reliable birth control. For the first time in human history, women had a choice on whether or not to become pregnant—and that would transform absolutely everything.

Organized feminism revived in the 1970s, and women won many political goals, including laws against discrimination in employment, credit, and other areas. Court rulings also contributed to female freedom, especially *Eisenstadt v. Baird* (1968), which struck down a state ban on sales of birth control pills, and *Roe v. Wade* (1973), which struck down Texas' strict law on abortions.

The 1980s brought political backlash, as the Republican Party rescinded its previous support for the Equal Rights Amendment: It had gained the necessary two thirds of both houses of Congress in the 1970s, but died in state legislatures in the 1980s. The 1990s saw the election of many more women to office, with 1992 being dubbed "The Year of the Woman." As the century ended, however, women's average wages remained stuck at about 76 percent of those of men, and much remained to be done.

Eleanor Roosevelt—an author and newswoman, as well as First Lady— is strongly and properly associated with the Great Depression of the 1930s and World War II in the 1940s, but her leadership continued into the 1960s. She chaired the Presidential Commission on the Status of Women, a wholly new governmental agency that President John F. Kennedy created during his first year in office. The commission conducted thoughtful research and pondered important questions, such as why the percentage of female college students had slipped from 47 percent in 1920 to 35 percent in 1958. Its first report in 1961 was only seventy-five pages, but its 1963 report, *American Women,* would weigh in at three hundred pages and feature an introduction by Margaret Mead. Among other things, the report revealed that only 7 percent of the nation's attorneys were women, and fewer than 4 percent were physicians.

The commission led directly to formation of the National Organization for Women (NOW). Although author Betty Friedan (*The Feminine Mystique,* 1963) was widely seen as NOW's founder, its first chairwoman was Kathryn Clarenbach of the University of Wisconsin. The work that she and others did for the presidential commission made them keenly aware of women's needs, but because that body was publicly funded, their political action was limited. The result was NOW, with thirty out of three hundred charter members attending the first organizational meeting in

The National Organization for Women (NOW), founded in 1966, is one of the most enduring outgrowths of second wave feminism. NOW has helped mobilize activists throughout its long history, including, as pictured here, those at a protest in December of 2000 in Washington against the Supreme Court ruling that decided the 2000 presidential election in favor of George W. Bush.

Washington, D.C., on October 29, 1966. Soon the organization had chapters throughout the nation, and within a few years, NOW had absolutely revolutionized American thought on women.

Bookwomen in the Sixties

The decade began with a significant change: In 1961, for the first time in nineteen years, a woman won the Pulitzer Prize in Fiction—and Harper Lee's *To Kill a Mockingbird* would go on to have a powerful impact even in the twenty-first century. To be sure, she didn't use her first name, Nelle, and many thought that the author was a man. Moreover, almost every publisher in New York had rejected the manuscript by the unknown Alabaman, until Tay Hohoff, who was a senior editor at Lippincott, took a serious look.

Helen Gurley Brown's *Sex and the Single Girl* (1962) had only an obscure publisher—until it stayed on the *New York Times* best-seller list for twenty-six weeks. Her candidly cheerful celebration of the unmarried state came before the serious feminism and scholarly research of Betty Friedan's *The Feminine Mystique*, which found a home at W.W. Norton. An Arkansas native, Brown later impressed the magazine industry by completely revolutionizing *Cosmopolitan* magazine.

The feminist revolution of the 1970s was real and would soon accomplish much, yet women won fewer Pulitzer Prizes than in any other decade, past or future. Compared with the 1920s and 1930s, when women won in ten of the original categories that date to 1917, there were just six female winners in those categories during the 1970s—and half were for writing in newspapers, not books. Two women did win in general nonfiction, a category that began in 1962. They were Annie Dillard in 1975 for *Pilgrim at Tinker Creek*, and Barbara Tuchman, who won her second prize in 1972 for *Stilwell and the American Experience in China, 1911–1945*. Her previous award had been in 1963, also in general nonfiction, for *The Guns of August*, on the origins of World War I. As of 2016, Tuchman remains the only woman to have won two Pulitzer Prizes. Several men have been so honored, with the first being novelist Booth Tarkington, who won in 1919 and again in 1922.

Women rebounded with Pulitzer Prizes in the 1980s, with winners in fifteen of the original categories. The newer prize for general nonfiction went to Susan Sheehan for her study of mental illness, *Is There No Place on Earth for Me?* (1983), published by Houghton Mifflin. Elizabeth Frank won the 1986 prize for biography with *Louise Bogan: A Portrait.* Louise Bogan was the first female poet laureate at the Library of Congress, appointed in 1945—and her biography was the first written by and about a woman to win the prize since 1917, when Julia Ward Howe's daughters, Laura Richards and Maude Howe Elliott, wrote about her. Although published by Knopf, both Frank and her subject remained obscure to most readers. Instead, the publishing phenomenon of the 1980s was "*... And the Ladies of the Club.*" Its author, Helen Hooven Santmyer, was nearly ninety years old and a retired librarian and English professor. At almost twelve hundred pages, the novel featured an Ohio women's club that began in 1868; initially published by Ohio State University Press, Putnam made it an unlikely commercial success.

Newspapers and Magazines Help Define an Era

Without a doubt, Katharine Graham of the *Washington Post* was the most influential newspaper publisher of either gender, as she courageously empowered investigative journalists who brought down the Nixon administration in 1974. Her male colleagues had already rewarded her courage in 1972, when they elected her as the first female president of the American Newspaper Publishers Association because of her publication of the secret Pentagon Papers that revealed the dark side of the Vietnam War. Graham was also the first woman on the board of the Associated Press—something that demonstrates women's traditionally inferior place, given that AP had employed countless women since its inception in 1846.

It was under Graham's leadership, too, that the *Post's* Meg Greenfield became the first female editor of the paper's editorial page. Greenfield was also the first woman *at a major paper* to win the Pulitzer Prize for editorial writing—even though that prize began in 1917. The only other winner had been Hazel Brannon Smith of *The Advertiser* in Lexington, Mississippi, who was recognized in 1964 for her brave editorials on racial integration. As the Pulitzer committee began to create more and more prizes in journalism—categories such as spot news photography and investigative reporting, women won more attention, especially for news that hadn't been previously reported, such as domestic violence.

Graham also made a major donation that allowed journalist and author Gloria Steinem and co-founder Dorothy Pitman-Hughes to begin *Ms.* magazine in 1972. Like Lucy Stone's *Woman's Journal* in the nineteenth century, *Ms.* managed to be both revolutionary and a long-term financial success. It is still in business in 2017, and the indefatigable Steinem still travels the country with her feminist message. Although Steinem is most strongly associated with *Ms.*, Elizabeth Fosling Harris, formerly with *Newsweek*, was its publisher. Letty Cottin Pogrebin, also a founder, wrote widely on feminist issues, including *Getting Yours: How to Make the System Work for the Working Woman* (1975).

Ms. successfully withstood competition from several feminist publications. Among them was *Up From Under*, a mail-only periodical that had a socialist ideology, while also issuing advice on everything from fixing toilets to understanding ovulation. *Off our backs* deliberately used lowercase for its name; published by a collective and often called *oob*, it included several lesbians on its proudly unpaid staff. *New Woman*, which *Saturday Review* called the *Playboy* of the new magazines, was intended to be shocking—even under consulting editorship from Caroline Bird, a serious scholar. *Progressive Woman*, published in Indiana, was for "the mature woman who is working…to achieve." *You* targeted a young audience assumed to be white, while *Essence* was aimed at black women. Even *Feminist Speeches* sought a place in this new market, emulating *Vital Speeches*, a magazine that long had communicated the thoughts of international leaders.

Cathleen Black joined *USA Today* in 1983, the year after it was founded, serving as both president and publisher. Black had already made her mark as the publisher of *New York* magazine. Many people were skeptical of a newspaper aimed at travelers that lacked any specific geographical identity—but, like Alicia's Patterson's *Newsday*, Black's model worked. Her colleagues would show their respect by electing her the first female president of the Newspaper Association of America in 1991.

Despite the popularity of meaningfully titled *Ms.* magazine, it wasn't until 1986 that the *New York Times* was willing to use that term when the marital status of a woman was unknown. Not surprisingly, women at the *Times* were not as happy as those at Katharine Graham's *Washington Post*, and they went on strike in 1978. Part of the settlement was a promise to fill 25 percent of the *Times'* senior news positions with women. Even

The cultural and intellectual influence of Katharine Graham—at the helm of the *Washington Post* from the early 1960s to the early 1990s— is hard to overstate. She is pictured here in 1966 at a masked ball at the Plaza Hotel in New York with Truman Capote.

more strikingly, Le Anne Schreiber was named sports editor, where she supervised a fifty-five-member, mostly male, writing staff. The late 1970s also marked the first appearance of the term "glass ceiling," representing the limits on women's advancement.

"If Wonder Woman Were Alive Today, She'd Probably Be in the Typing Pool"

This was the title Rita Black chose for her 1973 article in the trade publication *Book Production Industry*. Even the women who had worked their way to the top of the profession acknowledged its truth, saying that

GLORIA STEINEM
ON HOW
WOMEN VOTE

MONEY FOR
HOUSEWORK

NEW FEMINIST:
SIMONE
DE BEAUVOIR

BODY HAIR: THE
LAST FRONTIER

WONDER WOMAN FOR PRESIDENT

PEACE AND JUSTICE IN '72

Launched by Gloria Steinem and Dorothy Pitman-Hughes, *Ms.* magazine has been at the forefront of the women's movement since its founding in 1972. Pictured here is one of the magazine's first covers.

they were often expected to do their own typing—something that was never the case for male executives of that era. Businessmen were proud of their inability to type, and they dictated their correspondence to a female stenographer. If they were up to the technology, they might speak to a Dictaphone or tape recorder, from which the secretary would type. Male authors typed, but executives did not. Typing was a symbol of status in the office, and the broader message was that gender limited business careers.

Ursula Nordstrom had risen to senior vice president at Harper & Row—in charge of juvenile books, of course—and commented on what it was like to be a woman in publishing in the 1970s:

> *You are going to have to live constructively, trying to never let feelings of bitterness and resentment damage you, and you are going to have to fight for the things in which you believe. I feel that women have just begun to scratch the surface of finding their rightful place in all aspects of the book world. I think the prejudices are deep, deep, deep. Our conditioning is very different from what men's has been and this makes it hard for women.... [Prejudices] have been there for many centuries. They will not be overcome in a few years.*

Mary V. Gaver, a former American Library Association president, president of the WNBA-NYC chapter, and a 1973 WNBA Award winner, began her career as a school librarian and had wide knowledge of the industry when she said in a speech: "I'm not a so-called women's libber specialist, but I am very much aware of the problems and needs of equality." She went on to cite demonstrable statistics, including the fact that just four women were head librarians at the nation's eighty-four research-level university libraries. Her most salient example of commercial success was Helen Honig Meyer, then president of Dell, which specialized in paperbacks. Unlike most women in publishing, Meyer never went to college, but rose to the top job after forty-nine years with Dell.

Gaver's speech also noted a phenomenon that others were only barely beginning to grasp: In traditionally female fields such as teaching and librarianship (and nursing), affirmative action in the 1970s could mean more bias against women, not less. She said, "In a few states, I have been told by the editor of *School Library Journal*, the certification regulations are being deliberately rewritten so as to discriminate against the qualifications of most of the women in the state so that the top jobs are going to men."

Dealing with daily discrimination was reality, of course, for women in every field, not just publishing or librarianship. And often it was not the job title or even the paycheck that mattered as much as expectations of behavior. One female executive at a major house summarized the problem well when she said: "It's not that I want a bloody refrigerator in my office. I just don't see why he can have one and I can't."

Office refrigerators and other machines often are clues to the status of women. Throughout history, men raced to be the first to use new machines—until that was no longer exciting, and then using them became women's work. The first "typewriters" were men, for instance, as were the first telephone operators. The best indicator of progress for women near the end of the twentieth century, therefore, may be that the typing pool disappeared as men learned word processing. Even Wonder Woman wouldn't be needed in the typing pool.

In an article from the early 1970s titled "The Publishing Business: Still a Gentleman's Game?" novelist and social historian Stephen Birmingham pointed out that Nan Talese, wife of future best-selling author Gay Talese, had risen to senior editor at Random House, where she shocked her colleagues by offering a good advance to a poet—and Rod McKuen soon surprised them with books that sold in the millions. At Harper & Row, Genevieve Young (whom Birmingham described as "a tall and willowy Chinese girl") had *two* of her books on the *Times'* best-seller list, a feat almost unheard of. Yet, Birmingham added, "on the sixth floor of Harper, where the senior editors' offices are, there wasn't even a ladies' room."

Women continued to head children's book departments in many trade houses. Jean Karl was the founding editor of Atheneum Books for Young Readers from 1961 to 1985; authors she edited won two Caldecott and five Newbery medals. In addition, she published the work of the noted young adult science-fiction authors Ursula LeGuin and Anne McCaffrey. In 1974 Susan Hirschman established Greenwillow Books at publisher William Morrow, publishing such luminaries of the children's book world as Ezra Jack Keats, Anita and Arnold Lobel, Jack Prelutsky, and Virginia Hamilton. Charlotte Zolotow began as an assistant to the legendary Ursula Nordstrom at Harper & Row; when Nordstrom retired in the mid-1970s, Zolotow succeeded her as head of Harper Junior

Blazing Trails in Publishing Houses

One of the few women who rose to a management position in publishing in the mid-twentieth century was Helen Honig Meyer. In 1923, when she was sixteen years old, she was hired by George T. Delacorte, two years after he started Dell Publishing. She rose to become president and chief executive in the 1950s and remained in that position until the company was sold to Doubleday & Co. in 1976, when she continued on as a consultant. When Meyer started at Dell it was publishing pulp magazines. Under her guidance, Dell began publishing comics, paperbacks, and, later, hardcover books. The family-friendly comics that Dell chose to publish were enormously lucrative: *Bugs Bunny*, *Woody Woodpecker*, and the wildly popular Disney line sold three hundred million copies a year, making Dell the largest comic book publisher in the world by 1953. Meyer led Dell into paperback and hardcover publishing, establishing the Delacorte Press, with such popular authors as Kurt Vonnegut, James Baldwin, Danielle Steel, and Belva Plain.

Meyer inspired other women in the publishing world, and as chief executive of Dell she was an influential presence in the publishing community. Those who knew and worked with Meyer remember her acute business sense and her forceful personality. Esther Margolis, who worked briefly at Dell during Meyer's tenure, credited Meyer's influence

Books. During her tenure, she published books by Karla Kuskin, Robert Lipsyte, M.E. Kerr, and Paul Zindel. She was a prolific and successful picture book author as well; many of her own books were illustrated by award-winning children's illustrators. Zolotow was a beloved figure in the publishing world whose understanding of the interior landscape of childhood never faltered. She wrote that, "We are all the same except that adults have found ways to buffer themselves against the full-blown intensity of a child's emotions." She retired in 1991 and was named publisher emerita.

In the 1970s women began to join the all-male Association of Book Travelers (ABT), founded in 1884 and probably the oldest book trade organization in the U.S. ABT members were book salesmen who called on bookstores on behalf of publishers. Some were "commission reps" and some were "house reps" but all were male until Bebe Cole was admitted

on her own career. Margolis spent seventeen years at Bantam, where she became a vice president—the youngest in the industry—and turned her attention to publicity and marketing, sending such authors as Peter Maas and E.L. Doctorow on author tours, something that was not yet standard practice. In 1981, she founded Newmarket Press, where one of her successful innovations has been film tie-in books.

By the 1960s there were a handful of women editing adult books and that decade would see them gain acclaim and welcome additional women to their ranks: Nan Talese, Betty Prashker, Judith Jones, Ann Harris, Toni Morrison, Genevieve Young, and Lisa Drew were among them. They were stellar editors with taste and insight who discovered and advanced the careers of commercial and literary authors. Nan Talese published Margaret Atwood's novels; Betty Prashker championed Kate Millet's *Sexual Politics*; Judith Jones published Julia Child's first cookbooks and found Anne Frank's *Diary of Young Girl* in the reject pile; Ann Harris published Colleen McCullough's *The Thorn Birds*; Toni Morrison edited books by Toni Cade Bambara and Angela Davis. Many of the women in this generation went on to executive positions, some with their own imprints. Joan Kahn, who was at Harper & Row from 1946 to 1980, became the doyenne of suspense; the Joan Kahn/Harper Novels of Suspense imprint was sought after by both writers and readers. These women blazed the trail for other women in succeeding decades.

in 1971. By 1984, when the ABT celebrated its centennial there were more than sixty women in the organization. The WNBA honored Bebe Cole with the WNBA Award in 1987 for her many contributions to the industry, including her role as president of the ABT from 1979 to 1980.

Rocking the Publishing Boat

Women at Grove Press ignited a feminist revolution when they seized the president's office in 1970 after several women had been unfairly fired. They were arrested, but with support for the women from the AFL-CIO, the National Labor Relations Board conducted an election on whether or not to unionize. Proponents lost that election—but four of the five women who had been fired were reinstated. Other companies, including Scholastic, Macmillan, and Holt, avoided similar negative publicity by creating informal women's groups that allowed them to voice concerns. In March of that year, *Newsweek* ran a cover story on feminism titled "Women in Revolt," but the real story was about *Newsweek* itself, as that same day women employees announced they were suing the magazine for gender discrimination. Only one woman, Lynn Povich, wrote for the magazine at that time.

Two years later, in 1972, women at Harper & Row voted to go on strike after management ignored the objective study they commissioned by an outside auditor. The WNBA archives contains a copy of the study and also the letter sent to Harper & Row president Win Knowlton announcing the upcoming strike. Among the inequalities the study showed: 50 percent of women with college degrees were asked to take a typing test before being hired at Harper, while only 12 percent of similar men were; 78 percent of men were assured that their jobs would be a training ground for promotion, while 47 percent of women got that encouragement; and, perhaps most revealing of the industry's biases, 52 percent of men with degrees started in sales, compared with 1 percent of women. Specific numbers in top positions showed 17 men and 4 women, with no women at a higher level than "department manager."

Macmillan staff picketed the company in October, 1974, when 179 employees were dismissed. Two editors, Susan Hirschman, editor in chief of the children's book department, and Ada Shearon, managing editor in the same department, resigned in protest. The WNBA newsletter,

The Bookwoman, reported that "The year 1974 will be remembered as one seething with labor troubles for the book industry. June saw a strike by the Association of Harper & Row employees with union members and management in deadlock for several weeks over the terms for a new contract." Meetings were held at a number of publishing houses about unionization. Nor was feminist agitation limited to New York City. Five Boston-based publishing companies—Addison-Wesley, Allyn & Bacon, Ginn, D.C. Heath, and Houghton Mifflin—were sued by female employees alleging discrimination in hiring, pay, and promotion policies.

Feminist agitation wasn't limited to the Northeast or to book publishing. The *San Diego Union* and other newspapers around the country published a 1973 story about discrimination against women in the book industry that quoted Ann Heidbreder, president of the WNBA: "The greatest annoyance for career woman in responsible positions is to be left out of the decision-making process. We are also ruled out of sales, financial and budgetary decisions that relate vitally to our own effectiveness." She said that 65 percent of the total work force in the book industry was made up of women—about fifty thousand women. "The book industry recruits very able and intelligent women. But while the young men are trained and guided upward, the young women rarely are. The only way most women can get to a high-level position is by moving from publishing house to publishing house. And if and when the woman finally reaches a position of authority, she has less clout than the man. The industry, indeed, is notorious for hiring young college graduates as 'editorial assistants,' a euphemism for 'secretary.'"

Just as with the alternative periodicals of the era, alternative publishers sprang up, supporting women's lives and viewpoints. Some of these "underground" businesses delighted in such attention-getting names as Shameless Hussy Press (1969–1989) and Booklegger Press (1972–1985). By far the most successful of these new publishers was Feminist Press. Begun by Florence Howe in 1970, it found its niche by republishing works by women that other houses had allowed to go out of print. The press's best sellers were usually authors who hadn't been recognized in their own lifetimes, including Zora Neale Hurston, Charlotte Perkins Gilman, Anzia Yezierska, and Agnes Smedley, a journalist whose ashes were buried with honors in communist China.

Before beginning Feminist Press, Howe had tried to interest academic presses in women's classics, but was rebuffed. Seeing her example, though, some of the presses began to take women's history seriously, and at the millennium, it would be academic presses that published most of the new books in women's history. Gerda Lerner at the University of Wisconsin pioneered that field, while the University of North Carolina probably claims top place today. Some of these books, especially those aimed at girls, were distributed via the catalog of the National Women's History Project, which began in California in 1980.

Indeed, no political movement in history benefited as much as 1970s feminism did from the positive influence of women in the literary and publishing industry. They promoted an avalanche of thoughtful books that readers eagerly bought—clearly, times were changing. At least six books that would become best-selling classics were published in just the first two years of the decade: Caroline Bird, *Born Female* (McKay, 1970); Kate Millett, *Sexual Politics* (Doubleday, 1970); Robin Morgan, *Sisterhood Is Powerful* (Random House, 1970); Elizabeth Janeway, *Man's World: Woman's Place* (Morrow, 1971); Gerda Lerner, *The Woman in American History* (Addison-Wesley, 1971); and *The Female Eunuch* (McGraw-Hill, 1971), by Germaine Greer, an Australian who was featured prominently on American television.

Both men and women at major houses in the 1980s were caught up in the Reagan-era economic trend of mergers and conglomeration. Beyond that, more and more publishers were sold to an alphabet soup of mega-corporations, sometimes with little or no connection to publishing. Random House acquired Alfred A. Knopf, for example, and then both became part of RCA, which had begun in the 1920s as Radio Corporation of America. Little, Brown sold out to the Time-Life empire, while CBS (originally Columbia Broadcasting System) bought other houses. Prestigious Prentice Hall became part of the giant Gulf & Western in 1984: That name was inscrutable, but the company originally built car bumpers in Michigan.

From Bookselling Challenges to Feminist Strongholds

Bookstores were under extreme threat, as giants Barnes & Noble (B&N) and, to a lesser extent, Borders and Books-A-Million, gobbled up smaller

Argosy Bookstore

In 1925, Louis Cohen opened the Argosy Bookstore on Fourth Avenue in Manhattan, in a neighborhood that for many years was known as Book Row. In its heyday, forty-eight bookstores lined the street from Union Square to Astor Place. Of those bookstores, today only the Strand remains. In 1953, Cohen moved the business uptown to Fifty-Ninth Street. His three daughters, Judith, Naomi, and Adina, all came to work in the store after college, and in 1991, the sisters inherited the business. Today, the Argosy still occupies all six floors of the brownstone Louis Cohen purchased, a mecca for book lovers interested in rare and used books, as well as maps, prints, autographs, and paintings. Argosy exemplifies Madge Jenison's ideas about the "personal bookshop" with an old-world atmosphere and personal service. Janet Malcolm, in a 2014 *New Yorker* profile of the shop and the sisters, mindful of the changing landscape of the book business, concluded her article with these words: "Godspeed, wonderful bookshop, on your journey into the uncertain future."

chains such as Little Professor, Cole's Bookstores, and Brentano's. Many independents went bankrupt, although a surprising number of well-established stores with loyal customers and niche markets, particularly rare books, would survive the onslaught.

The 1970s also brought an explosion of alternative newspapers, magazines, and journals with a lively feminist viewpoint: *Ain't I a Woman* (Iowa City, Iowa); *Kalamazoo Women's Newspaper* (Michigan); *New Broom* (Boston); *The Amazon* (Milwaukee); *Big Mama Rag* (Denver); and *Lesbian Tide* (Altadena, California) are just a few of the many titles. Some were ephemeral—photocopied notes that circulated among small groups; some had national circulation. As women met in consciousness raising groups, at conferences, and at demonstrations, the notes, pamphlets, and newsletters they wrote and printed began to circulate; eventually some became magazines or books. Small presses were created to publish the material; Shameless Hussy Press, Naiad Press, Seal Press, Cleis Press, Kitchen Table: Women of Color Press, Calyx Books, and Daughters, Inc. are a few among many. Women who were denied access to mainstream publishing—especially women of color, lesbians, and

Louisa Solano and the Grolier Poetry Bookshop

When Louisa Solano stepped into the Grolier Bookshop in Boston at the age of fifteen, she sensed that she had come home. At that time it was a general bookstore owned by the beloved but cantankerous Gordon Cairnie. Solano became a frequent visitor, then an employee, and when the store was up for sale in 1974, she managed to find the funds to purchase it. Five years later, she gave the shop a new focus: poetry. Donald Hall, Robert Bly, Marianne Moore, Robert Creeley, and other well-known and aspiring poets had already been frequent visitors. Solano introduced physical changes that made the shop more welcoming and stocked books by women, gays, African-Americans, and others who hadn't been welcomed by her predecessor. It was hard work to make a profit and Solano claims to have subsisted on "peanut butter and rice and beans for five or six years." She ran a poetry contest to recognize young poets, held autograph parties and readings, all in service of her goal to bring poetry to the general public and expand opportunities for poets of diverse backgrounds. The store became a gathering place for poets and book lovers to find rare or obscure titles. Still, it was always a struggle to turn a profit and Solano sold the store in 2004 to the Nigerian poet Ifeanyi Menkiti, the current owner.

In 1989, Solano gave a talk to the Boston chapter of the WNBA titled: "The Changing Position of Women in the Poetry World." She spoke of how women poets have become more visible but have yet to receive adequate recognition from the publishing community. She said, "Recently, I received the new Macmillan catalogue, which contains a blurb for the Best Poetry of 1988...the blurb listed the names of twelve poets, all male, followed by the curt phrase 'and others.' That says it all. Basically, we are still 'and others.' If we are not careful, we shall be voiceless and invisible again."

working-class women—found an outlet for their opinions and ideas at these magazines and small presses. Dissemination of the written word was integral to second wave feminism.

Women opened bookstores that served as community gathering centers for book discussion, self-help groups, meetings, and performances, with chairs and tables to sit at and bulletin boards to advertise local events. The bookstores stocked nonsexist children's literature, lesbian fiction, books that portrayed nontraditional families, writings on women and violence, and, as women's history developed into an academic discipline, they were sources of feminist scholarship. They were also safe spaces for women leading nontraditional lives. Publishers, ever conscious of the marketplace, recognized that these bookstores meant there were new opportunities in the field of feminist literature.

In the 1970s and 1980s there were at least one hundred feminist bookstores around the country. The first two were Amazon in Minneapolis and ICI in Oakland. They were soon followed by New Words in Boston, Bookwoman in Austin (Texas), and Charis in Atlanta, among many others. Carol Seajay, one of the founders of Old Wives' Tales in San Francisco, started the *Feminist Bookstore News*, creating a way for the bookstores to exchange news and ideas. In 1994, there were still one hundred feminist bookstores, but by the late 1990s, with the arrival of chain bookstores and online sales, the number declined, and by 2014, there were only fourteen.

Librarians Stand Up for Civil Rights

ALA's pioneering Office of Intellectual Freedom (OIF) was established in 1967 and "charged with implementing ALA policies concerning the concept of intellectual freedom as embodied in the Library Bill of Rights, the Association's basic policy on free access to libraries and library materials." Judith Krug was the OIF's first director, remaining in that position for more than forty years, supporting libraries in fighting censorship and all attempts to limit access to materials under the First Amendment. A fierce champion of free access to information for all, Krug started Banned Books Week in 1982 to draw attention to the dangers of censorship. Her achievements in the fight against censorship were unparalleled and she received numerous awards. After her death in 2009, a tribute from the ALA stated that "Judith Krug inspired librarians and educated government officials and others about everyone's inviolable right to read. Her leadership in defense of the First Amendment was always principled and unwavering."

In 1969, the Freedom to Read Foundation (FTRF) was established to challenge censorship and other First Amendment threats. The Foundation's first action, in 1970, was to support librarian Joan Bodger, who was fired from the Missouri State Library for writing a letter to her local newspaper protesting the suppression of an underground newspaper. ALA's Office of

Virginia Steele and the Freedom Libraries

"We have about 50,000 books scattered....Would you be in charge of one of these Freedom Libraries for the summer? Your job would be to recruit some local students or whomever you can to help you catalogue the books, fix up the library room, set up some kind of workable sign-out system, and, in general, publicize and run the library. Could you just drop me a line soon to tell me if you would like to do this?...P.S....try to get some 3x5 cards."

Virginia Steele was a library science student at University of California, Berkeley in 1964 when she responded to this request from a student civil rights worker in Jackson, Mississippi. Steele drove her VW bus to Mississippi with two other volunteers. The local children dubbed it the "Freedom Bus" as it was used to take books to local stores, barber shops, and other public places for free distribution. At the age of forty, Steele was one of the oldest volunteers in the project.

By then the impact of the civil rights movement was spreading across the U.S. The fight was centered in the Jim Crow South, but support came from all over the country. The key issues were desegregation of schools, public transportation, and facilities, and the right to vote. Myriad state and local laws mandating testing, literacy, poll taxes, and other requirements were used to deny voting rights to African-Americans.

In 1964 the Council of Federated Organizations, Student Non-Violent Coordinating Committee, and other groups organized an ambitious response called the Mississippi Summer Project. Hundreds of students from northern colleges were recruited to come to Mississippi for the summer to participate in voter registration projects and to establish Freedom Schools for the local population. Freedom Libraries were also an important part of the project, where literacy classes were open to children and adults who had been denied education and excluded from public libraries.

Thousands of books had been donated to the libraries, and Steele

Intellectual Freedom issued a fact-finding report exonerating Bodger. In the years since, the FTRF has provided support to individual librarians and in book censorship cases, often filing *amicus curiae* briefs.

Women librarians were only slowly making inroads into the boardrooms and corner offices of public and academic libraries when this era began, but significant gains would come soon. The political and social movements of the 1970s and 1980s, especially second wave feminism, would spark organized volunteers to sort and distribute the books to the Freedom Schools across the state. Steele says the volunteers had no library training, but she came to value more their chief qualifications: "enthusiasm, the capacity to respond to challenge and the capacity for hope."

Steele was based in Greenville, where, in addition to organizing the school, library, and voter registration projects, she and others had to handle keeping everyone involved safe from racist violence, as all of them were at risk of violent retaliation. By the end of the summer the volunteers had established twenty-five libraries. One was destroyed by bombing, and another was destroyed when the church housing it was burned to the ground. Volunteers were often harassed and arrested.

In a letter to her Berkeley classmates at the start of the summer Steele wrote: "I go through double shock all the time—first, that this is my country and I'm afraid...and secondly, that this is what a whole group of people have lived in all their lives."

They learned not to separate or label children's and elementary books, so the many adults and teens who could not read could borrow them without embarrassment. She described the "confusion of a swarm of young people, real contact with books and genuine library activity." The Freedom Libraries made books available to the local African-American population in a setting where they felt comfortable and the books were of particular interest to them. The libraries became an essential part of the community and Freedom Schools.

Steele's work in Mississippi included setting up library systems and local book distribution, teaching, working with local children, participating in voter registration activity, and helping to organize the continued functioning of the libraries after the summer volunteers left. The following year, a number of librarians formed a group to continue to promote libraries and literacy in the state.

Steele later taught in Berkeley schools and supported a leadership program for girls in West Virginia, where she died in 2006.

—Andrea Baron

demands for pay equity with other professions and representation in library management and ALA leadership. Younger librarians were no longer content with the traditional image of the retiring librarian and were not shy about expressing their feelings. Booklegger Press, founded in the Bay area by three librarians, Celeste West, Sue Critchfeld, and Valerie Wheat, expressed their rebellious nature. The first publication by the new press, an anthology titled *Revolting Librarians*, was meant to shake up the way libraries had been doing business, proposing alternative models of library service. *Booklegger Magazine*, published by the same women from 1973 to 1976, continued the revolt.

In response to the demand for a more progressive agenda within ALA, the Social Responsibilities Round Table (SRRT) was formed in 1969, an activist group that birthed a number of significant subgroups to deal with issues of race, gender, feminism, and political and economic issues. The Feminist Task Force (FTF) was created by SRRT in 1970 to address issues of sexism in libraries. The FTF fostered the creation of other groups in ALA, notably the Committee on the Status of Women in Librarianship, still in existence, which supports the growth of women inside and outside librarianship, sponsors research projects and publications, and creates subcommittees for special needs. In the 1980s, the Women Studies Section (now the Women & Gender Studies Section) came into being to support and promote women's studies collections and programs in academia.

In the 1970s and 1980s, women began to take over the helm at some of the larger urban libraries. Clara Stanton Jones became the

Celeste West, one of the three librarians who founded Booklegger Press, in the mid-1970s.

director of the Detroit Public Library from 1970 to 1978 and the first African-American president of ALA in 1976; Regina Minudri was the director of the Berkeley Public Library in California from 1977 to 1994, and then headed San Francisco Public Library from 1997 to 1999; Allie Beth Martin headed the Tulsa City-County Library from its inception in 1963 until her death in 1976. These three, as well as many other women in director and management positions, moved the profession forward in a variety of ways: expanding access to services, opposing censorship, securing library funding, and educating the next generation of librarians.

The WNBA Supports Women in Publishing

The Women's National Book Association joined other publishing organizations in 1962 in offering a $1,000 annual award to the undergraduate student who, in the opinion of the judges, had collected the best personal library. It was named the Amy Loveman Award in honor of a longtime

Effie Lee Morris

Effie Lee Morris (1921–2009) was a pioneer in public library services for children, and an advocate for minorities and the visually impaired. After obtaining a master's in library science from Case Western Reserve University she began work in 1946 at the Cleveland Public Library, where she established the first Negro History Week celebration for children. In 1955, she joined the staff of the New York Public Library where she served as the children's specialist at the Library for the Blind from 1958 to 1963. In 1963, Morris joined the San Francisco Public Library (SFPL) as its first children's services coordinator, where she remained for fifteen years. While at SFPL she created the Children's Historical and Research Collection for out-of-print children's books, featuring titles that depicted the changing portrayals of ethnic and minority groups in the twentieth century. In 1981 the collection was renamed in her honor. An activist throughout her career, Morris received many honors; she was particularly active in the American Library Association, served on the Advisory Board of the Library of Congress's Center for the Book, and was president of the National Braille Club. Her vision and advocacy for children's services touched and inspired all who knew her.

—Kate Farrell

WNBA activist; Loveman was an associate editor for *Saturday Review* and a judge for the Book-of-the-Month Club. The young winners would have to prove that they had at least thirty-five books in their individual collection, offer advice on building a home library, and reveal what their next ten purchases would be.

Several new chapters came on board in this period: San Francisco in 1968, Los Angeles in 1975, and Washington, D.C., in 1978. The westward expansion was significant, as a study showed that more writers lived in Southern California during the 1970s than in any other part of the country.

Virginia Mathews was the youngest woman yet to be honored with the Constance Lindsay Skinner Award in 1965, when she was forty. According to *Newsday,* she was an author, editor, and literary critic, as well as a link between the written word and the broadcast word on radio and television. The early 1960s were indeed glory days for speakers at the WNBA's annual awards dinner, as popular authors Pearl S. Buck, Catherine Drinker Bowen, Eleanor Roosevelt, and Rachel Carson were honored in the years between 1960 and 1963. Carson's work *Silent Spring* (1962) was reaching permanent best-seller status, despite its scholarly subject of the dangers of pesticides.

The Women's National Book Association celebrated its fiftieth anniversary in 1967, with President Victoria S. Johnson in charge. To honor the occasion, the WNBA issued an eighty-five-page commemorative booklet entitled "Women in the World of Words." Its first feature was a timeline of progress in the field of children's literature, beginning with 1918. Many of the pages were copies of programs from previous annual dinners, with men noted at least as much as women, and many congratulatory ads from publishers. It also included a history of then-extant chapters in Chicago, Cleveland, Detroit, Nashville, and Binghamton, New York—as well as Boston, which cited its recent work with the pioneer educational television station WGBU. The most important feature of "Women in the World of Words," though, was its brief bios of the first winners of the Constance Lindsay Skinner Award, complete with photographs of the women honored between the 1940 beginning of the award and the WNBA's Golden Anniversary in 1967.

Congratulations
to the
Women's National
Book Association
on its Fiftieth Anniversary.

May your fine contribution
to the world of books continue
throughout the years to come.

THE SEABURY PRESS

Publishers of the Book of Common Prayer, *religious books for the general reader, and children's books.*

**Happy Birthday
WNBA**

Parents' Magazine Press

The WNBA celebrated its fiftieth anniversary in 1967. To commemorate the milestone, the organization published "Women in the World of Words," which included many good wishes from publishers and other book-related companies, as these examples show.

WNBA took an active role in supporting the women who were striking and picketing at publishing houses. President Virginia Matthews, in 1971, said of the fifty-six-year-old organization:

> *The WNBA has 1,000 members, divided into 10 chapters across the country. It prides itself on activities to further the careers of women in the publishing field. It tries to help women identify prominent roles for themselves and to aid them in making a contribution to the book industry. WNBA is a professional organization. I stress the word professional.*

In the early 1970s the New York chapter started a newsletter called "Did You Know," written by the Status of Women Committee. It reported on progress in promoting women to management positions in publishing, sources of information about women's rights in the workplace, and related WNBA activities and programs. Around the same time the WNBA partnered with the Anti-Defamation League to record a series of twenty-five simulated scenarios of workplace discrimination and distribute them to members. And in 1972, the New York chapter undertook a survey of women in the publishing world regarding workplace issues. The survey was initially distributed to WNBA members as a pilot program, then to almost three hundred heads of publishing houses. More than five hundred questionnaires were returned, but this was a small portion of what was expected. Very few publishers distributed the questionnaires to all the women in their employ. Despite disappointment with the numerical results, the conclusion stated that "some of the responses to the open-ended questions on the form were painful to read and contemplate. Over and over again women revealed that the kinds of treatment that harmed them most (and which they found it most difficult to combat) lay in the areas of education and upgrading....Men seem to move into management-level positions more easily than women."

Interest in the subject was intensely debated through the 1970s and into the 1980s, and the WNBA continued to offer programs on the status of women in publishing. In 1975, the New York chapter sponsored a panel discussion that included feminists of two generations. Elizabeth Janeway had written on women's issues since World War II, and young Nora Ephron was beginning to make her reputation with *Wallflower at the Orgy* (1970); she would follow up with a string of popular books and woman-centered screenplays. At another panel discussion on women in the publishing business, however, the *Boston Globe* reported that Anatole Broyard of the *New York Times* "took the brunt of most of the questioning.... His comment that man's control in the past was usually nominal, that women were the power behind the throne, brought some good-natured hisses." In all probability, some of those hisses were not intended to be good-natured, as many women were tired of being patronized.

The front-page article of *The Bookwoman* in the summer of 1985 was an interview with Margaret Laurenson from the Lynne Palmer Agency, an employment agency that specialized in publishing and media. Laurenson said: "Women in the past were a kind of captive body of low-paid workers who could be counted on to pour into the publishing houses when they were fresh out of Vassar, work for a couple of years until they got married, and then make way for the next tide of young women. But that body of women doesn't exist anymore and probably won't exist in the future, one hopes. Therefore, new opportunities must be made." (For more information about the WNBA and second wave feminism, see Chapter 2: "From the Archives.")

In 1981, the Pannell Award was created to honor Lucile Micheels Pannell, longtime WNBA member, librarian, and manager of the Hobby Horse Bookshop in Chicago. Since then, the Pannell Award has been given to a general bookstore and a children's specialty bookstore to recognize the value of booksellers in their communities. The award is given out at Book Expo, the trade show for the publishing industry; the Pannell Award has become a prestigious event.

The seventieth anniversary of the WNBA, in 1987, was an exceptional event, honoring seventy women in the book world who have made a difference in bringing authors and their readers together. Nominations for the citation were open to the entire publishing industry and chosen by a panel of distinguished judges. The seventy women who were chosen represented a diverse range of roles and responsibilities, including booksellers, editors, authors, educators, publishers, and literary agents. Fifty-seven of the honorees gathered at the Celeste Bartos Forum at the New York Public Library to celebrate.

A NETWORKED WORLD, A FAST-CHANGING WORLD

The 1990s were an era of consolidation, with less dramatic feminist action than in the 1970s, but also less regression than in the 1980s. Acknowledgement of that regression, however, was a necessary first step, and perhaps more than anything else, it was Susan Faludi's *Backlash: The Undeclared War Against American Women* (1991) that created consciousness of the reversal. Political backlash, indeed, was largely due to one woman, Illinois' Phyllis Schlafly. Supported by conservative interests and by promotion of her own books, she organized Republican women so effectively that they killed the proposed Equal Rights Amendment to the U.S. Constitution. Schlafly's work was self-published or essentially so, while major houses continued to publish feminist books. Still, many women saw the death of the ERA as the death knell of feminism, and organizations such as NOW lost membership and influence.

The 1990 death of ninety-eight-year-old Iphigene Ochs Sulzberger, "the matriarch of the *New York Times*," marked another kind of change that would appear in the decade. Her father had passed the title of publisher to his son-in-law, not his daughter, but "I.O.," as she was called, played an active role at the internationally influential paper, and columnist James Reston deemed her "the most remarkable woman our profession has seen in my lifetime." In the future, however, the *Times* and every other medium in the circulation of thought would have to deal with an electronic revolution comparable to the invention of the telegraph, telephone, and television. Newspapers, magazines, and printed materials would lose readership, as the world switched to other forms of communication.

Elections are the way we measure our social and cultural trends, and the political pendulum swung to the left in 1992, when Democrat Bill Clinton defeated incumbent Republican president George H.W. Bush and put an end to twelve years of Republican dominance in the White House. Clinton renewed the commitment to women that President Kennedy had begun in the 1960s, creating the White House Office on Women's Initiatives. He also appointed more women to Cabinet offices than ever before, including the nation's first female attorney general, Janet Reno. Labeled "The Year of the Woman," 1992 was highlighted by the election of two Democratic women to the U.S. Senate from the giant state of California, a major historical milestone.

Both the Violence Against Women Act and the Freedom of Choice Act passed in 1994, but public acceptance of feminism remained ambivalent, and First Lady Hillary Clinton was widely criticized for attending the 1995 United Nations conference on women's rights in Beijing. Congress continued to ignore ratification of the UN treaty that would ban all forms of discrimination against women, and every election brought rhetoric—but no real congressional action—on abortion rights. Republican attempts to impeach President Clinton for sexual misbehavior brought further attention to gender issues, much of it negative, and for the first time in political history, a few congresswomen embarrassed other women: Republican representative Helen Chenoweth-Hage of Idaho, for example, vehemently criticized Clinton while conducting an extramarital affair herself. She personified a new and negative viewpoint for women with her comment, "it's the white Anglo-Saxon male that is endangered today." Congresswomen in the past generally had supported other women and their goals for women, but as partisanship intensified, this feminist pattern was no longer true. Voters in both parties failed to nominate moderates, and bipartisan organizations such as the National Women's Political Caucus and The White House Project, which aimed to elect a woman as president regardless of party, fell apart and disappeared.

Organizations in general lost membership because people increasingly communicated through social media, especially after the 2004 launch of Facebook. Ironically, while their organizations declined, many women felt empowered by the change. They no longer had to find time in their busy work/home lives to go to meetings or pay dues or otherwise make sacrifices to network with other women. Instead, the computer and cell phone allowed them to e-mail, text, and blog, aiding the formation of online communities about all issues, including feminist issues. The Internet would also encourage increased communication because it was

Women senators, and candidates for the U.S. Senate, at the Democratic National Convention in 1992; "The Year of the Woman" saw an unprecedented number of women running for and elected to the Senate. Pictured here, in the front row (left to right), are Carol Moseley-Braun from Illinois, Barbara Boxer from California, and Barbara Mikulski, from Maryland.

infinitely cheaper than postal delivery. Groups such as the League of Women Voters stopped the expensive monthly newsletters it had mailed for decades. Electronic communication was also highly advantageous in nearly instant notifications of needed action, especially with lobbying for feminist issues. Unlike in the past, new groups such as Women's E-News and Ultra Violet could quickly expand their audiences with relatively little investment.

These innovative ways of targeting an audience meant that fewer and fewer people were influenced by traditional mainstream news, with the result that elections showed a nation increasingly divided by age and gender. The 2000 presidential election was historic, as Democrat Al Gore won the popular vote, but narrowly lost the Electoral College when the Supreme Court ordered an end to the recount in the tight race in Florida. George W. Bush, brother of Florida governor Jeb Bush, moved into the White House in 2001, and the Office on Women's Initiatives again died. On September 11 of that year, an airplane attack by Middle Eastern men—most of them from Saudi Arabia, an ally of the U.S.—killed thousands of people in the Northeast.

One consequence of the resulting "war on terror" was the passage of the Patriot Act, which attempted to limit free speech, something that would become a particular concern to librarians. The 2002 election brought two Republican women to the U.S. Senate, giving that party a historic high of five—but 2004 was the first presidential election year in decades that saw no new female senators. In 2006, however, Democrats won a majority in the U.S. House, which meant that California's Nancy Pelosi became America's first female speaker of the House. As of 2017, though, that precedent has not been repeated—and it was not a genuine victory for organized feminists, as few voters realized when they voted for their individual representative that this would result in a woman holding the nation's third-highest position of power.

In 2008 voters chose the first African-American president, Barack Obama. He defeated Republican John McCain, who had named Alaska governor Sarah Palin as his running mate. She was the first female vice presidential nominee in either major party since the Mondale-Ferraro campaign of almost a quarter century earlier. Neither woman was elected, however, and Palin soon proved a disappointment to her supporters. After several scandals, she resigned from her governorship and faded from the scene. (Earlier, however, her autobiography was a best seller.) During Obama's two terms in office, the civil rights of the lesbian, gay, bisexual, and transgender communities were recognized. "LGBT" entered the language as a word, and the publishing industry did much to promote information on sexuality that had not been available in libraries or most bookstores before the twenty-first century.

In 2010, with Obama in the White House, House Speaker Nancy Pelosi was able to push through the Affordable Care Act, arguably the most important economic reform in a half-century, but when Democrats lost the House majority in that November's election, she lost her position. Obama won re-election in 2012, and Michelle Obama remained one of the most popular first ladies in history as she prioritized better health practices, especially among children. With children's issues highlighted, it became clear that most people believed quality of life was more important than quantity of offspring, and even grocery stores put contraceptives on their shelves—something unimaginable a few decades earlier.

At the same time, though, women's reproductive lives were a constant wedge issue in elections, and attacks on Planned Parenthood were a factor in Democrat Hillary Clinton's loss in 2016. It nonetheless was a milestone, as she was the first female presidential nominee of either of the two major parties in the nation's history, and she won the national popular vote by a margin of almost three million. But Republican nominee Donald Trump, a billionaire with no experience in government, successfully appealed to largely male voters in the swing states of Pennsylvania, Ohio, and Michigan, and thereby won the Electoral College. Millions of women responded by joining protest marches all over the world on the day after his inauguration. As the Trump administration began in 2017 with travel bans and attacks on the news media, organizations and individuals showed their determination to fight censorship in the circulation of thought.

Authors Connect with Readers

President Clinton invited fellow Arkansan Maya Angelou, an African-American author, to read a poem at his 1992 inauguration, and sales of her autobiography *I Know Why the Caged Bird Sings*, first published back

Pulitzer Prize Milestones

The issues of the 1990s were reflected in the 1991 Pulitzer Prize for Meritorious Public Service, which went to Jane Schorer of the *Des Moines Register* for raising objections to the longtime publishing practice of not naming rape victims. The year also marked the first time ever that the history prize went to a woman for a book on a woman, as Laurel Thatcher Ulrich won for *A Midwife's Tale* (1991), based on the diary of an eighteenth-century midwife in New England. This, too, was an example of a cultural trend, as modern women insisted on much more involvement in their pregnancies and deliveries than had been the case for their mothers.

Perhaps the most significant Pulitzer was that awarded to Signe Wilkerson of the *Philadelphia Daily News*, who won the prize for editorial cartooning in 1992—the first female winner since the award began in 1917. Drawing has always been considered appropriate for women, but drawing cartoons in a newsroom apparently was different. Finally, Susan Faludi, writing for the *Wall Street Journal*, won the 1991 Pulitzer Prize for exploratory journalism, a prize that began in 1985.

in 1970, would skyrocket to 3.5 million by 1995. The most important African-American woman of the decade, though, doubtless was Chicago television star Oprah Winfrey. The publishing industry gained a real bonanza with Oprah, who introduced many TV watchers to the habit of reading. Beginning with her book club in 1996, she influenced sales for all genres of books by both men and women. Books that Winfrey picked often sold millions of copies; in the industry the phenomenon was dubbed the "Oprah effect." The first three books Oprah chose were by women: Jacquelyn Mitchard's *The Deep End of the Ocean*; Toni Morrison's *Song of Solomon*; and Jane Hamilton's *The Book of Ruth*. Mitchard's book went from one hundred thousand copies in print to over nine hundred thousand. *Song of Solomon* sold well over one million copies. In the course of its fifteen-year existence, Winfrey's book club recommended seventy books. As a result, book clubs began to flourish again, with most hosted by and for women in their homes.

Some women belonged to several book clubs at the same time, since each book club had a distinct personality. Libraries sponsored book clubs

Maya Angelou reciting her poem "On the Pulse of the Morning" at President Bill Clinton's inauguration on January 20, 1993. She was the second poet, after Robert Frost who spoke in 1961 at John F. Kennedy's swearing in, to take the podium at a presidential inauguration, and she was the first woman and African-American to do so.

and bought multiple copies of books favored by discussion groups and often packaged them in bags with discussion guides—a handy "to go" service. Publishers inserted discussion guides into the trade paperback editions of books and several websites such as www.readinggroupguides.com offered discussion guides. These new kinds of reading groups were akin to the old women's study clubs, and the *New York Times* would estimate in 2015 that some five million Americans belonged to book clubs. Publishers saw additional opportunities for sales with cookbooks pairing recipes and wines with books and even with fiction about book groups, like *The Jane Austen Book Club* by Karen Joy Fowler. In 1997, Shireen Dodson's book *Mother-Daughter Book Club* told the story of ten African-American mothers who discussed books with their preteen daughters; Dodson's book became the inspiration for many parent-child book groups.

A new genre, "chick lit," became popular in the late 1990s: lighthearted commercial fiction about young women in their twenties and early thirties finding love, jobs, and friendships. *Bridget Jones's Diary*, by Helen Fielding, is generally credited with starting the craze.

Publishers were happy to jump on the bandwagon as, despite the lack of critical acclaim, sales were high. The genre has many defenders and critics, with much lively debate centering on the use of the term chick lit and whether it devalues the women who write it and the readers who love to read it. The popularity of memoirs (and memoir writing workshops), which began in the 1990s with Mary Karr's *The Liars' Club* and peaked around 2012, provided catharsis and community for women with difficult life stories.

Upheavals in the Publishing Industry Bring New Opportunities

By the year 2000, there were 122,000 books published annually in the U.S. More copies of individual titles were sold than ever before: E.L. Doctorow's best-selling novel *Ragtime*, published in 1997, sold 230,000 copies, while Jonathan Franzen's best seller *The Corrections*, published in 2001, sold 720,000 copies. This was partly due to the growth of chain bookstores and warehouse stores that made books available in areas of the country previously underserved by bookstores. Marketing to those two outlets became paramount in driving sales for publishers.

There was more consolidation of publishing houses in this period as longstanding American publishers became part of European conglomerates. Hachette Livre purchased Time Warner, which included Warner Books (renamed Grand Central), and the venerable Boston publishing company Little, Brown and Company. The resulting company was renamed Hachette Book Group. Macmillan, one of the oldest independent publishing houses, was acquired in 1995 by the German company Holtzbrinck. In addition to the Macmillan imprints, other formerly independent publishers became part of the Holtzbrinck Group: Farrar, Straus and Giroux; Picador; St. Martin's Press; Tor; and Henry Holt, among others. In 1998, the German media giant Bertelsmann AG acquired Random House, which joined previously acquired Bantam Doubleday Dell. In 2013, Penguin added its imprints to the mix, forming the giant Penguin Random House.

The corporate changes reflected the ongoing challenges of the publishing market, as readers found new ways to acquire and access books. The expansion of broadband gave more people access to the Internet, changing the way everyone communicated and shared information. According to the Pew Research Center, "as people adopted those higher-speed, always-on connections, they became different internet users: They spent more time online, performed more activities, watched more video, and themselves become content creators." This led to the explosive rise of self-published books—in print or as e-books—between 2006 and 2011, with the assistance of new, nontraditional companies to serve that market: Smashwords, Lulu, XLibris, AuthorHouse, CreateSpace, and others. In 2015, more than seven hundred thousand books were self-published in the U.S.; for authors there was no longer the stigma of the "vanity press" when so many were following this path. Stories of authors whose self-published works were "discovered" by trade publishers, going on to best-seller status, encouraged many writers. The erotic *Fifty Shades* trilogy, originally self-published, was picked up by Knopf/Doubleday and became a huge success. *Publishers Weekly* began to devote a section each month to listing and reviewing self-published titles, adding additional legitimacy. Most librarians, however, resisted purchasing self-published titles unless readers requested them.

Traditional publishers went heavily into the e-book market, where the profits were high. As of 2017, the dire predictions that e-books would drive print books out of the market haven't been realized, as e-book sales have been declining since 2013. The audiobook market, once restricted solely to the sight-impaired, also expanded as part of consumers' demands for books in multiple formats playable on multiple devices. "Talking books" were first launched by the Library of Congress in 1934, as an alternative to Braille reading. Some authors were initially opposed to audio versions of their books; Willa Cather was among those who found the idea distasteful, and critics were sure that listening instead of reading was a sign of laziness. But audiobooks found a huge audience, first with commuters, as audiotape and CD players became ubiquitous in automobiles. Narrators such as Barbara Rosenblat developed loyal followings: People were willing to listen to any book that she narrated. With the proliferation of inexpensive portable playing devices and better headphones, and the vogue for "multitasking," the Audio Publishers Association was able to announce in 2011 that 46 percent of consumers had listened to an audiobook, most as an adjunct to another activity.

In many ways, the world was turning from print to other forms of media, something that Arianna Huffington understood when she began the online liberal news site Huffington Post, in 2005. Initially scorned by the business and journalistic communities, it soon garnered respect for gathering news that no one else did—and in 2012, would become the first electronic newspaper to win a Pulitzer Prize. During the same years, the term "blog" entered the language. It derived from Web log, in the sense of a ship's log or diary, and soon thousands of women were circulating their thoughts online. "Mommy blogs," in particular, raised serious competition to longtime magazines such as *Parents*, which traditionally were headed by women.

Publishers Weekly, the industry's Bible since its beginnings just after the Civil War, finally had its first female editor-in-chief, Nora Rawlinson, in 1993. Rawlinson, a former librarian, served twelve years and then became *PW*'s vice president for library services; later she was cofounder of www.earlyword.com, a valuable resource for connecting publishers and librarians

VIDA: Women in Literary Arts

Although the founders of VIDA weren't the first to notice gender disparity in popular literary review sources, they were the first to turn a statistical lens on the subject. In 2010, VIDA members began an annual survey to count the number of books written by women that were reviewed in popular review sources and the number of women reviewers in those sources. The survey revealed that women's books were chosen for review at a much lower rate than men's and that reviewers were predominantly male. The VIDA Count has taken place annually since 2010 and now includes thirty-nine literary magazines and periodicals, including the *New York Times Book Review, Harper's, The New Republic, The Atlantic, Poetry,* and the *Times Literary Supplement.* The count for 2015 was expanded to identify "race, ethnicity, gender, sexual identity, and ability." A scan of the results from 2010 to 2015 shows that there has been improvement in many of the review sources. Chair of the VIDA Executive Committee and WNBA Award winner Amy King writes on the VIDA website, "If certain women's voices are absent or poorly represented in mainstream publications, how does that deficit shape public thought?...Do stereotypes take the place of lived women's thoughts, ideas and experiences? To what extent is the status quo rendered bankrupt by such glaring absences?"

to forthcoming books. Rawlinson was followed at *Publishers Weekly* by Sara Nelson, in 2005. The time was not propitious, as the economy was collapsing under the administration of George W. Bush, and the digital industry was overtaking print. Nelson brought innovations such as the Quill Awards, which allowed buyers to make nominations for favorites in bookstore kiosks, but she was dismissed in 2009, along with executive editor Daisy Maryles, who had worked for *Publishers Weekly* for four decades.

As the larger trade publishers fought for space on the best-seller lists, smaller niche-oriented publishing houses arose in the 1990s, some of them headed by women. Easier production because of computers was a factor in the rise of independent presses, as well as wider book distribution because, as the Internet developed, many readers would browse in bookstores and order their books online. The Internet became a reality for ordinary people in the 1990s. Writers found research infinitely easier—but also found their words more easily plagiarized.

Women were moving up the corporate ladder in trade publishing houses, no longer just in the children's departments, and some started their own publishing concerns. Dominique Raccah used retirement savings to begin Sourcebooks in suburban Chicago in 1987. When she was named *Publishers Weekly*'s Person of the Year in 2016, thirty years later, Sourcebooks was publishing around five hundred books a year and had passed the one hundred million units sold mark. Raccah, with a background in business analytics, was open to new technology and innovative multimedia formats. Erika Goldman became publisher and editorial director of the new Bellevue Literary Press in 2007—and to the surprise of almost everyone, would win a Pulitzer Prize in 2010. Bellevue has an unusual focus: It is a project of the New York University School of Medicine, housed in Bellevue Hospital, and it seeks to publish books at the intersection of science and the humanities.

Although women greatly outnumber men in the publishing workforce, the significant gap between their wages has persisted. Annual surveys in *Publishers Weekly* demonstrate the industry's resistance to change in this area. The salary survey for 1997 showed that men's median total compensation was 30 percent higher than women's. The same survey in 2007 showed no improvement. The median salary for men in editorial positions was roughly 39 percent more than women; the figures for

In 1987 Dominique Raccah launched Sourcebooks, which is now one of the country's most successful independent publishing houses. In recognition of her achievements, *Publishers Weekly* honored Raccah in 2016 with its Person of the Year citation.

sales and marketing were worse: Men's median salaries were 62 percent greater than women's. In 2015, with women holding 84 percent of all editorial positions, men in those positions were making 60 percent more than women. In sales and marketing men were making 57 percent more. Understandably, *PW* reported that year that women were frustrated with the pay gap; the job satisfaction statistic of 47 percent reflected those feelings. Women, however, continue to enter the publishing job market in greater numbers than men.

Women have also been successful literary agents, negotiating the terrain between author and publisher. Elisabeth "Bessie" Marbury (1856–1933) may have been the first, a pioneer in the field who was an early promoter of the writers of the Harlem Renaissance. Much of her career was spent in the theater, where in England she worked as an agent for Oscar Wilde and George Bernard Shaw. In the U.S. in the early twentieth century, she was instrumental in developing the modern Broadway musical. Virginia Kidd (1921–2003) had a long career specializing in science fiction; Ursula LeGuin and Anne McCaffrey were among her clients, and the Virginia Kidd Agency, founded in 1965, is still in existence. Marie Freid Rodell (1912–1975), who founded a literary agency in 1948, worked with Rachel Carson and Rev.

Martin Luther King, Jr. Patricia Schartle Myrer (1923–2010), after a career as editor-in-chief at Appleton-Century Crofts, became president of McIntosh & Otis literary agency where she worked with Mary Higgins Clark and Patricia Highsmith, among other very successful writers. Frances Goldin, who founded a very successful agency in 1977 is equally well known for her decades of activism on behalf of social and political causes.

These early literary agents were followed by many others: Marly Rusoff, Jenny Bent, Nicole Aragi, Amanda "Binky" Urban, Esther Newberg,

Women Editors and Executives, Selected Highlights

Children's Trade Books

Ellie Berger, president of Trade Publishing, Scholastic Inc.; responsible for the production and manufacturing of the Harry Potter books.

Jean Feiwel, senior vice president and publisher of Feiwel and Friends, Square Fish, and Swoon Reads at Macmillan; for many years Feiwel was publisher at Scholastic Books.

Margaret Ferguson, editor at Farrar, Straus and Giroux for thirty years; gained an eponymous imprint, Margaret Ferguson Books, in 2011.

Valerie Garfield, vice president and publisher, Simon & Schuster Children's Publishing Division.

Kate Jackson, senior vice president, associate publisher, and editor-in-chief, HarperCollins Children's Books.

Susan Katz Radin, president and publisher of HarperCollins Children's Books, from 1996 to 2015.

Jennifer Loja, president of Penguin Young Readers Group (PYRG); she joined PYRG in 2009, as associate publisher.

Barbara Marcus, president of Random House, Children's Division, since 2012.

Suzanne Murphy, president and publisher of HarperCollins Children's Books; formerly vice president, group publisher, trade publishing and marketing, Scholastic Inc.

Megan Tingley, executive vice president and publisher, Little, Brown Books for Young Readers, Hachette Book Group.

Women Editors and Executives, Selected Highlights

Adult Trade Books

Ellen Archer, president, trade publishing group, Houghton Mifflin Harcourt, formerly president and publisher of Hyperion.

Reagan Arthur, senior vice president of Little, Brown and Company; editorial director, Reagan Arthur Books, Little, Brown and Company, Hachette.

Margo Baldwin, cofounder, president, and publisher of Chelsea Green, which specializes in books on the politics and practice of sustainable living.

Lee Boudreaux, vice president and editorial director of Lee Boudreaux Books, Little, Brown and Company; formerly editorial director at Ecco (HarperCollins).

Karen Braziller, cofounder of Persea Books, since 1975 an independent, literary publishing house.

Gina Centrello, president and publisher, The Random House Publishing Group; formerly president of Pocket Books, a division of Simon & Schuster.

Judith Curr, executive vice president, publisher, and founder, Atria Books, Simon & Schuster.

Barbara Epler, joined New Directions as an editorial assistant after graduating from college in 1984; became editor in chief in 1995; named publisher in 2008, and president in 2011.

Jane Friedman, CEO and cofounder of Open Road Integrated Media, e-book publisher. Friedman was president and CEO of HarperCollins Publishers Worldwide from 1997 to 2008. Friedman was named Person of the Year for 2006 by *Publishers Weekly*.

Erika Goldman, publisher and editorial director of Bellevue Literary Press; formerly at St. Martin's Press, Charles Scribner's Sons, Simon & Schuster, and W.H. Freeman.

Phyllis Grann, senior editor at Doubleday; formerly president, chairperson and CEO of Putnam.

Julie Grau, senior vice president and publisher, Spiegel & Grau, Random House Inc., cofounded with Celina Spiegel.

Donna Hayes, publisher and CEO, Harlequin Enterprises Ltd. Hayes moved Harlequin from magazine-style publications to single-title books

Esther Margolis, president and owner, Newmarket Publishing and Communications Co. and Newmarket Press, acquired by HarperCollins in 2012.

Brenda Marsh, managing director of Abrams & Chronicle Books, the sales and marketing joint venture of Abrams and Chronicle Books; formerly an executive at Barnes & Noble.

Fiona McCrae, publisher of the literary Graywolf Press since 1994.

Jeanne M. Mosure, senior vice president and publisher, Disney Global Book Group, Disney Publishing Worldwide, 1998 to 2016.

Jamie Raab, president and publisher, Grand Central Publishing, Hachette Book Group.

Dominique Raccah, founder, president, and publisher, Sourcebooks; *PW*'s Person of the Year in 2016.

Julia Reidhead, president of W.W. Norton since December 2016.

Carolyn Reidy, named president and CEO of Simon & Schuster. In 2008, responsible for all the publishing and operations of Simon & Schuster worldwide.

Mary Beth Roche, president and publisher, Macmillan Audio, Macmillan.

Marji Ross, president and publisher, Regnery Publishing, since 2003.

Tracy Sherrod, editorial director at Amistad, the HarperCollins imprint that publishes books for the African-American market.

Vickie Stringer, CEO, Triple Crown Publications, an urban fiction publisher. Stringer started Triple Crown with the fictionalized story of her life, *Let That Be the Reason*, which she wrote in federal prison.

Diane Wachtel, executive director and cofounder of the New Press (with André Schiffrin), founded in 1992; formerly an editor at Pantheon.

Susan Weinberg, senior vice president and group publisher, Perseus Books Group, which includes the imprints Basic Books, Nation Books, and Public Affairs.

and Betsy Lerner, to name only a very few of the many currently active now. Agents are grappling with the changes in the publishing industry; some have begun to offer e-book publishing services to their clients.

Changes in the Bookselling Landscape

Well into the mid-twentieth century, department stores like Macy's sold the lion's share of retail trade books and women often ran those book departments. Books carried prestige and it was thought they would attract educated customers who had money to spend. Chain bookstores entered the market in the 1960s and 1970s: Among the largest were B. Dalton Booksellers, which began in 1966 in Minneapolis, and Borders, which began in Ann Arbor in 1971. By the 1990s, those two companies, along with Walden Books and Barnes & Noble, had numerous locations. In that same decade, however, mergers, bankruptcies, and consolidations disrupted the market and today only Barnes & Noble remains of those large chains.

The arrival of Amazon in the late 1990s caused major changes once again, when its founder, Jeff Bezos, saw the future in online bookselling and discounted prices. The rise of the warehouse clubs, which also sold books at an attractive discount, offered consumers the convenience of purchasing books with their groceries. These two developments, coming after the expansion of the chain bookstores, drove many independent bookstores out of business. In an example of *plus ça change, plus c'est la même chose*, the successful independent bookstore today has much in common with Madge Jenison and Mary Horgan Mowbray-Clarke's Sunwise Turn: They are comfortable places to browse for books, talk about them with the staff (who are happy to provide recommendations and personal service), attend author programs for children and adults, and even enjoy a latte. In short, the "personal bookshop" that Jenison wrote about is the model for success. Women have been at the forefront of successful bookselling today. Joyce Meskis built Denver's Tattered Cover Book Store into an icon of independent bookselling until she retired in 2017, and Carla Cohen and Barbara Meade were the force behind Politics and Prose in Washington, D.C. (Cohen died in 2010 and Meade sold the store to new owners in 2011). Other notable women booksellers, among many others, include Ann Patchett and Karen Hayes at Nashville's Parnassus

Parnassus Books owner Ann Patchett with co-owner Karen Hayes (right) and shop dogs, Opie and Sparky (left to right). Parnassus and other contemporary stores carry on a proud tradition of women booksellers since the WNBA's founding by women bookstore owners in 1917.

Books; Louise Erdrich at Minneapolis' Birchbark Books; and Rebecca Fitting and Jessica Stockton Bagnulo at Greenlight Books in Brooklyn. Another woman, Sessalee Hensley, the main fiction buyer for Barnes & Noble, has become a powerful player in the publishing industry. As the remaining retail book chain, B&N's purchasing choices are important to publishers. Hensley's decisions matter; publishers consult her about book covers and hope for B&N's promotional clout.

Judith Rosen, in an article in *Publishers Weekly* titled "What's Ahead for Bookselling in 2017?" predicted that 2016 would be a record year for independent bookstores, edging out 2015 for that spot, despite Amazon's discounting. Independent booksellers have entered the online market, although as Roxanne Coady of R.J. Julia's told Rosen, "I still feel that none of us have quite figured out what experience online people want from an independent." At Winter Institute, a booksellers' conference that has been held since 2006, Oren Teicher, CEO of the American Booksellers Association, had an optimistic report, citing increased sales, an increase in independent bookstores, more bookstores opening branches, and bookstores on the market finding new owners more easily than in past years. Teicher

Joyce Meskis and Ann Patchett: A Tale of Two Bookstores

Joyce Meskis purchased the Tattered Cover Book Store in Denver in 1974. It was a small store with two employees. Between 1975 and 1983, as Tattered Cover became a beloved Denver gathering place, Meskis expanded the store seven times and later moved into additional locations, with a four-story building opening in 1986. Additional locations around Denver followed, as the business expanded. She was an early adopter of author events and of computerized inventory, and successfully faced down the competition with the inevitable big-box stores and online retailers. The Tattered Cover became one of the largest independent bookstores in the U.S; it's a beloved fixture in the life of the city, with hundreds of author events each year, an emphasis on customer service, and comfortable surroundings. In a 2015 interview with National Public Radio reporter Scott Horsley, Meskis said that from the beginning she designed a bookstore with her own comfort in mind. "Yes, I was there to buy a book.... But I also wanted to be comfortable. I wanted service sometimes. Sometimes I just wanted to be by myself. It's nothing more than treating the customer as you'd want to be treated."

A strong proponent of First Amendment rights and freedom to read, Meskis successfully challenged lawsuits that would have prevented the bookstore from displaying books that might be harmful to minors and

was also heartened to see younger and more diverse bookstore owners. The bookstore landscape may change once again as Amazon is entering the bricks and mortar arena, extending its competitive edge.

Libraries in the Digital Age

Women began to routinely take the helm at larger library systems in this time period, overseeing expansions and technological innovations. The Library Services and Technology Act, passed in 1996, helped provide funding to bring libraries into the new digital era. At the Nashville Public Library, director Donna Nicely was responsible for a new downtown main library and additional branches during her tenure from 1995 to 2011; Susan Kent was city librarian at Los Angeles Public Library from 1995 to 2004; Ginny Cooper was director of the Brooklyn Public Library from turning over purchase records of a suspected drug dealer. After serving as a faculty member of the University of Denver Publishing Institute for many years, she became director in 2008. In 2015 Meskis began the two-year process of turning over the bookstore to its new owners, Len Vlahos and Kristen Gilligan.

Ann Patchett and Karen Hayes opened Parnassus Books in 2011 after the last remaining independent bookstore in Nashville had closed. While Hayes designed the store's interior, popular novelist Patchett was touring for her latest book, *State of Wonder*, and in talking about the forthcoming opening found that she had become a spokesperson for independent bookstores. On opening day for Parnassus, there was a front-page article in the *New York Times*; even the BBC carried the news. In an article that appeared in *The Atlantic Monthly* in December 2012, "The Bookstore Strikes Back," Patchett wrote: "They are lined up outside most mornings when we open our doors, because, I think, they have learned through this journey we've all been on that the lowest price does not always represent the best value. Parnassus Books creates jobs in our community and contributes to the tax base. We've made a place where children can learn and play, where they can think those two things are one and the same. We have a piano. We have two part-time store dogs. We have authors who come and read; you can ask them questions, and they will sign your book. The business model may be antiquated, but it's the one I like, and, so far it's the one that's working."

2003 to 2007, and then director of Washington, D.C., libraries from 2007 to 2013 where she oversaw the building of fourteen new branches.

In 2003, Seattle librarian Nancy Pearl inspired an action figure, a shushing librarian created by the company Accoutrements. As usual in the library world, response was divided between those who were dismayed at the stereotype and those who found it humorous. Pearl, a popular book reviewer on Seattle radio, came to national prominence with her books *Book Lust* and *More Book Lust*, recommended lists of books by topic that would help readers choose what to read next based on their preferences. Another initiative by Pearl, "If All Seattle Read the Same Book," spread to cities and towns around the country. Pearl won the WNBA Award in 2004.

The Patriot Act, passed in the wake of the 9/11 attacks, obligated libraries to turn over patron circulation records when ordered to do so by law enforcement; the law also forbade librarians to tell patrons about these requests. Protecting the privacy of patrons and the confidentiality of library records has been a longstanding library tradition. librarians responded by adding additional privacy provisions to their catalogs and informing patrons of the possibility of subpoenas. In 2005, ALA fought the gag order in court and it was no longer enforced.

After the 2016 election, when proposals for eliminating funding for libraries through the Institute for Museum and Library Services and other agencies were circulating, ALA issued a conciliatory statement saying that it was looking forward to working with the new administration. The response from the membership was immediate and vitriolic—an example of the tightrope ALA walks with its members when it comes to political issues that affect libraries.

President Obama's appointment of Carla Hayden as librarian of Congress in 2016 was well received by librarians; this was the first time that a woman, a professional librarian, and an African-American would head that august institution. Hayden's career as a librarian is filled with stellar accomplishments, most notably her commitment to equal access to library services for all. Immediately before becoming Librarian of Congress, she was CEO of Enoch Pratt Free Library, Baltimore's venerable twenty-two-branch library system, from 1993 to 2016. While there she opened the first new branch library in thirty-five years and renovated the central library. She developed after-school programs to provide homework assistance and career counseling to Baltimore teens. *Library Journal* named her Librarian of the Year in 1995 for this effort. During the protests following the death of Freddie Gray in 2015, Hayden kept the libraries in Baltimore open at a time when many stores were closed. She said, "We knew that [people] would look for that place of refuge and relief and opportunity." From 2003 to 2004 she was president of the American Library Association, where she chose as her theme "Equity of Access." She used that position to speak out about the abuses in the newly passed Patriot Act that failed to safeguard the privacy of library users. Hayden was concerned about the Justice Department and the FBI having access to patron borrowing records and she often argued publicly with John Ashcroft, then U.S. attorney general. As a result of these actions, she became *Ms.* magazine's 2003 Woman of the Year. She wrote: "Libraries are a cornerstone of democracy—where

Librarian of Congress Carla Hayden (left) with actress Lynda Carter, who played Wonder Woman in the 1970s TV series, at the opening of the exhibit, the *Library of Awesome*, celebrating comic books.

information is freely and equally available to everyone. People tend to take that for granted, and they don't realize what is at stake when that is put at risk." As of the spring of 2017, legislation was in process in Congress to limit the Librarian's term of office to ten years and to remove the Copyright Office from the jurisdiction of the Library of Congress.

WNBA at the Millennium and After

In these tumultuous years of change in the publishing, bookselling, and library worlds, WNBA prospered, expanding to Seattle in 2008, Charlotte in 2009, New Orleans in 2011, Philadelphia and South Florida in 2015, and Greater Lansing in 2017. Some chapters folded during this time, but at the end of 2017, there were eleven very active chapters. Budgets for postage vanished as websites and electronic newsletters took the place of paper mailings. Webmasters, graphic designers, and social media mavens became critical to the organization in the new millennium. Carolyn Wilson, president of the WNBA from 1992 to 1994, commented, "I believe one of the most significant changes of recent time has been the onset of the digital environment…I think how we work within [that] framework…requires a good sense of balance and careful planning looking both backward and forward." Former National president Margaret Auer echoed some of those sentiments when she wrote: "The Women's National Book Association in its long history has faced numerous challenges but it seems none so compelling as today's changes in the publishing and library worlds. With advances in technology, publishing company mergers, right-sizing of company workforces, and outsourcing of jobs, the work and networking of the WNBA is more crucial than ever."

WNBA Award winners in this period have continued to represent the organization's diverse interests: First Lady Barbara Bush for her work in highlighting illiteracy; Carolyn Heilbrun for her groundbreaking feminist scholarship; Doris Kearns Goodwin for her historical research; Masha Hamilton for her cross-cultural novels and activism; novelist Ann Patchett for championing the independent bookstore; and Amy King for her work with the VIDA Count are among the winners. The Pannell Award continues to applaud bookstores that encourage young people's interest in books, and the Eastman Grant supports training for librarians. Several chapters have their own awards named in honor of local bookwomen.

For many chapters, the changing times have required exploring new types of programming. Members have expressed interest in programs about marketing, self-publishing, and e-book publishing as the publishing world changes around them. Chapters sponsor writers' groups and events where authors meet agents. Members with jobs in the publishing community have flocked to programs on career development. Increasing networking events and tutorials about social media serve the needs of our very communication-conscious times. Partnerships with other local organizations and events expand each chapter's reach. Kate Farrell, National Board member and former San Francisco chapter president, commented, "Our local network in the literary community has expanded greatly, from its first partnership with the San Francisco Writers Conference in 2004, to now include events cosponsored with Litquake, San Francisco Public Library, Northern California Book Awards, Oakland Book Festival, Books, Inc., the Women's Building, and Afghan Women's Writing Project. It is this combined connectivity, both in person and online, that has benefitted SF chapter members and created a higher profile for WNBA in the very literary San Francisco Bay Area."

One of the most important program innovations undertaken by the WNBA during this period was National Reading Group Month

The WNBA launched National Reading Group Month at the "signature event" in New York City on October 29, 2007, at the General Society for Mechanics and Tradesmen. Pictured here are three of the featured authors—from left to right, Matthew Sharpe, Adriana Trigiani, and Wally Lamb. Authors not shown are Laura Dave and Beverley Swerling, as well as moderator Carol Fitzgerald.

(NRGM) in October of 2007. Based on the original groundwork laid by Martha Burns and Alice Dillon, the WNBA developed the program to help promote shared reading. Book clubs really took off as a trend at the end of the last century, and the WNBA saw NRGM as a crucial way to support the literary community—especially publishers and booksellers. Every year, for National Reading Group Month, a committee of members from around the country selects a group of books to recommend for book groups called Great Group Reads. Publisher recognition and support of Great Group Reads have been wholehearted, and the list is also sent to independent publishers to help them serve their reading groups. Many chapters use that list to form reading groups. Chapters support literacy programs, always a part of WNBA's mission statement. A later section of this book, containing chapter histories, illustrates the diversity of programs and initiatives undertaken around the country.

In 2009, a unique partnership was formed with the Boston Public Library (BPL). Author-members of the WNBA can send copies of their published books to BPL for deposit in a special reference collection. If a second copy is donated, it will go into the circulating collection. A bookplate identifies the book as a WNBA donation. The collection was started off with an initial donation of one hundred books.

Strategic partnerships have become increasingly important to the WNBA in this period—and will continue to be in the second century. The organization links up every year with the Southern Festival of the Book for its celebration of National Reading Group Month in Nashville, a relationship that has long been important to the WNBA chapter in that city. The Association of American Publishers, *Publishers Weekly*, Pen + Brush, and VIDA are other partnerships established in the years before the Centennial. And nearly all chapters have independent bookstores that they partner with, with many of the stores offering home bases for chapter programming. For instance, the Greater Philadelphia chapter, newly formed in 2015, was able to kick-start its programming with a home base at Town Book Center in Collegeville, Pennsylvania. Current president Jane Kinney-Denning has noted how critical it has been to "establish working ties with organizations that share our mission, since the work of supporting the world of books and the literary community cannot be done in a vacuum, especially now, as resources for cultural activities seem to compete with so many other aspects of contemporary life."

One hundred years ago, before women had the vote, and as World War I threatened European stability, a determined, optimistic group of female booksellers stood up to take their place in the literary world together and to offer support, encouragement, and camaraderie to women who, like themselves, made their living from books. If the men who refused to admit them to their all-male organizations wouldn't change their minds, then the WNBA would go on without them. It didn't take long for the rest of the publishing community to see that they had an important contribution to make to the literary-cultural dialogue. The WNBA's remarkable one-hundred-year history, filled with the dedication of so many gifted women, inspires members to continue this remarkable legacy for another hundred years.

This history, stretching back to the earliest days of our country, reveals the talent, persistence, and contribution of women to what the WNBA's founders called "the circulation of thought." From colonial printers, publishers, and writers in the seventeenth and eighteenth centuries, to the pioneering journalists and magazine editors of the nineteenth century, to the crusading and innovative booksellers, librarians, and editors of the twentieth century, to the women of the twenty-first century who continue to demand a place at the literary table, there is no doubt that our cultural dialogue has been enriched by the contributions of these remarkable women. For the past one hundred years, the Women's National Book Association has shared this journey, using our expertise to connect women in the literary community, support their education, advocate for their interests, and lead them to ever greater successes.

------------ ✦ ------------

Notes on Sources
Doris Weatherford

When I was asked by Valerie Tomaselli, past president of the Women's National Book Association and chair of the WNBA Centennial Committee, to write a bibliographic essay for this work, I was initially perplexed. Most of the information in its basic chronology has been rattling around in my head for more than three decades; it's hard to narrow down which of the many books, articles, and other resources is worthy of inclusion in a bibliography on "women in the literary world."

Additional suggestions from Valerie were helpful: "Five hundred to seven hundred words on the nature of the sources…how you used online sources, how you went about your research and how someone might conduct further investigations. Then a list of whatever you used and what you might recommend." I knew that this assignment would take more than seven hundred words but given the expectation of serious readers, extra ink certainly is worthwhile.

To expand on that: My first two books, *Foreign and Female: Immigrant Women in America, 1840–1930* (1986) and *American Women and World War II* (1990), had sound bibliographies, but those topics don't closely relate to WNBA's goal of "women in the book world." My third, however, had some four hundred entries on individuals and organizations, and thus axiomatically included many authors, journalists, publishers, and other women in the word world. That was *American Women's History:*

An A–Z (1994)—but Prentice Hall did not require a bibliography, and I thus avoided the source issue.

Facts on File, the publisher of my fourth work, *Milestones: A Chronology of American Women's History* (1997), wanted a "Selected Bibliography," and so that book has nine pages listing books and major periodical articles. I had by then visited forty-six institutions to use primary documents— archives, libraries, museums, and more. In alphabetical order, the list started with the Adams National Historical Park in Quincy, Massachusetts, and ended with the Women in Military Service for America Memoria (WIMSA), which has its museum in Arlington Cemetery and extensive archives in a corporate office tower in Arlington, Virginia. WIMSA didn't officially open until October 1997, but it continues to accumulate wonderful records from thousands of women who have written about their wartime experiences.

Geographically, the 1997 *Milestones* list of institutions ranged from the beautiful Huntington Library in Pasadena, California, which houses artifacts on the 1911 victory for the California vote, to the northeastern seaport town of Gloucester, Massachusetts, home to Judith Sargent Murray, who penned "Equality of the Sexes" in 1790. In the Deep South, the Historic New Orleans Collection provides information on French nuns who began working there in 1727, and going far north, the Minnesota Historical Society has a modern, user-friendly archive in St. Paul that includes such women as Civil War journalist Jane Swisshelm.

Although the Internet often makes it unnecessary to travel to such places now, I still find excuses to do so. There simply is no feeling like that of sitting in Harvard's Houghton Library and reading Mercy Otis Warren's history of the American Revolution in her own handwriting. It's thrilling to find countless photographs I'd never seen before in Susan B. Anthony's Rochester attic. I'm very grateful to the archivists and museum curators—often volunteers—who properly treasure such things.

My fifth book, undertaken with Valerie's MTM Publishing, was written for the 150th anniversary of the 1848 Seneca Falls Convention, the world's first formal call for women's rights. Because *Milestones* came out in 1997, I wrote *A History of the American Suffragist Movement* in a hurry, to have it ready for the big days of July 19–20, 1998—which included a speech by then First Lady Hillary Clinton. Partly because of this manuscript rush, but mostly because I thought it was underappreciated, I depended on just one source: the massive six-volume *History of Woman Suffrage* that was written between 1881 and 1922 by Elizabeth Cady Stanton, Susan B. Anthony, Matilda Joslyn Gage, and Ida Husted Harper.

If the latter two names are unfamiliar, there's your beginning point for further research. Ida Husted Harper would not have called herself a pioneer of public relations writing, but in fact, she shaped the image of the mainstream women's movement in the early twentieth century and was a particular acolyte in creating Susan B. Anthony's historical persona. Matilda Joslyn Gage should also be better known, and you could start by reading her *Woman, Church, and State* (1893). Its feminist theory was so advanced that, as an older woman, she was rejected by organizations she had founded in her youth. With four authors and dozens of other contributors, the approximately five thousand pages of *History of Woman Suffrage* introduced me to countless "women in the circulation of thought." Periodical publisher Miriam Leslie is just one example. Always called "Mrs. Frank Leslie," she was so successful that when she died in 1914 she left $2 million to Carrie Chapman Catt to be used for the cause of female enfranchisement.

That 1998 book was my last without aid from the Internet, which changed everything. Electronic access to information made it much easier and faster to find specific facts—but the Internet has also spread a great deal of erroneous history that is caught only if one already is familiar with the facts. Within a few years, of course, it completely remodeled the publishing industry, and Valerie and I soon realized that the *Women's Almanac* we issued in 2000 and 2002 would not have a sustainable market.

Instead we launched a much more ambitious project, what turned out to be a four-volume *History of Women in the United States: A State-by-State Reference.* Plus Washington, D.C., and Puerto Rico, covering women from prehistoric tribes to 2004—when publisher Scholastic/ Grolier snatched it before I could add still more. Its bibliography is thus hard to determine, as after each state narrative and a biographical section on prominent women in that state, we added "Prominent Sites," "Further Reading/History," "Further Reading/Biographies and Autobiographies," "Useful Websites," and "Selected Organizations and Institutions." With essays and sidebars by other authors, it totaled 1,626 pages, at least fifty of which probably are lists of resources. My library card for the University of South Florida showed that I checked out literally thousands of books to write these state histories.

When I did a second book on World War II, an encyclopedia published by Routledge in 2010, I was pleased to discover considerable improvement since my first experiences with research. That was particularly true of the National Archives, which had moved its primary sources out to suburban Maryland and left the downtown building to tourists. Working there on my first book in the 1980s had been absolutely Kafka-like, and if my agent, Fran Collin, hadn't already obtained a publishing contract, I might have given up on ever writing about immigrant women or anything else.

The Library of Congress has also become more user friendly. I remember a male librarian in the Prints and Photographs Division during the early 1990s who sneered when I said I wanted images on women, and if it hadn't been my third purchase of illustrations from that office, I might just have gone to the ladies' room and cried. But I knew that he had a female boss—and she reprimanded him. Since then, women in the Manuscript Division at the Library of Congress have begun conducting monthly gatherings so that researchers can exchange information with each other. Even if you can't travel to Washington, it's worthwhile to get on the library's e-mail list for the updates of who is researching what.

My last work for a national audience, again with Valerie, was a two-volume *Women in American Politics: History and Milestones* (2012). It was arranged by office—women as governors, Cabinet members, congresswomen, state legislators, etc. The most difficult chapter to research was mayors: It turned out that neither the National League of Cities nor the U.S. Conference of Mayors had kept records by gender. I knew from previous work (*Milestones*) that the first big city female mayor was Bertha Landes in Seattle in 1926, but it was hard to fill in the blanks after that. E-mail inquiries to librarians and archivists were absolutely invaluable for this work, which was published by Congressional Quarterly Press, as well as for the earlier state histories.

I especially remember e-mailing with a man in New Mexico who was an expert on Soledad Chacon; she became the nation's first female secretary of state in 1922. I knew that North Dakota was first to elect a woman to statewide office (Laura Eisenhuth, 1892, state superintendent of schools), but a man with the North Dakota Historical Society introduced me to two other precedents: North Dakota was the first state to have a woman as House speaker (Minnie Craig, 1933), and it holds the record for the longest tenure of a woman in a legislature (Byrnhild Haugland, fifty-three years).

Women in American Politics also owes a huge debt to an obscure book by Elizabeth M. Cox, *Women State and Territorial Legislators, 1895–1995,* which was published by McFarland Press in Jefferson, North Carolina. It has rosters of more than six thousand women who served in legislatures prior to 1996—and the used copy that I bought online now looks like a rainbow, as I color-coded data by legislature chamber, decade, and more. Analyzing such data is the important part—and the fun part, as I frequently discover patterns only after I've created a table of statistical categories. One of the things I uncovered with the CQ work, for example, is that capital cities are much more likely than others to elect women as mayors. My own state capital, Tallahassee, headed the 2012 list with six women.

More recently, I've published a history of women in Florida and another about my hometown of Tampa, both with university presses. I've also researched local (deceased) people for statues on Tampa's Riverwalk. Local history is an entirely different kettle of fish, and most professional historians avoid it, not only because of a lack of resources, but because of the difficulties of dealing with both outsized egos and family secrets. That aside, I generally enjoy local history, especially being able to place women in their national and even international context. For instance, in doing the Florida history *They Dared to Dream* (2015), I realized that women had been on every one of the six exploratory voyages between 1513 and permanent settlement in 1565.

These expeditions sailed from Puerto Rico, Cuba, Mexico, and Spain, and that reminds me: interesting clues to American history often can be found abroad. An English-language newspaper in a Budapest archive, for instance, covered the international suffrage convention there in 1913. Another great and too-often overlooked resource is cemeteries. I've read the tombstones of American women from Korea to Greece to Belize and elsewhere. Put cemeteries at the top of your next travel agenda.

Finally, to summarize the request for "a list of whatever you used and what you might recommend," let me recommend that you go back through Chapter 1 of this book and highlight the titles that appeal to you, preferably original works such as Lydia Maria Child's *The History of the Condition of Women* (1835) and Margaret Fuller's *Woman in the Nineteenth Century* (1845). Vital though such works are, however, you won't find them listed below, as this bibliography aims to avoid repetition of titles used in the text. Instead, with a few exceptions, the books below are secondary books. All were published after women won the vote in 1920, and most after women's history began to be recognized as a legitimate academic field in the 1970s. Please be aware that the list includes only one title per author, but many of these scholars have produced multiple works—enough to supply both research ideas and bedtime reading for a lifetime.

⸙

Resources and Further Reading

Note: Works cited in the text are not repeated here; only one work per author is listed.

Allen, Agnes Rogers. *Women Are Here to Stay*. New York: Harper & Co., 1949.

Anthony, Katherine. *Susan B. Anthony: Her Personal History and Her Era*. New York: Doubleday, 1954.

Aronson, Amy. *Taking Liberties: Early American Women's Magazines and Their Readers*. Santa Barbara, CA: ABC-Clio, 2002.

Banner, Lois. *Women in Modern America: A Brief History*. New York: Harcourt Brace Jovanovich, 1974.

Baxandall, Rosalyn, Linda Gordon, and Susan Reverby. *America's Working Women: A Documentary History, 1600 to the Present*. New York: Vintage Books, 1976.

Berkin, Carol R., and Mary Beth Norton, eds. *Women of America: A History*. Boston: Houghton Mifflin, 1979.

Butcher, Patricia Smith. *Education for Equality: Women's Rights Periodicals and Women's Higher Education, 1849–1920*. Westport, CT: Greenwood Press, 1989.

Catt, Carrie Chapman, and Nettie Rogers Schuler. *Woman Suffrage and Politics: The Inner Story of the Suffrage Movement*. New York: Charles Scribner's Sons, 1923.

Cott, Nancy, ed. *No Small Courage: A History of Women in the United States*. New York: Oxford University Press, 2000.

Degler, Carol. *At Odds: Women and the Family in America*. New York: Oxford University Press, 1981.

DuBois, Ellen Carol. *Feminism and Suffrage: The Emergence of an Independent Women's Movement in America, 1848–1869*. Ithaca, NY: Cornell University Press, 1978.

Evans, Sara. *Born for Liberty: A History of Women in America*. New York: The Free Press, 1989.

Flexner, Eleanor. *Century of Struggle*. New York: Athenaeum, 1974.

Haber, Barbara. *Women in America: A Guide to Books*. New York: G.K. Hall, 1978.

Harvey, Sheridan. *A Library of Congress Guide for the Study of Women's History and Culture in the United States*. Washington, D.C.: U.S. Government Documents Office, 2001.

Hewitt, Nancy, ed. *No Permanent Waves: Recasting Histories of U.S. Feminism*. New Brunswick, NJ: Rutgers University Press, 2002.

Hine, Darlene Clark, ed. *Black Women in America*. 3 vols. New York: Oxford University Press, 2005.

James, Edward T., Janet Wilson James, and Paul S. Boyer, eds. *Notable American Women: A Biographical Dictionary, 1607–1950*. 3 vols. Cambridge, MA: Harvard University Press, 1971.

Kerber, Linda, and Jane Sherron De Hart. *Women's America: Refocusing the Past*. New York: Oxford University Press, 1995.

Kessler-Harris, Alice. *In Pursuit of Equity: Women, Men, and the Quest for Economic Citizenship in the Twentieth Century*. New York: Oxford University Press, 2001.

Lerner, Gerda. *Living With History/Making Social Change*. Chapel Hill: University of North Carolina Press, 2009.

Lutz, Alma. *Crusade for Freedom: Women of the Anti-Slavery Movement*. Boston: Beacon Press, 1968.

Martin, Theodora Penny. *The Sounds of Their Own Voices: Women's Study Clubs, 1860–1910*. Boston: Beacon Press, 1987.

McKerns, Joseph P., ed. *Biographical Dictionary of American Journalism*. New York: Greenwood Press, 1989.

Mead, Margaret. *Male and Female: A Study of the Sexes in a Changing World*. New York: William Morrow, 1949.

Parks, Maud Wood., ed. *Victory: How Women Won It: A Centennial Symposium, 1840–1940*. New York: H.W. Wilson, 1940.

Roosevelt, Eleanor, and Lorena Hickok. *Ladies of Courage*. New York: G.P. Putnam's Sons, 1954.

Ross, Ishbel. *Ladies of the Press*. New York: Harper & Co., 1936.

Rothman, Sheila M. *Woman's Proper Place: A History of Changing Ideals and Practices, 1870 to the Present*. New York: Basic Books, 1978.

Ryan, Mary P. *Mysteries of Sex: Tracing Women and Men Through American History*. Chapel Hill: University of North Carolina Press, 2006.

Scott, Anne Firor. *Natural Allies: Women's Associations in American History*. Urbana: University of Illinois Press, 1991.

Sicherman, Barbara, and Carol Hurd Green, eds. *Notable American Women: The Modern Period*. Cambridge, MA: Belknap Press of Harvard University Press, 1980.

Sinclair, Andrew. *The Better Half: The Emancipation of the American Woman*. New York: Harper & Row, 1965.

Smith, Jessie Carney, ed. *Notable Black American Women*. 3 vols. Detroit: Gale Research, 1992–1996.

Smith, Page. *Daughters of the Promised Land: Women in American History*. Boston: Little, Brown, 1970.

Solomon, Barbara. *In the Company of Educated Women*. New Haven, CT: Yale University Press, 1985.

Tyler, Alice. *Freedom's Ferment*. Minneapolis: University of Minnesota Press, 1944.

Wadsworth, Sarah, and Wayne A. Wiegand. *Right Here I See My Own Books: The Woman's Building Library at the World's Columbian Exposition*. Boston: University of Massachusetts, 2012.

Ware, Susan, ed. *Notable American Women: A Biographical Dictionary Completing the Twentieth Century*. Cambridge, MA: Harvard University Press, 2004.

Weimann, Jeanne Madeline. *The Fair Women*. Chicago: Academy Press, 1981.

Wertheimer, Barbara Mayer. *We Were There: The Story of Working Women in America*. New York: Pantheon, 1977.

Zuckerman, Mary Ellen. *A History of Popular Women's Magazines in the United States, 1792–1995.* Westport, CT: Greenwood Press, 1998.

———— ◌〜 ————

Notes on Sources
Rosalind Reisner

My contributions to the research and writing of this chapter specifically targeted book publishing, librarianship, and WNBA history. The research was challenging due to the dearth of secondary historical material available through library catalogs and periodical indexes. For an industry that publishes so many books that explain so much, there are few histories of publishing. There is the incomparable four-volume *A History of Book Publishing in the United States* by John Tebbel and Leonard Marcus' wonderful *Minders of Make-Believe*, about the development of children's book publishing in the twentieth century. Those books and others consulted about publishing history are detailed below. Magazine and journal articles, websites, and published theses were extremely helpful. Many of these are listed below for those curious to learn more.

Publishers Weekly, which has reported on the industry for so many years, was an indispensable source of information for this narrative. I was lucky to be able to visit its offices and consult the hard-copy versions of the magazine from the early 1900s, a trove of information, just as lively and informative then as it is today. Articles from those early issues made that time come alive. For many years, *PW* reported on WNBA meetings and programs. It was very helpful to have access to all the back issues of *Publishers Weekly* at the *PW* offices since not all the material in the magazine is indexed in the standard online research tools.

The research process is alternately structured and serendipitous. Days spent combing through *Retrospective Readers' Guide* in a serious manner are upended by the publishing friend who says, "Well, you have to include Helen Venn from the Radcliffe Publishing Course," a name that might have been overlooked and then, of course, researching Venn led to Lindy Hess, her successor at Radcliffe and a figure of great influence to publishers and job seekers alike. A stray comment at lunch by Blanche Wiesen Cook changed the direction of research once again. A friend's husband, who was part of the Freedom Summer in 1964, gave me an article by Virginia Steele, whose remarkable work with the Freedom Libraries would have been lost to me otherwise. Online reference sources, including *Wikipedia* and *Encyclopedia Britannica Online*, were helpful in verifying elusive facts about the lives of many of the women in the chapter, as were organizational websites with detailed histories.

The WNBA's own archives, dating back to that first meeting in 1917, are held at the Rare Book & Manuscript Library at Columbia University, part of a much larger collection of archives about the publishing industry. The founders and early members of the WNBA were diligent about saving materials and there are several amazing scrapbooks, neatly organized, containing all minutes, flyers, memos, copies of speeches, and the other odds and ends generated by an organization. Searching through those archives is a reminder of how our lives have changed where information is concerned. There are numerous copies of typewritten speeches with handwritten notes and corrections. Someone who knew stenography must have always been on hand, since minutes from the early years recount verbatim what was said and by whom. The archives are filled with letters between chapters, between board members of chapters, even telegrams. Articles from *The Bookwoman* and documents from the archives are not cited here individually but are the source of information of most of the WNBA activities described in these pages.

———— ⋄ ————

Resources and Further Reading

Albanese, Andrew Richard. "Making ALA Great Again." *Publishers Weekly*, February 20, 2017.

———. "The Top 10 Library Stories of 2016." *Publishers Weekly*, December 19, 2016.

The Aldersonian, "Virginia Steele—Obituary." n.d. http://www.min7th.com/ahs/ovs.html.

American Library Association. Press release. "Judith Krug, librarian, tireless advocate for First Amendment rights, dies." April 13, 2009. http://www.ala.org/news/news/pressreleases2009/april2009/oifkrug.

Barcelona, Leanna. "Activism and Advocacy in ALA: Women's Organizations," October 19, 2016. https://archives.library.illinois.edu/ala.

Barnes, Earl. "A New Profession for Women." *Atlantic Monthly,* March, 1915.

Barry, Rebecca Rego. "Is Audio Really the Future of the Book?" Review of *The Untold Story of the Talking Book* by Matthew Rubery. November 16, 2016. https://daily.jstor.org/the-future-of-the-book-is-audio/.

Battles, David M. *The History of Public Library Access for African Americans in the South, or, Leaving Behind the Plow.* Lanham, MD: Scarecrow Press, 2009.

Bliley's Funeral Homes. "Bebe Nance Cole." August 31, 2002. http://www.blileyfuneralhomes.com/obituary/Bebe-Nance-Cole/Richmond-VA/13204.

Black, Rita. "If Wonder Woman Were Alive Today, She'd Probably Be in the Typing Pool." *Book Production Industry,* n.d., 1973.

Book Business Magazine. "50 Top Women in Book Publishing." May 1, 2009. http://www.bookbusinessmag.com/article/i-book-business-i-honors-leading-female-executives-helping-shape-industry-406759/all/.

Burger, Pamela. "Women's Groups and the Rise of the Book Club." *JSTOR Daily,* August 12, 2015. https://daily.jstor.org/feature-book-club.

Cott, Nancy, ed. *No Small Courage: A History of Women in the United States.* New York: Oxford University Press, 2000.

Cox, Erin. "On Being a Woman in Publishing." *Publishing Perspectives,* July 23, 2015. http://publishingperspectives.com/2015/07/on-being-a-woman-in-publishing/.

Digital Public Library of America. "A History of US Public Libraries." https://dp.la/exhibitions/exhibits/show/history-us-public-libraries.

Dodson, Shireen. *The Mother-Daughter Book Club.* New York: HarperCollins, 1997.

Donadio, Rachel. "Promotional Intelligence." *New York Times,* May 21, 2006, Sunday Book Review. http://www.nytimes.com/2006/05/21/books/review/21donadio.html.

Eddy, Jacalyn. *Bookwomen: Creating an Empire in Children's Book Publishing, 1919–1939*. Madison: University of Wisconsin Press, 2006.

Feldman, Gayle. *Best and Worst of Times: The Changing Business of Trade Books, 1975–2002*. New York: National Arts Journalism Program, Columbia University, 2003.

Finchum, Tanya Ducker, and Allen Finchum. "Not Gone With the Wind: Libraries in Oklahoma in the 1930s." *Libraries and the Cultural Record* 46, no. 3 (2011): 276-294.

Flock, Elizabeth. "Why These Librarians Are Protesting Trump's Executive Orders." *PBS Newshour*, Public Broadcasting Service, February 13, 2017. http://www.pbs.org/newshour/art/librarians-protesting-trumps-executive-orders/.

Garrison, Dee. *Apostles of Culture: The Public Librarian and American Society; 1876–1920*. New York: Macmillan Information, 1979.

Geller, Evelyn. "ALA Centennial Vignette No. 2: Tessa Kelso: Unfinished Hero of Library Herstory." *American Libraries* 6, no. 6 (June 1975): 347.

Graham, Patterson Toby. *Right to Read: Segregation and Civil Rights in Alabama's Public Libraries, 1900–1965*. Tuscaloosa: University of Alabama Press, 2002.

Grosse, Anisse. "Head of the House." *Publishers Weekly*, May 1, 2017.

Guthrie, Priscilla. "The Bookshop—Pittsburgh." *Publishers Weekly*, May 26, 1917.

Hall, R. Mark. "The 'Oprahfication' of Literacy: Reading 'Oprah's Book Club.'" *College English* 65, no. 6 (July 2003): 646–667.

Hogan, Kristen. *The Feminist Bookstore Movement: Lesbian Antiracism and Feminist Accountability*. Durham: Duke University Press, 2016.

Howard, Pamela. "*Ms.* and the Journalism of Women's Lib." *Saturday Review*, January 8, 1972.

Hymowitz, Carol. *A History of Women in America*. New York: Random House, 1984.

Independent Publisher. "Audiobook Industry Surveys Show Growth." n.d. http://independentpublisher.com/article.php?page=1611.

Japanese American National Museum. "Internment Camp Libraries and Clara Breed." http://www.janm.org/exhibits/breed/breed_t.htm.

Jenison, Madge. "Bookselling as a Profession for Women." *Women's Home Companion,* June 1922.

Joan, Polly, and Andrea Chesman. *Guide to Women's Publishing.* Paradise, CA: Dustbooks, 1978.

Knight, Brenda. *Women of the Beat Generation: The Writers, Artists and Muses at the Heart of a Revolution.* Berkeley, CA: Conari Press, 1996.

Lepore, Jill. "The Lion and the Mouse: The Battle that Reshaped Children's Literature." *New Yorker,* July 21, 2008.

Malcolm, Janet. "The Book Refuge: Three Sisters Keep a Family Business Going." *New Yorker,* June 23, 2014.

Markowitz, Miriam. "Here Comes Everybody." *The Nation,* December 9, 2013.

Mangione, Jerre. *The Dream and the Deal: The Federal Writers' Project, 1935–1943.* Boston: Little, Brown and Co., 1972.

Marcus, Leonard. *Minders of Make Believe: Idealists, Entrepreneurs, and the Shaping of American Children's Literature.* Boston: Houghton Mifflin, 2008.

Miller, Laura. "The Librarian Who Changed Children's Literature Forever." *Slate,* August 5, 2016. http://www.slate.com/blogs/ nightlight/2016/08/05/anne_carroll_moore_the_new_york_ librarian_who_changed_children_s_lit_forever.html.

Milliot, Jim. "Dominique Raccah: Publishing Person of the Year." *Publishers Weekly,* December 19, 2016.

———. "Jane Friedman: Publishing Person of the Year." *Publishers Weekly,* December 11, 2006.

———. "Salary Survey: A Small Bump in Pay." *Publishers Weekly,* September 19, 2016.

———. "Salary Survey: Tough Times to Get Ahead." *Publishers Weekly,* July 28, 2008.

Milliot, Jim, and Susan Connolly. "Salary Survey: The Bigger the Company, Bigger the Paycheck." *Publishers Weekly,* July 6, 1998.

Mowbray-Clarke, Mary. "The Sunwise Turn Bookshop—New York." *Publishers Weekly,* May 26, 1917.

National Public Radio, *Morning Edition.* "Denver's Tattered Cover Bookstore Is Focused on Succession, Not Just Survival." September 9, 2015. http://www.npr.org/2015/09/09/437473687/denvers-tattered-cover-bookstore-is-focused-on-succession-not-just-survival.

Oklahoma Library Commission. "Reports of the Oklahoma Library Commission and Survey of Libraries of Oklahoma, 1932–1934." Oklahoma City, Oklahoma, 1934.

Patchett, Ann. "The Bookstore Strikes Back." *Atlantic*, December 2012. https://www.theatlantic.com/magazine/archive/2012/12/the-bookstore-strikes-back/309164/.

Patrick, Diane. "Behind the Pannell Award." *Publishers Weekly*, August 17, 2004, 18.

Poetry Foundation. "Harriet Monroe." https://www.poetryfoundation.org/poets/harriet-monroe.

Publishers Weekly. "APA Survey: Audiobook Sales, Production, Still Growing." August 16, 2015.

———. "Margaret McElderry Dies at 98." February 15, 2011. https://www.publishersweekly.com/pw/by-topic/childrens/childrens-industry-news/article/46150-margaret-k-mcelderry-dies-at-98.html.

———. "The Rise of Women in Publishing (plus some other useful statistics for the manager planning ahead)." February 15, 1971.

———. "Women in Bookselling." October 13, 1928.

Relke, Diana. "Constance Lindsay Skinner." In *Dictionary of Literary Biography, Canadian Writers,* vol. 92, Detroit: Gale Research Inc., 1990.

Ronda, Bruce A. *Elizabeth Palmer Peabody: A Reformer on Her Own Terms.* Boston: Harvard University Press, 2002.

Rosen, Judith. "What's ahead for bookselling in 2017?" *Publishers Weekly,* January 2, 2017.

Shelf Awareness. "Accomplishments and Challenges: ABA's Oren Teicher on Indie Bookselling." March 2, 2017. http://www.shelf-awareness.com/issue.html?issue=2948#m35654.

Silverman, Al. *The Times of Their Lives: The Golden Age of Great American Publishers, Their Editors and Authors.* New York: St. Martin's Press/Truman Talley Books, 2008.

Steele, Virginia. "Freedom Libraries: Mississippi Summer Project 1964." *Southeastern Librarian* 15, no. 2 (July 1965): 76–81.

Stuart, Nancy Rubin. "Empress of Journalism." *American History* 49, no. 6 (February 2015): 42–49.

Tebbel, John. *A History of Book Publishing in the United States.* 4 vols. New York: R.R. Bowker Co., 1972–1981.

Thompson, John B. *Merchants of Culture: The Publishing Business in the Twenty-First Century.* Malden, MA: Polity, 2010.

Walker, Belle. "The Women's National Book Association." *The Bookman: A Review of Books and Life,* July 1921, 53.

West, Celeste. *Words in Our Pockets: The Feminist Writers' Guild Handbook on How to Gain Power, Get Published & Get Paid.* Paradise, CA: Dustbooks, 1985.

Wiegand, Wayne. "ALA's proudest moments." *American Libraries* 47, no. 6 (June 2016): 32–39.

———. "The Freedom to Read: The History of ALA's Vital Statement on Intellectual Freedom." *American Libraries,* March 15, 2016.

Wiegand, Wayne, and Sarah Wadsworth. *Right Here I See My Own Books: The Women's Building Library at the World's Columbian Exposition, Studies in Print Culture and the History of the Book.* Amherst, MA: University of Massachusetts Press, 2012.

Wikipedia. "New Words Bookstore." https://en.wikipedia.org/wiki/New_Words_Bookstore.

———. "Virginia Kidd." https://en.wikipedia.org/wiki/Virginia_Kidd.

The Woman Citizen: A Weekly Chronicle of Progress IV, no. 20 (December 6, 1919): 545. "Woman and the Stream of Thought."

CHAPTER 2

BOOKSELLING THEN AND NOW

In 1916, friends Madge Jenison (1874–1960) and Mary Horgan Mowbray-Clarke (1874–1962) opened a bookstore on 31st Street near Fifth Avenue in midtown Manhattan called the Sunwise Turn Bookshop. The unusual name came from a Celtic belief that following the motion of the sun brought good fortune. As Jenison wrote in her 1923 memoir, *Sunwise Turn: A Human Comedy of Bookselling*: "Our theory was that we meant to sell books in a more modern and civilized way than they were being sold, and carry them, if the powers were in us, into the stream of the creative life of our generation." With the judicious use of paint, pillows, upholstered chairs, and wall hangings, they created a cozy place for readers and book buyers. Theodore Dreiser was the first author to give a reading; other well-known authors followed, and exhibits by avant-garde painters and sculptors soon rounded out the picture of a welcoming bookshop dedicated to literature and the arts. The Sunwise Turn quickly became a popular gathering place for artists and writers who were interested in the modernist movement. Peggy Guggenheim was an intern in those early years; she found her calling as an art collector there (as well as her first husband).

Jenison was an idealist and a dreamer, a member of the original group of women booksellers who met at Sherwood's Book Store in lower Manhattan in the fall of 1917 to form the Women's National Book Association. It was these women booksellers, closed out of the all-male American Booksellers Association (ABA) and the Booksellers' League, who believed that the reading and circulating of books was of vital importance to a civilized society. As Jenison wrote in her memoir, *Sunwise Turn*: "Books! Do I make too much of them? They knock at the future." She was the repository of much WNBA history and we are grateful for the many years of her spirited support.

On the afternoon of March 1, 1957, the WNBA held a tea in honor of Jenison and her many contributions to the WNBA. Jenison had remained an active member for many years, had seen the organization thrive and expand, and often served as its institutional memory. At the time of the tea, she was eighty-one. A scroll was presented to her that afternoon in honor of all her accomplishments. In 1957, according to notes in the WNBA archives, she was "a very frail but alert old lady." She died three years later.

Engraving of the interior of the Sunwise Turn, the bookshop co-owned by Madge Jenison, one of the WNBA's cofounders, and Mary Mowbray-Clarke; the print was published in Jenison's memoir, *Sunwise Turn: A Human Comedy of Bookselling.*

The WNBA members who have spent time reading Jenison's articles and notes in the WNBA archives or reading her memoir have found it impossible not to miss her presence among us. Her buoyant personality shines through in everything she wrote. She was remarkable for her enthusiasm, idealism, and devotion to her family, friends, and the literary world. In addition to her work as a bookseller and WNBA member, she was the author of several novels, including *Dominance* (1928), *Invitation to the Dance* (1929), and *Roads* (1949).

In her article "Bookselling as a Profession for Women"

which appeared in the *Women's Home Companion* in the early 1920s, Jenison wrote about the joys and challenges of running a bookstore. So much of what she described remains true for booksellers today. In this chapter, we've reprinted her article followed by the comments of Joyce Meskis, another pioneering woman bookseller, retired owner of Denver's Tattered Cover Book Store.

Since the WNBA was founded by a group of women booksellers, their concerns and interests were always on the WNBA agenda. In an early issue of *The Bookwoman*, the WNBA's newsletter that began in 1937, there appeared a Booksellers Quiz, asking women booksellers to provide answers to questions commonly fielded in bookstores. The questions—and the answers—are hilarious and true, another reminder that *plus ça change, plus c'est la même chose.* In later issues of *The Bookwoman*, in a section called "Bookwomen Speak Their Mind," booksellers commented on the challenges they faced. Both the quiz (with answers) and the booksellers' comments are reprinted in this chapter.

"BOOKSELLING AS A PROFESSION FOR WOMEN"
Madge Jenison, "Bookselling as a Profession for Women,"
National Business Woman, *February, 1926*

Once a woman came to talk to me about opening a bookshop in Montclair. She said that she had three children to educate and five thousand dollars in the bank. What did I advise her to do? I told her that I could not possibly even guess for her. I did not know how much imagination she had, or will, or culture, or power to work. It takes a great deal of all these to keep a bookshop. But she was insistent, and she was plainly in need of a helping hand from somewhere to keep her from being simply a mother of three children with an uneasy heart. She went away, saying that she would come back in two weeks. Would I think it over and tell her what I thought then?

It gave me three headaches and spoiled a performance of "Il Pagliacci" for me, but when she came back I advised her to do it. Five thousand dollars would not educate three children. It would not educate half a child, or buy their clothes or keep them in overshoes. But if she would get out in the world of affairs, even if she failed, somebody would be watching her, and she would get an experience which would help her to do something else.

Probably five hundred women and a hundred men in the United States are at this moment planning to open bookshops, and thirty or forty thousand more regard them as one of the romantic possibilities of life, like sitting on a stone in the moonlight or finding that there is oil on the farm your grandfather left you, appraised in the last bill for taxes at one thousand dollars.

There is some golden spell about bookselling. If you love books you can check, dust, label, wrap, bill them, and still they give you out some phantom joy. I have loaned books, sometimes ten at a sitting; I have bought them, and spent evenings rearranging them after various theories; but to sell anybody one hundred and eighty—pile them up so that all the surrounding chairs and tables are toppling with them, is a kind of fever dream. "The work is the wages" in bookselling more than in most things with which we occupy ourselves, I think.

Women in "making room for their feet" have overrun bookselling. They are at the head of virtually all the book departments of the large department stores in New York. These are the big "merchandising women"—who can buy competently, turn over stock at the required rate, get space from the advertising manager, and handle a large sales force with judgment. The number of women at the national Booksellers' Convention increases markedly each year. One half the attendance at the convention last year was women.

The small, expert shops, where there is something of that experienced professional relation to your material which we associate with a physician or lawyer, are in a marked degree the enterprises of women.

Eight such shops were opened in New York in one winter—five by women. One was a children's bookshop and one of the two members of the firm was a pediatrist (children's physician) and it aimed to provide as expertly for children's reading as physicians do for their physical development and health. The Sunwise Turn in New York, which was visited during the war by all the high commissions from abroad for material on education and labor, is the project of two women. It is hard to think that women sell books any differently from men but it seems to be true that most of the experimental creative things in bookselling are being done just now by women.

One of the romantic subjects of conversation for years in the book trade has been the peddling of books from door to door. We have all talked about a bookshop on wheels winding over the hills and far away. But nobody did it. It remained for Miss Bertha Mahoney of Boston to convince sixteen publishers that a Book Caravan would be a practical advertising project which could be crossed off on their publicity budget even if it did not entirely pay for itself. A special truck was built for Miss Mahoney. It cost fifty-five hundred dollars. The ends let down to give as much space as possible when it stops for business. It carries a thousand books. The plan of its administration is roughly as follows: An itinerary was laid out in advance, and the woman's club, or some interested organization, was asked at each stop to act as hostess and give the Caravan some advance publicity. It drew up in a town square or the court of a hotel, and opened its doors for business. Every night accounts were cast, and a postal order and the orders for books not in stock returned to Boston. At certain points along the route the stock carried was renewed by packages sent from Miss Mahoney. During the first summer, the Caravan sold eight thousand dollars' worth of books. Miss Mahoney's venture was subsidized by the Women's Educational and Industrial Union of Boston.

A later venture was that of Appleton's. Mr. Hiltman, president of this publishing house, sent out a truck to sell Appleton publications alone. This was a standard truck which cost twelve hundred and fifty dollars, and made no pretensions beyond carrying two tons. Instead of two women at salaries of fifty dollars a week each, it was driven by a single salesman; and instead of making a long tour it ran close to New York and used the home office as a base for restocking. But the fundamental departure it made was that it peddled from door to door instead of selling to those who came to an established stand. The Appleton truck paid from the first week, although it tilled an infinitely more restricted territory than the Book Caravan—the list of a single publisher. But most publishers have a rounded list: fiction, business books, children's books, poetry, biography, travel. At one house, where the driver of the Appleton truck found a sick man he sold thirty novels, not all new by any means, but all new to his buyer.

Any woman whose husband or father would lend her a truck, and who could find a friend to go along for the ride, so that the overhead would not rise too seriously, could try out this experiment. A little ingenuity, and some steps to let down, would make any standard truck a place to stand around and talk of books. And what a chance for headliners the walls of the truck would offer! "Books are food, air, light, love, hope, common sense, information—Buy."

It is startling to think what the effect on the next generation would be if fine books were carried to the intellectually starved communities of the country. There are states beyond the Mississippi which are almost bookstore-less. The Book Caravan sold forty dollars' worth of books in one hour on one farm in Massachusetts. One woman could do more in a summer by talking about and selling *The Story of Mankind*; the Lives of Pasteur, Benvenuto Celini, J.J. Hill, and Elizabeth Blackwell; Evelyn Dewey's *New Schools for Old*; Carpenter's *Love's Coming of Age*; Stanley Hall's *Jesus in the Light of Modern Psychology*, and a dozen or two of the best contemporary novels and volumes of poetry—or anything else she loved, and could present with zeal—than by writing all the checks a fountain pen can sign. She would put in the hands of hundreds of people large models of things about which they think in small, and stories of how people did what they longed to, instead of looking at the horizon and thinking about little poems on resignation.

It has been proved that it is the "quality books," as the publishers call them, that sell from caravans, and that, when people seldom have a chance to buy books, they buy the best. The last United States census shows that nearly one-half of the population of the United States is on farms and probably not in the trading radius of a good bookstore; and such a book truck would bring, especially to youth, the world of the gods.

The Hampshire Bookshop, of Northampton, organized and financed by Smith Alumnae and managed by Miss Marion Dodd, is an experiment in a different milieu. There is a place in every college community in the country for a shop such as this. Such a shop does not compete with the textbook bookstores. Let these stores keep the textbook trade, and all strength to their elbows. These college-town bookshops are shops with a feeling, and with a look of being lived in. Miss Dodd has proved that such centers are wanted. She has tripled her staff in four years and is doing now a business of seventy thousand dollars a year.

One of the most magnetic figures in the book trade is Miss Marcella Burns, now Mrs. Hahner, head of the book department of Marshall Field's, in Chicago. Miss Burns conducts at Marshall Field's an annual book fair of national importance, where all the publishers show exhibits. America will have in time a book fair conducted by the book trade itself; but in the meantime Miss Burns is doing it.

The important step in a bookshop is to get it started. A bookshop is so important to a community that it will not be allowed to die if it is once started.

"What did you do?" I asked a woman who had found fifteen thousand dollars capital for her shop in the worst period of the financial depression of 1920.

"What didn't I do?" she answered, and clapped a hand to the forehead that had served her well.

She had written to everyone she heard of, who might help, followed up every idea, every suggestion, devised a plan by which friends of the shop could take each a small hand in helping it; with every turn she made, learned to put her case more and more vividly. One must be able to talk about any idea, to sell it.

To get the shop started, the first great necessity, after the will to do it, is capital. The financing of anything more than a velvet hat frightens very many women; but if women are to realize their business visions they must learn to find the money for what they believe in, take the hazards, and then get the returns, if there are any.

"Desiring isn't everything. The chief thing is to have a straight backbone." Perhaps you can capitalize it yourself. The husband of one woman I know financed hers, an aunt helped another. The Detroit Arts and Crafts Society partially subsidized its bookshop. In some states the State Federation of Women's Clubs has funds for public-spirited enterprises. The Hampshire Bookshop and the Radical Bookstore in Chicago are both cooperative organizations. They rebate back to all members of the company a percentage of profits.

A bookshop can be begun on a very small capital. Miss Marion Cutter, owner of The Children's Book Shop, in New York, walked along

Fifth Avenue thinking how tall the buildings were and how small she was and that she knew nothing about business, and then she went into a little sliver of a room partitioned off from a laundry, which looked to her like a bookshop, and signed a lease for it. She had a capital of $2,000 made up of a small legacy and the savings of a librarian's salary. At the end of four years she has a capital invested of $12,000. The Sunwise Turn began with $2,500. But an adequate capitalization is $5,000 to $12,000, and it saves one many a sleepless night to have it. No business is expected to be on an assured basis in less than three years, and a sinking fund for these problematic three years will go partly for rent and partly for publishers' bills, and provide a fund of peace and leisure for constructive effort. The accepted amount of yearly business which a bookshop must do to be on a paying basis is $20,000. The Sunwise Turn did $12,192 the first year, $12,874 the second; $18,259 the third; $37,782 the fourth.

Any place will do for a bookshop if one gives it individuality. If you have an idea, you do not have to pay rent. I never see on the main street of any small city one of those old gubernatorial or justice-of-the-supreme-court-looking houses, which always stand somewhat above the car line, without wishing that some daughter of the house would set up a bookshop in the little reception-room which is sure to be at the right hand of the front door. Stables make big studio-like rooms in which it is easier to set up a bookshop than it is not to. In New York the small bookshops are sometimes down a few steps in the old brown-stone houses, sometimes up a few steps, sometimes on the second floor. They can be anywhere that you can put yourself, a few books, a customer—and a chair to fall into when publishers' bills come in.

The safest first buying is the things one likes. One is sure sometime to sell a book one likes. The problem of bookselling is not to sell books but to sell the books one has. Merchandising is not a matter of buying five hundred books and selling them, and then taking the money to buy seven hundred and fifty more, as I thought in the naïve days when I first planned a bookshop; it is keeping a set of Jane Austen five years on the shelf, and then selling it at rare book prices because that edition is out of print, or entering more unfortunate items year after year on the stock list until the sight of them makes one's breast give forth a moan.

A good card catalogue of customers is one of the richest assets a bookseller can have, and she should begin from the first to create it. Good card catalogues with information about clients are coming to be recognized in every profession and business as a routine part of equipment. They have sold for as much as ten thousand dollars. The greatest insurance salesman in the world, who sells more than a million dollars' worth of insurance a year, has in his files notes on his clients and those whom he regards as candidates, which includes their relations to their wives and children, their investments, tastes, clubs, careers, and character sketches to rival Margot Asquith's autobiography.

What you want to know to sell a man a book is not where he lives but whether he wants Ulster to have a separate Parliament, loves the sea, or likes stories best where the young man gets rich and marries the daughter of the owner of the mill, and whether he prefers Airedales or Cocker spaniels. You get this information day by day from people who lean their elbows on the tables opposite you and lay before you their tastes, hates, needs, and sometimes stories out of their lives more poignant and brilliant than anything you have in print. Your window, your technique of selling, your organization, your policy of advertising grow up and change, month by month, within the engrossing movement of human beings in and out of the shop.

Bookselling is the most fascinating thing in the world to do. But with the best management in the world there always remains, especially in the small shop, the difficulty of making it pay—that almost irreducible gap between the overhead of selling books and the profits to be made on them. The big commercial bookstores fill this gap by selling stationery, old and rare books, typewriters, office furniture, even linoleum and automobiles. The small shops which are trying to keep within their walls the feeling of creative, imaginative life sell textiles, pictures, publish, and take orders for printing. One is supported by its English importations.

Sometimes a bookstore is an adjunct to another business. Several gift shops carry a wall of books. Occasionally tea-rooms undertake this, and more could. Any tea-room could add a thousand or two dollars a year to its income with its left hand, by having a shelf of books to let out to solitary diners, and copies of a few of the popular contemporary books for sale. Books bring people.

There is a great untapped possibility for fine bookselling in modern life—the leisure-class woman. Women of family could sell books preeminently well. They have the equipment. It ties up to their traditions. Many of them could do that, and use their powers, who would not do anything else. Every book one sells opens a door into a new life, and a woman's perception could fling open with generous hand the way to a brighter and more spacious world to many a person too busy, or young, or unaspiring to find it for himself.

EDITOR'S NOTE: This article is reprinted by the gracious permission of the author and the "Woman's Home Companion." It appeared in that magazine several years ago, but it is just as pertinent to women's interests now as it was then. Those of our readers who like the easy charm of Miss Jenison's writing will be delighted to know that E.P. Dutton has recently published her book, "The Sunwise Turn," for which, she says, this article was merely a "preliminary canter."

Madge Jenison, "Bookselling as a Profession for Women," National Business Woman, 2/10 (1926), 6–7, 26. Used by permission from ProQuest Information and Learning Company, Copyright 2006, all rights reserved. All spelling and punctuation from the original has been preserved.

RESPONSE TO MADGE JENISON'S ARTICLE, "BOOKSELLING AS A PROFESSION FOR WOMEN"
Joyce Meskis, Retired Owner, Tattered Cover Book Store, 1974–2017, Denver, Colorado

Madge Jenison (1874–1960) was an author, publisher, and bookseller. Given her work as a founding member of the Women's National Book Association in 1917, and her subsequent long tenure of involvement with that organization, it seems appropriate on the eve of the WNBA's Centennial celebration to make some observations and comparisons about bookselling then and now, and on how she and others may have influenced its evolution.

Jenison's article "Bookselling as a Profession for Women" gives us insight into the changes that were occurring in the marketplace, how her own experience had evolved, and the encouragement she so freely offered to women who had the need and/or desire to make their way into the world of business—particularly, the book business.

Jenison's bookshop, the Sunwise Turn, co-owned with Mary Horgan Mowbray-Clarke, opened in 1916, in New York City on 31st Street. It is hard to imagine now what it must have been like in those years— really not so very long ago—when women were denied membership in the all-male American Booksellers Association. It was during that era, in 1920, that the women's suffrage movement finally won access to the voting booth! And it was thanks to women's activism and the efforts of so many others, that the talent, entrepreneurial spirit, and contributions of women were brought to light, shining on our institutions, cultural endeavors, and business interests—not the least of which was the bookshop.

During the ten years it was open the Sunwise Turn Bookshop made its mark on the culture of a nation. At the same time, it must have been gratifying to witness the transformation in the roles women played in the book industry. As Jenison observed, "Women...have overrun bookselling." Stores were being opened in greater numbers by women; women were managing the book departments in major department stores; and they were opening bookshops, lots and lots of bookshops. Through various means, these women found the capital, locations, inventory, and the knowledgeable staff to sell books to a welcoming audience of readers.

By 1923, Jenison had written a book, *Sunwise Turn: A Human Comedy of Bookselling*, which documented her own development as a bookseller, capturing the pleasures and confusions inherent in the business of books. As a well-connected observer, she chronicled the unique creative expressions of her sister booksellers in their efforts to bring books to the people: through her own intellectual soirées; a focus on the political anarchistic interests of the day; books by mobile caravan; books for children; good books of all kinds.

All of this is not to say that there are no more hurdles to overcome. To stay in business requires constant oversight of market trends; creative enterprising attentiveness; unflagging attention to financial detail; and a passion for the business of books as strong as the passion for the creative construct of the words and ideas presented in them.

Bookselling today is not an endeavor for the hobbyist. There is too much at risk, too much to do and too much to lose, individually and collectively. Even to accomplish one's lofty philosophical goals, a viable business plan must be in place to support such a noble endeavor. Yet today, as before, there remains a kind of dreaminess about owning a bookshop. I have heard hundreds of times the refrain, "Oh, it must be wonderful owning a bookstore, doing nothing all day long but sitting on a stool and discussing the great books with your customers." Well, of course, there is some of that, but in reality it's cleaning the bathrooms, shoveling the snow, dealing with a leak in the roof that the landlord is slow to fix; it's tax forms, labor laws, censorship challenges from right and left; keeping an eye on the budget, not letting the inventory of the store get ahead of its sales; it's paying the bills, or at least worrying about paying them. It's hard work, heavy work requiring a strong back and a fertile mind, the latter to serve as a repository for the minutiae so necessary to answer the myriad questions from a diverse clientele in search of information, answers, edification, relaxation, or a favorite bedtime story to read to the children. Then and now, serving the critical thinkers and interests of those readers residing in a pluralistic society is a demanding job.

And it is just as difficult today to make it a profitable enterprise with the high cost of doing business, given escalating commercial rents (particularly in urban areas); wages that are too low for the employees, yet too high for the business to bear; and health insurance premiums on an increasing continuum. That and more are too much for the insufficient margins to cover, with too little if any profit left over.

Technology has become a necessity to the work of today's successful bookshop: in managing and selling inventory; placing orders to wholesalers and publishers; and marketing. Keeping the connection with customers through the Internet has largely but not entirely replaced print communication.

Jenison noted that women were increasingly involved in attending the book conventions and trade shows. Certainly, women today are very much a part of the American Booksellers Association, not only as members but as leaders. It took a while, but Joan Ripley, owner of Second Story Bookstore in Chappaqua, New York, was its first woman president, from 1980 to 1982. More have followed, and others have provided guidance

The Tattered Cover Book Store location in the historic LoDo (Lower Downtown) district in Denver.

as teachers, mentors, and advisors for members of both national and regional bookseller associations.

Current bookselling challenges are multifaceted. The negative economic effects of the Great Recession of 2008 are finally being overcome; e-book sales have leveled out, giving assurance that the print book is not dead; terms of trade are being reevaluated; net pricing is back in discussion (the lack thereof played a role in the formation of the American Booksellers Association in 1900); and social media has become a strong marketing option.

The bookselling landscape has changed dramatically since the 1990s rollout of the superstores Barnes & Noble and Borders (with Borders gone twenty-five years later). Amazon has proved to be a dynamic and fierce competitor online and with its new efforts to open bricks-and-mortar stores.

And independent stores are experiencing a revival in the marketplace with creative innovation: Bookstores with coffee shops are making way for bookstores with wine and beer bars; literary travel tours are being offered; summer book camps for children and myriad other adventures, such as expanded author programs, are in the schools; and smaller satellite stores are also being established in combination with a larger parent store. The Buy Local First movement is gaining a lot of traction with increased bookseller participation.

Basically, however, then as now, it's all about the connection between the customer and the bookseller—the delight of putting the right book in the hands of the reader. There is nothing like it.

A QUIZ FOR BOOKWOMEN, FROM *THE BOOKWOMAN*
Vol. 3, no. 1, November, 1938

Are you employed in a bookshop? And how good are you at finding a solution to such vital questions as those given below? To each of the three bookwomen who send in the most convincing answers to the following questions, THE BOOKWOMAN offers a year's membership in the Women's National Book Association. Send no money—buy nothing. Simply write your answers and sign your name, business address, and position held, on any paper (letterhead preferred but not required) and mail to the editor, Alice Klutas, 98 Woodruff Ave., Brooklyn, N.Y., on or before January 15, 1939. The judges are the staff of THE BOOKWOMAN. The winnahs! will be announced in the February 1939 issue of THE BOOKWOMAN, and the winning answers will be printed as rapidly as space will permit. The questions, as you may have guessed, are by those master quizzers—RoseJeanne Slifer and Louise Crittenden. Let's go!

QUIZ

1. What is the correct answer to the pompous "I want to talk to someone who knows the stock"?

2. Is it better to be truthful and lose the sale or be evasive and make it when the customer asks if you have read every single book you suggest?

3. What line of action do you pursue when you are told of a book you recommend, "Oh, but that got an unfavorable review"!

4. What age level is advisable to suggest to the customer who says, "My son is nine, but he has the mentality of an eleven-year old"?

5. Are more books damaged or is more customer goodwill gained by allowing a customer to copy recipes from cookbooks or to look up her latest dream in *100,000 Dreams Interpreted*?

6. How old can a latest book be, when a customer says, "Oh, that's not new. I saw that reviewed three weeks ago"?

7. When Junior wants a certain book and his mother wants him to have a different one, what do you say?

8. What is the wisest thing to do with an author who repeatedly offers to autograph her books— which you never stock?

9. What do you answer when Madame says, "I can't see why you don't have that book. Every other store in town carries it"?

10. How can you dispose of the browser, who having spent the afternoon "just looking" shows no sign of leaving, twenty minutes after closing time?

ANSWERS

1. The correct answer to the pompous "I want to talk to someone who knows the stock" in my case is "I believe I shall be able to help you Madame (or Sir) as I ordered the entire stock myself and I am in the book business because I do want to help people select books."

2. It IS better to be truthful and lose a sale than be evasive and make it when the customer asks if you have read every single book you suggest. Why? Because in not too many years of trouping or bookselling, as you will, you will recommend the wrong biography of Mary Baker Eddy to a devout Christian Scientist; you will sell Asbury's *French Quarter* to the sweet old lady who

wants something interesting on New Orleans; and you will sell a good author's pot-boiling contract-filler to someone who has liked his earlier and better things. And that is all very well if you have let the buyer know you have not read the books and are not responsible personally for his disappointment.

3. When the retort is "Oh, that got an unfavorable review!" my answer is (depending on the book), "Well, reviewers are human, you know, and perhaps the reviewer whose opinion you read did not like whimsy (or satire, or Texas, or realism in inland Mississippi, or whatever it may be) but I really believe that this is a book you will enjoy. Frankly, it demands a discriminating reader."

4. When the proud mother says, "My son is nine but he has the mentality of an eleven-year old" the best age level is 8 to 10. To be very sure you may inquire as to the things he has just read and if he liked *Westward Ho* or if he's read *The Wind in the Willows*. If you can get the mother to talk sensibly about his reading that will be a clue. However, the mother who pulls the mentality IQ stuff usually doesn't talk sensibly.

5. Although I believe that more books are damaged in allowing customers to check on their dreams or copy recipes than goodwill is gained, I do not know the answer when you decide to say "No!" Then there is always the story of the old man who read about his dream and was so encouraged by it that he bought the $4.50 book on sex rejuvenation.

6. The answer to "Oh, that's not new. I saw that reviewed three weeks ago" is "Isn't it funny, though, that books like *Gone With the Wind*, *Green Light* and *Anthony Adverse* are years old and still selling like new books. You know it doesn't matter how old a book is, if it is worthwhile it continues to sell and to please its readers. I think if you have not read _____ you will enjoy it thoroughly."

7. When Junior wants a book and his mother wants a different one, either bring out a third book (preferably a dollar more) or side with the mother in a delicate way and bring out a point about the mischievous nature of the young boy in the book the mother has selected. Or you might fall back on Tom Sawyer.

8. When the author repeatedly offers to autograph his books which you have never stocked, the wisest thing to say is, "But, sir, I am just not able to keep your books in stock—the customers buy it for gifts and don't wait to get it autographed." Or, you might say "Shall I order the books from you or your publisher?"

9. When Madame says, "I can't see why you don't have that book. Every other store in town carried it!" the bookseller can at least come back with "I have had such remarkable sales on _____ that I have been forced to re-order several times. At the present moment I have a shipment coming in and I shall be glad to send a copy out to you tomorrow."

10. When the browser—who has spent the afternoon "just looking" shows no sign of leaving twenty minutes after closing time, you might say, "I'm so sorry to have to disturb you, but a man from the termite company is coming to spray the floors. I'm afraid the odor will be terrific. But you WILL come back."

BOOKWOMEN SPEAK ABOUT BOOKSELLING
These comments are taken from an article titled
"Bookwomen Speak Their Mind." They appeared in
The Bookwoman, *vol. 10, no. 3, Spring 1947.*

The problems of bookwomen are many, but seem to be similar in nature. To open the discussion, we have asked a number of sellers to "speak their minds."

Lura B. Cummings, Everyday Bookshop, Inc., Burlington, Vermont

From the buying angle I protest against wildly extravagant blurbs—"the book of the century"—"the best novel of 1947"—"the most authoritative treatment of the subject." Words have lost their meaning by misuse. Also, as a buyer I protest the policy of some publishers on returns. As the manager of a small book shop I'd like to return one, two or three copies of a "leftover." I am pleased that some publishers are becoming more liberal.

As a seller of books I am very wroth that reputable publishers continue to issue "uninhibited" books. And when, as one salesman openly stated recently, they feel justified in building up sales of a "rich and lusty" book so they can publish better books that might not make a profit, I find myself wondering what has become of the honor of "the happy profession." Women have sold their honor to buy bread for their children but I cannot believe that there are no crusts left in the cupboards of some publishers who have put out books that once they would have been ashamed to acknowledge.

Also, as a seller of books. I wish the "best-seller" lists had never been started. I find it irritates me to put on a smile when a customer chooses a worthless "best-seller" in preference to a book of merit. But, of course, the customer has a right to choose so we keep our "peevers" to ourselves.

And, last of all, how overworked my adrenal glands are when I've shown a customer every book in the shop—well, almost every one—and she says, "Thank you. I don't see just what I want."

But I'm not so peeved that I'd change my job for any other!

Nesta C. Edwards, The Little Book Shop, Milwaukee, Wisconsin

We deal entirely in books for children. From little tots, on through high school, and this shop has become something of a laboratory for parents, teachers and children.

I think it would be a good thing for the book business in general if you could be instrumental in getting a few more of the writers out in this part of the country. The East needs the West and the West needs the East. The two authors which we have had at this shop have been a tremendous stimulation to our customers. I am willing to admit that maybe New York is the hub, and that it takes a long time for some things to trickle down through the spokes to the rim.

Esther Bates, The Book Nook, Daytona Beach, Florida

In such a small personalized book shop much satisfaction comes from having books of unusual interest. One's ego is inflated when a customer finds just the books wanted and adds that she knew she would when she drove from another town for her purchases. Yes, it gives one a wonderful feeling but it also often adds up to not turning that stock as often as modern merchandising demands. Is the day of the personalized bookshop on the wane? Should a small shop close books out at a discount just to make that turnover and not await the chance of selling at full price? Of course I refer to books of lasting value.

Katharine Flower, McClelland's Bookstore Inc., Columbus, Ohio

After you have been in the book business as many years as I have, many of the pet peeves of earlier days don't seem sufficient cause for peevishness any more. I suppose it is just a matter of growing up and not letting molehills be made into mountains. Nowadays, the most unreasonable customer hardly gets under my skin at all. Customers, for the most part, are fun, and are decent and likeable—and we sure have to have them.

CHAPTER 3

FROM THE ARCHIVES

Nancy Rubin Stuart

The Women's National Book Association (WNBA) archives date back to the very first organizational meeting, in the fall of 1917. In an era of handwritten minutes and letters, the first generation of members made sure that their meeting minutes, financial records, program planning documents, newsletters, and memos were collected in scrapbooks. As the chapters were established, they, too, sent their news and records to the archives at Columbia University's Rare Book and Manuscript Library. A curious researcher can experience firsthand the excitement, soul-searching, creativity, and friction that made the organization thrive. WNBA members were engaged with the social and political issues of the day, and those concerns are reflected in a century of activities and initiatives. Many well-known, accomplished women in the book world believed in the value of the organization and its mission; their intelligence, energy, and commitment were essential to its early survival and current vitality.

For this section, Nancy Rubin Stuart, WNBA member and author, copresident of the Boston chapter, explored archival materials to offer a look at some interesting personalities and events from the organization's history.

THE FOUNDING STORY
"Dear Madam: You are cordially requested to attend an informal meeting to be held at Sherwood's Book Store, No. 19 John Street, New York City,

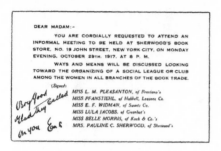

The invitation sent to women booksellers in 1917 that launched the Women's National Book Association.

on Monday Evening, October 29, at 8 p.m. Ways and Means will be discussed looking toward the organization of a social league or club among women in all branches of the book trade," read an invitation that marked the founding of the Women's National Book Association.

Not coincidentally, the request arrived in the mailboxes of thirty-five booksellers soon after the large suffrage march on Fifth Avenue on October 27, 1917. Contemporary reports noted that twenty-five thousand people marched in the parade, some carrying posters with the signatures of one million New York women who wanted the right to vote.

The signers of the invitation were six prominent women booksellers whose gender prohibited them from membership in the American Booksellers Association (ABA) and the Booksellers' League. They were: L.M. Pleasanton of Brentano's; Josephine Pfanstiehl of Hubbell, Leavens Co.; E.F. Widman of F.A.O. Schwarz Co.; Lula Jacobs of Greenhut's; Belle Morris of Keche & Co.; and their gracious hostess, Pauline C. Sherwood of Sherwood's Book Store.

Given their exclusion from the ABA, women's seven-decade battle to achieve the vote, and the National American Woman Suffrage Association's alignment with the war effort, the 1917 creation of a women's organization of booksellers with an activist agenda seemed justified. So they came—about fifteen women—to No. 19 John Street and sat around on high stools. No one seems to remember just who these women were, beyond the committee members who signed the invitation, plus Madge Jenison of The Sunwise Turn Bookshop and Effie Hubley of Loeser's.

Madge Jenison, one of the WNBA's founders and its second president, wrote in later years about the idealistic fervor that informed the group:

The Women's National Book Association was founded when great ideas were about. It was in the years of the First World War, toward the end of it. Big ideas of civilization and what we wanted of it; how we could keep all we have and get some more. It seemed to us that books are power—that if we could create a working body of all those who have to do with the circulation of ideas in books…if we could start up such an organization, we would have a mechanism, through which we could throw our weight en masse behind anything in which we believed; that we could even stop war if our organization became complete and vigorous enough. Books are a step above the newspapers, magazines and radio. They are the cream of the crop. And it seems to us logical that women should undertake such an enterprise as this.

Enthusiasm for the organization continued to rise. Two weeks later, by which time the New York State Legislature had granted women residents the vote, "They met again, with thirty-five women present, on November 13, 1917, and formed a permanent organization. The first President was the little woman with the big idea—Mrs. Pauline Sherwood, of Sherwood's Book Store," recalled Belle Walker in a July 21, 1921, *Bookman* report.

By the time of Belle Walker's article, women's political status had changed. Not only had American women achieved the vote with the 1920 ratification of the Nineteenth Amendment, but the WNBA was so widely "recognized as a factor in the book business," that the ABA invited the organization to become a member.

The WNBA considered that invitation warily. Possibly that was because of its tone. As the new organization's second president, Madge Jenison, noted in a September 2, 1920, meeting, the ABA had not merely issued an invitation but "urged that the WNBA be merged" within the men's organization. Subsequently, "it was voted that the president reply expressing appreciation of the invitation but courteously declining to merge at the present time." Nevertheless, "there was further discussion of the relations between the two Associations…especially for the necessity for getting women appointed in the future to all Committees of the ABA instead of only one or two committees as at present." In short, the women of the WNBA believed that one condition for joining the ABA would be that its members would have an important voice in the formerly all-male organization. Already that representation had been achieved in a related industry event. As Walker noted in her 1921 *Bookman* report, two WNBA members had been elected officers at the Booksellers Convention in the past two years. Walker wrote, "And so the Women's National Book Association feels that, young and imperfect as it is, it has a place in the fallow fields of book distribution. For its desire is to be both pupil and guide in the literary Labyrinth, to be with those who are building for the great future of the limitless possibilities of the book business." Almost two decades after the organization was formed, the inaugural issue of its newsletter, *The Bookwoman*, reprinted the WNBA Creed linking the importance of women in the world of books to the democratic spread of human thought:

> *Believing that it is impossible to isolate any single instrumentality in the great arterial circulation of thought, this Association is created to include in a single working body, women writers, women booksellers, women critics, women editors, women librarians and women advertisers, together with women employed in the printing and bookmaking trades and in publishing houses, as a means to education to more consciousness in ourselves and as an organized power to further in every instance we can make use, the freer movement of life and truth.*

THE EARLY DINNERS

From the start, the WNBA understood the importance of raising funds through social events. On January 30, 1919, the organization invited members to attend its first banquet at the literary-minded Aldine Club at 200 Fifth Avenue, New York. Among the speakers was Kate Douglas Wiggin, author of *Rebecca of Sunnybrook Farm*, who described a chance meeting with Charles Dickens on a train when she was only eleven years old. Wiggin was followed by Ida C. Bailey Allen, who addressed the then controversial issue of "the professional woman and her home." (Allen was the popular author of more than fifty cookbooks; in 1924 she became the food editor of the Sunday *New York American* and later had her own radio show.)

At the time no one knew how many guests to expect, but the first dinner drew such an overflow crowd for its third speaker, novelist Edna Ferber, that there weren't enough chairs for all the attendees. Another early dinner at the Aldine Club, however, produced a different type of embarrassment when the WNBA treasurer, Josephine Pfanstiehl, found she didn't have enough money to pay the bill, since the crowd was far larger than anticipated. Consequently she had to sign an IOU for the organization "until the crisis was resolved."

Humor was an integral part of those first banquets. The archives revealed that Bob Sherwood, co-owner of Sherwood's Book Store and the husband of WNBA cofounder Pauline C. Sherwood, who was a circus clown for P.T. Barnum in his youth, often delighted audiences with his capers. Memorable too was a 1922 dinner during which WNBA leaders prepared a skit in which they played marionettes representing prominent figures in the book trade. However, during a rehearsal that afternoon, the current WNBA president, Belle Walker, got stuck in a barrel and "had to be pulled out by the legs." And that, as Madge Jenison, one of the organization's founders, drily recalled in her memoir, "put a damper on the marionette show."

Fortunately, the entertainment section of that evening was rescued by Doubleday author Dorothy Spears, who, having previously studied singing with Caruso, left the speakers' table for the piano and sang to the guests. Other speakers included a prominent journalist from the *Manchester Guardian*, novelist Fanny Hurst, and best-selling Canadian author Martha Ostenso. The event was chaired by author Alexander Black, "the most hilarious toastmaster ever born," who introduced Belle Walker as Mr. Harold Belle Walker in a sly reference to the male-dominated publishing profession.

By March 5, 1925, the WNBA's banquet was so popular it was moved to the Hotel McAlpin at 34th Street and Broadway to accommodate its 465 guests. Among the speakers were Kathleen Thompson Norris, a popular journalist and best-selling author, who amused the audience with a personal account of bookselling in San Francisco; and short story author Edward J. O'Brien, who predicted those tales were the wave of the future.

O'Brien was the founder of the annual anthology *The Best American Short Stories*. By then the publishing industry so enthusiastically supported the WNBA that guests received copies of books as souvenirs of the evening.

Musical accompaniment was always part of earlier WNBA banquets but by 1927, at the peak of the Jazz Age, the tenth anniversary dinner included dancing to the Edwyn Allen orchestra. That year the speakers included noted authors Honore Willsie Morrow (novelist and wife of the founder of Wm. Morrow and Co.), novelist Hervey Allen, Dorothy Canfield Fisher (author, educational reformer, and social activist), and poet Edmund Vance Cooke. To the astonishment of the WNBA, 700 guests appeared for the event and made the banquet room feel overcrowded. As a consequence, by November 1928, the secretary reported that the banquet required larger accommodations. A report from that era observed, "WNBA saw no black cloud on the horizon in 1928." The invitation for March 6, 1929, was headlined "Make Way for the Ladies" at the "Grand Ball Room of the Hotel Commodore," at Lexington Avenue and East 42nd Street. Tickets included "dinner, souvenirs [books] and dancing, four dollars and fifty cents each."

Then came the stock market crash of October 29, 1929, followed by the Great Depression. In 1930 the despairing WNBA president wrote that only "three speakers, two reporters from *Publishers Weekly*, and eleven members attended the meeting that year. In that grim economic climate, the WNBA banquets immediately became more modest. While the fifteenth anniversary dinner of 1932 still included five speakers, the event was relocated to the less costly Hotel Pennsylvania. And by the organization's eighteenth anniversary of March 11, 1935, tickets were reduced to three dollars and fifty cents. Two years later on March 12, 1937, at the WNBA's twentieth dinner, the price was only twenty-five cents higher. Tellingly, a *Bookwoman* report praised one of its author-speakers, Morris Ernest, by observing that "the book trade has reason to be grateful…for his alert and sympathetic interest in its problems."

Despite those strains, women were finally acknowledged as full-fledged members of the publishing industry. Proof of their inclusion happened on February 17, 1937, at the Booksellers' League's annual Ladies Night at the Aldine Club where the WNBA was represented by past president Alice E. Klutas. As a WNBA report chortled, "In passing we might say that it only took the American Booksellers Association three years to recognize the importance of the Women's National Book Association, but it took the Booksellers' League twenty years! Who knows, perhaps in another ten years we may hold our annual parties together!"

Three years later that partnership became a reality. On February 16, 1940, the WNBA's twenty-third dinner dance was held in partnership with the Booksellers' League of New York to celebrate its First Annual Dinner Dance.

> *For many years, the two organizations have held separate parties, and so near together that sometimes it was difficult to choose between them.... This year we seized the opportunity afforded by the Printing Anniversary to combine forces....the five hundredth anniversary of the invention of printing from movable type, the four hundredth anniversary of printing on the American continent, and the three hundredth anniversary of printing in the United States.*

Apparently worried that the program might be too long, its two speakers, the acclaimed author-educator Mary Ellen Chase and prominent Chinese author Dr. Lin Yutang, were monitored by a "very noisy alarm clock which acted as a brake on such speakers as might forget time limits."

After a dinner of filet mignon or lobster thermidor, the first Constance Lindsay Skinner Award was presented to Anne Carroll Moore, superintendent of children's work at the New York Public Library, and guests danced to the music of Harry Meyer and his orchestra.

> *So ended another successful party. We may continue to join forces in our annual party and we may not, but the committee of the WNBA wishes to express our appreciation of the enthusiastic help given by the committee from the Booksellers' League. To have a lot of good looking men doing all the heavy work was a most gratifying experience, and we're all for more combined parties.*

On March 20, 1942, in the wake of America's declaration of war against the Axis powers, the WNBA hosted its silver anniversary dinner dance. While it was "rather a small party" at the Hotel Pennsylvania, the WNBA reported it was "the most enjoyable in several years." The toastmaster was the publisher and punster Bennett Cerf, who delighted the audience with his introduction of the evening's author-speakers Rex Stout, Helen MacInnes, Margaret Lee Runbeck; and Princess Zophia Sapieha. A highlight of that event was WNBA past president Alice E. Klutas' presentation of the Constance Lindsay Skinner Award to Irita Van Doren for "dramatizing books to the masses." Despite that gala celebration, America's entry into World War II dominated the night. In honor of the WNBA's twenty-fifth anniversary, publishers had donated twenty-five books to the guests who, in turn, contributed most of them to the Victory Book Campaign, which collected books for American soldiers. That night members of the WNBA contributed "enough money to buy one $25.00 War Bond and two $5.00 books of War Stamps."

The WNBA Takes on the Status of Women in the Publishing Industry

Have women in the book industry been treated as equitably as men?

Almost certainly not, according to early members of the WNBA. As its outspoken second president, Madge Jenison, observed during a February 17, 1921, meeting at the Children's Book Shop on New York's West 47th Street, "We all know men whose work some woman is doing, for which he is taking all the credit and getting the returns. Women must come out in the open and do things in the way that the world requires them to be done….[and avoid] the not doing of anything we want to do because we are afraid."

While members of the Women's National Book Association continued to experience male bias for the next twenty-seven years, the organization first formally addressed that problem in 1948. A column in the spring issue of *The Bookwoman* that year entitled "What's Your Opinion: Is a Woman's Chance for Success in the Book Field Limited or Unlimited?" broached the subject by asking several booksellers across the country. Opinions varied. According to Rose Oller Harbaugh, who headed the Book Department of Chicago's Marshall Field & Co., "I think women have every chance in the book world, both in publishing and retail outlets. It is a world of detail, imagination, and initiative."

Mrs. L.S. Teeter from the Book Department of F&R Lazarus & Co. in Columbus, Ohio, agreed. "I would say that a woman's chance of success in the books field is unlimited." In contrast, Robert B. Campbell, president of Campbell's Book Store, Los Angeles, thought their opportunities limited. Admittedly "women seem to be at least on a par with men in the retail end of the books field in this part of the country," but "they are very limited in the field of publishers' representatives and...limited to second-string jobs in the publishing end of the business." George A. Hecht, general manager of the Doubleday Book Shops in New York, painted a still darker and probably more realistic picture. "A woman's success in the book world, particularly in that part which constitutes bookselling is restricted—the reason being...prejudice. That this factor is gradually being overcome is a tribute to those women who have succeeded in spite of that prejudice."

Two years later, in 1950, *The Bookwoman* ran a front-page story headlined "Are Women Holding Their Own in the Book World?" based upon a September 26 meeting at the English-Speaking Union. The talk was delivered by WNBA member Mary Elisabeth Edes, an assistant editor at *Publishers Weekly*. She referred to a report in the *Book and Magazine Guide* indicating that 80 percent of all employees in publishing were women, but few were "in top positions." In a reflection of ongoing post-World War II employment practices," Edes observed, "There is a trend... towards replacing women with men in the better jobs." In addition, the report found that men received almost twice the compensation as women in similar positions.

During the second wave of feminism some twenty years later, the WNBA made efforts to track that inequity more systematically. By early 1970 the New York chapter of the WNBA had a committee on the Status of Women in Publishing. That group mailed a test questionnaire to women with full-time publishing jobs. At an organization luncheon on November 17, the WNBA's guest speaker, Aileen C. Hernandez, president of the National Organization of Women, discussed the survey results with a large audience of members and nonmembers. Her tone was fiery. Not only did 57 percent of the women who answered the survey earn less than $15,000 but also "an amazing 55 percent said they thought they were fairly compensated for their experience and efforts."

Nevertheless 81 percent of those women had bachelor's degrees or better. "I wonder—do the women who responded...*truly* believe that they are being paid equally for their years of service?" Hernandez asked. While there were still no studies on the aggregate number of people employed in book publishing it was "estimated that women comprise well over 60 percent—and perhaps as much as 75 percent of that work force alone."

"What happens to women who enter the field? Do most...start as secretaries, and why?...only 2 percent started with responsible positions and an amazing 64 percent began with starting salaries of less than $4,500 per year. I suspect that you are NOT represented in top posts—and I wonder why..." From the test mailing it was revealed that only 11 percent of top management were women. Hernandez warned the audience, "I suspect that some heads of publishing firms and other communications organizations are not going to support you in this endeavor," but she nevertheless urged the WNBA to use "various techniques in order to gather the information you need."

Inspired by her talk, the New York chapter of the WNBA launched a new survey entitled *Status of Women in Publishing: A Survey 1972–73*. Introductory letters and questionnaires were mailed to nearly three hundred heads of publishing houses and personnel directors for distribution but fewer than a thousand people responded. A subsequent WNBA report about the findings listed three reasons for the disappointing results. First, publishing executives and personnel directors "withheld cooperation... distributing the questionnaires"; secondly, few women in book publishing responded and most that did were in middle-management; finally, the survey results had little meaning "because there is no comparative data on the status of men in publishing." Nevertheless, the survey was a start toward achieving a "full-scale survey of the working conditions of both men and women in publishing."

The April 1982 issue of *The Bookwoman* reported on a statistical study that appeared in *Publishers Weekly* by Stella Dong. Entitled "What's Happening with Women in Publishing?" the WNBA noted that Dong's report was a "golden opportunity" to obtain important information but failed to ask one crucial question—the gender of each respondent. "The inadequacies of this report are further proof of the need for real attention to the subject by the industry," opined *The Bookwoman*.

For example, one table of the Dong study listed salaries for specific job titles. Among them was a $50,000 average salary for a director of sales/marketing position and $35,000 for the VP of sales/marketing position. "One cannot help wondering if the person with the VP title is a woman who had been given the title as a sop to her vanity instead of the $50,000 reported [perhaps] by a man?" asked *The Bookwoman*. "An obvious conclusion seems to be that there is real need for an annual survey of salaries in publishing, as well as a basic study of overall employment problems."

Today such studies exist but there are still biases against women in the workplace. A *Publishers Weekly* report of October 7, 2013, entitled "Differences in Pay Between Men and Women" noted that the average compensation in 2012 for men in publishing was $85,000 compared to $56,000 for women—a 29 percent difference in their salaries. Still more recently, on October 7, 2015, a *Publishers Weekly*'s Salary Survey observed that inequities still exist but are smaller than in earlier years. The survey, which was conducted in 2014, attributed a salary decline for both sexes in publishing to the aftereffects of the Great Recession, the rise of e-books, and the increasingly youthful age of employees, down from forty-two to thirty-five. The average salary for men fell to $70,000 while for women it declined to $51,000—representing a significant 19 percent gap in compensation.

While that study reveals women in publishing continue to lag behind men in compensation, promotions, and visibility, the trend is positive. In contrast to their status in 1917, which Madge Jenison reminded readers was "zero," today's women continue to strive to close the gap and achieve full recognition.

Male Reaction to Women in the Publishing Industry

By the early 1970s the clarion call for female equity—or Women's Lib as it was then called—elicited strong emotions from both sexes in the publishing industry. Among those publicly expressed were ones by George A. Woods, children's book editor of the *New York Times*, whose interview appeared on the front page of the June 1971 *Bookwoman*. Bylined by Hazel Spiller, her introductory note read, "Mr. Woods graciously agreed to be interviewed for the benefit of members of the WNBA." The message

Woods delivered about the differences between men and women, their career paths, and the implications for literature was less than gracious. In defense of producing children's picture books with aproned mothers cooking in the kitchen, the critic insisted those books still "had validity" because they reflected the norm. "Change itself is a slow process," Woods observed. "If a book…has true literary value, and extends enjoyment to children, it belongs on library shelves and should not be discarded."

Citing one of his daughters' decisions to become a nurse rather than a doctor, Woods attributed it to the fact that more men "*choose* to study medicine than women because they are willing to invest that time and energy." That attitude accounted for the "discrepancy of numbers in male and female doctors," he said, rather than placing the reason at the door of 'cramped horizons.'" Admitting he was "convinced of the problem that women have," Woods predicted "the pendulum will strike in a perfect arc only after a great many excesses will have been committed." For that reason he opposed "the arbitrary setting up of anything that purports to be literary…to put people in terribly unnatural situations for the purpose of pleasing women liberationists. Works of art are not created through socialistic or propagandistic purposes."

Concomitantly, Woods objected to the feminist insistence upon the use of the word "humankind" in lieu of "mankind." After all, "We cannot turn our ways and our very existence around completely," he said. Nor did he intend to "change my semantics to please Women's Lib. I include women when I say 'mankind' and they will have to accept me on the basis of my integrity."

Despite that attitude the demand for a wider perception of women in books continued. Another well-publicized literary outcry occurred in April 1972 during a WNBA-NYC chapter-sponsored panel at a National Book Association conference. The tone of that meeting at the Waldorf-Astoria was decidedly feminist. According to an April 13 story in *Newsday*, the moment Anatole Broyard, book critic for the *New York Times* and the only man on the panel, spoke, he was reprimanded for male parochialism. Having addressed Nora Ephron, author of *Wallflower at the Orgy*, as "Miss Ephron," he was "smartly reminded…she was Ms. Ephron." When he referred to Carolyn Heilbrun, associate professor of English as Columbia University, as "Dr.," she, too, demanded to be addressed as Ms. "By the time he got around to the fourth panelist, English novelist Juliet Mitchell, author of *Women's Estate*, Broyard didn't call her anything." Superficially, the critic "came on as the quintessence of male-in-sympathy-with-the-principles-of-the-women's-rights movement [who]…said nice things." Not only did he agree there should be more female book critics but also admitted that the movement made him see women in a new light. Even so, "the panelists and audience quickly evaluated the lone man as a male chauvinist wolf in sheep's clothing." One member of the audience, for instance, accused Broyard of mouthing words "in support of the woman's movement, [but] you put into words exactly the opposite." Among her objections was that his remarks that "the so-called superiority of men as presented in literature and life has been nominal." Another was that "very often women have been portrayed as 'the power behind the throne.'" After a groan went up from the audience, panelist Mitchell suggested, "You take the power behind the throne and give us the throne." Wincing, Broyard admitted he "was concerned about what the women's revolution would do to men's sex life. One thing he didn't want women to lose was their 'mystery.'" To that, panel moderator Elizabeth Janeway, author of *Man's World, Woman's Place*, snapped, "Human beings spend more time out of bed than in it." Beyond the attack upon Broyard's sexual politics, the panel addressed the program's official subject, women in adult literature. Having reread the famous works of literature, Ephron said, "It's a shock to go back to the classics and look at them [from a women's liberation] point of view." While they were great writers, they were "sexist." In contrast, Heilbrun observed that many classic plays and novels by men portrayed women as if they were "written by members of the women's liberation movement yesterday." Among them were the Greeks, D.H. Lawrence, Henry James, and Shakespeare. In fact, she found extraordinary "the extent to which male writers outside of Americans, find the woman figure one which embodied imaginative impulses." Nevertheless, Mitchell observed that women's role has gradually evolved over time. This was epitomized in the work of George Eliot, the Brontë sisters, Doris Lessing, and Simone de Beauvoir, the last of whom wrote about "exceptional women trying to make it in a man's world." In contrast, today's literature of women's liberation presents "the dilemma of the ordinary woman."

Publishing and Literature Courses Offered by the WNBA

From its inception, the Women's National Book Association understood that if women were to achieve and maintain professional status in the publishing industry, they had to be well trained. With that in mind, the organization's second president, Madge Jenison, chaired a nine-session seminar in the early 1920s around a key question: "What does the reading public want and hope to find in a bookstore?" Hosted at the New York Public Library at Fifth Avenue and 42nd Street, the event was keynoted by Frederic G. Melcher of R. R. Bowker Company. That event was so well received that it inspired courses for college credit at Columbia University.

The Great Depression and World War II delayed the creation of new educational programs but by the late 1940s, the WNBA had revived its educational mission. In 1947, the Chicago chapter offered educational courses in publishing cosponsored with the *Chicago Tribune* Book Fair.

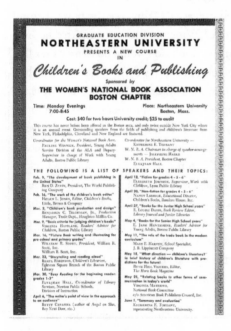

An ad for a WNBA-Boston course on children's books and publishing cosponsored with Northeastern University; as noted in the ad, the course traveled to various places across the county under WNBA auspices.

In the early fall of 1947 Virginia H. Matthews, head of children's books at Brentano's, was offering a course entitled "Selling Books for Children," cosponsored by the WNBA and the Association of Children's Book Editors. Matthews promoted the course to young women in an effort to help them protect their jobs and their financial independence. "As jobs become harder to get, and leveling off takes hold, girls are more apt to stay in their jobs and those in the sales end of children's books will be more inclined to make a career of it, instead of regarding it as a stop-gap either to marriage or a better paying job," she reasoned.

Officially it was promoted as a "course of lectures (six) planned for the young woman in a bookshop or book department, who displays, promotes and sells children's books...to familiarize her with the tools of her work, acquaint her with the best current practices of arranging and keeping stock, and help her form a general background knowledge of her subject."

Two years later the New York chapter of the WNBA partnered with the Booksellers' League of New York for six evening lectures on the techniques of specialized bookselling. The lectures were open to all interested men and women, "booksellers, their salespeople and those anxious to know more about the techniques of selling books," read the advertisement for "Selling More Books." The six lectures began on March 2, 1949, at the *New York Herald Tribune* auditorium on West 41st Street; each cost five dollars. At each session a different specialist discussed sales techniques for various kinds of books. The sessions were titled Books About the Home; Art Books, Press Books and Fine Bindings; Featuring Religious Books; Reference & Technical Books; Children's Books; and Current Trends on Our Book Counters.

In early January 1949, the WNBA's Chicago chapter, in cooperation with the University of Chicago, sponsored its own course on book-selling. Advertised as lectures on "merchandising print," the course's main speaker was Lloyd Wendt, literary critic of the *Chicago Tribune*, and also included literary agents and publishers. The following winter, in cooperation with the University of Chicago, the local WNBA chapter offered a second course, "Writing and Its Consequences." As its title implied, it provided an overview of current trends, editing, rewriting, and marketing.

In the summer of 1950 the WNBA offered its first full-tuition scholarship to the Summer Course in Publishing Procedures at Radcliffe College. The course, chaired by Nora Kramer, was directed by Helen Everitt, an editor for Houghton Mifflin. Marian Freda, an honor graduate of Barnard College and an employee at Harper Brothers, was awarded the WNBA scholarship. The scholarship continued to be offered for several years.

During the 1950s, local chapters stepped up efforts to educate their members and raise awareness about the importance of books. By 1952, the Cleveland chapter began cosponsoring books fairs and luncheons. The New York chapter presented programs in 1953 and 1956 as part of the Festival of Books, a WNYC radio annual event. During 1956 and 1957, it also partnered with Pauline Rivers, director of the *New York Times*' Organization Activities, to prepare a formal list of literary recommendations. The first was called "Books for Collateral Reading," and the second was presented to the annual Barnard Women's Forum.

Another example of outreach that began in the 1950s was the National WNBA's participation in projects to collect and distribute books to settlement houses, libraries, and centers serving underprivileged children and adults in poor neighborhoods here and abroad.

In the mid-1960s the New York chapter also hosted two Winter Workshops at the Sheraton-Atlantic Hotel on various aspects of publishing. The 1966 session covered subjects such as censorship, subsidiary rights, advertising, promotion and publicity, and design and production. The 1967 series was billed as "an Editorial Workshop which included Subsidiary Rights and Censorship." A panel on production demonstrating the practical use of silk-screen printing was one of the highlights of that session.

Other chapters, too, were creating other educational activities for their members. Starting in 1955 the Nashville, Tennessee, chapter initiated book fairs and sponsored events during National Library Week. In 1959 the Boston chapter, in partnership with the *Boston Herald*, began hosting Book and Author Luncheons each spring, and in 1966, drew a sell-out audience of nearly a thousand people. In 1961, the Binghamton, New York, chapter began hosting community service and book publicity programs, and in 1966 Detroit was offering similar programs. By June 1971, the *Bookwoman* report on chapter activities routinely listed educational events for each of the chapters.

As a *Publishers Weekly* article of November 27, 1967, observed, "one of the WNBA's most practical contributions has been setting up courses, workshops and lecture series to help heighten the professional competence and knowledge, not only of its own members, but of others who care to enroll."

Today, as the WNBA looks to the future, it remains proud of its educational legacy.

CHAPTER 4

SUPPORTING LITERATURE
AND LITERACY

The core of all of Women's National Book Association (WNBA) programming is support for literature and literacy, a mission that dates back to 1917, when the organization was established. The founding members believed that literature had the power to change the world. They reached high and they didn't shy away from the philosophical. The WNBA creed, agreed to at the start and affirmed in the 1936 inaugural issue of *The Bookwoman*, gives a flavor of these elevated goals:

> *This Association is created as a means of education to more consciousness in ourselves and as an organized power to further in every instance...the freer movement of life and truth.*

These principles guided the WNBA throughout our history. A grainy photograph in the archives shows a group of women packing books to send to India in the 1930s. From the 1950s on, the records show accounts of courses on children's literature and publishing developed to help professionals and parents alike engage young readers' interest in books.

Current programing is still have guided by these central goals. You will find in this section a description of existing programs through which the WNBA mission plays out, including the following:

- Since 1959, the WNBA has been a non-governmental organization with the United Nations Department of Public Information, specifically supporting the UN's literacy goals for women's literacy and education in Afghanistan. It was Pearl S. Buck, whose novels brought pleasure to so many readers, who encouraged the WNBA to take on this role.

- The Constance Lindsay Skinner Award, now known as the WNBA Award, was established in 1940 to honor a woman who, according to the announcement in *The Bookwoman*, "has done meritorious work in the world of books beyond the duties or responsibilities of her profession or occupation." The organization continues to give the award today. These winners are a stellar roster of women whose activism and writing have made significant contributions to our cultural life. Masha Hamilton, a winner who started the Afghan Women's Writing Project, inspired the San Francisco chapter to support the AWWP in its mission to amplify the voices of Afghan women.

- Other awards are important in fulfilling the WNBA mission. The WNBA Pannell Award, given annually since 1992, honors and supports bookstores that provide exceptional service to children, helping to create the love of reading at an early age. The Eastman Grant promotes the education of librarians through a grant to regional library associations across the country. The Amy Loveman Award, given from 1962 to 1969, was another initiative to foster the love of books in young people. That award, covered in a special feature here, honored college students and their personal book collections.

- In 2007 the WNBA took over sponsorship of National Reading Group Month (NRGM) from founders Martha Burns and Alice Dillon, and it later launched Great Group Reads, a program to celebrate the joy of shared reading. A group of WNBA members around the country selects a list of books each year to recommend to book groups. Author programs in October in each chapter celebrate NRGM and the GGR list. The publishing industry has welcomed this opportunity to join with the WNBA in spreading the word about books that promote discussion and community.

- In 2010, the WNBA started a national writing contest, open to members and nonmembers, initially in the categories of fiction and poetry, now expanded to include nonfiction. Plans are under way to publish the winning entries in an anthology.

- For several milestone anniversaries, the WNBA published lists of significant books by women. For the Centennial, two lists of books (fiction/poetry/memoir and nonfiction) were created by WNBA members to showcase the diversity of women's writing and ideas. From these lists, a presidential book-a-day program sent books to the president of the U.S. during Women's History Month in 2017. This program echoed another: In 1955, the WNBA had sent books to President Dwight D. Eisenhower when he was recovering from a heart attack.

- In honor of its Centennial, following a long tradition of WNBA service and support to literacy organizations, the WNBA awarded the Second Century Prize, a monetary award to a nonprofit organization that promotes literacy and lifelong reading. The Little Free Library, which encourages the sharing of books by individuals, was the honoree. From the early years, the WNBA has looked for opportunities to encourage reading and literacy.

WNBA chapters have pursued their own local literacy initiatives; many of those initiatives are described in Chapter 5, "The History of the WNBA Chapters."

THE WNBA AND THE UNITED NATIONS
Jill A. Tardiff

The Women's National Book Association has been a non-governmental organization (NGO) member of the United Nations since 1959 when Nobel Prize-winning author Pearl S. Buck encouraged the organization to take on an international role. As an NGO affiliated with the UN's Department of Public Information (DPI), we help to spread the UN's goals, particularly as they relate to our own mission, especially universal education and literacy, and women's equality and empowerment.

According to the "About Us" page on UN's DPI/NGO Relations website, an NGO is defined as "any non-profit, voluntary citizens' group that is organized on a local, national or international level. Task-oriented and driven by people with a common interest, NGOs perform a variety of services and humanitarian functions, bring citizens' concerns to governments, monitor policies and encourage political participation at the community level." As an NGO associated with the United Nations Department of Public Information, we adhere to the following four criteria in order to remain a member in good standing:

- Share the ideals of the UN Charter.
- Operate solely on a not-for-profit basis.
- Have a demonstrated interest in United Nations issues and a proven ability to reach large or specialized audiences, such as educators, media representatives, policy makers, and the business community.
- Have the commitment and means to conduct effective information programs about UN activities by publishing newsletters, bulletins, pamphlets; organizing conferences, seminars, and roundtables; and enlisting the cooperation of the media.

In short, the WNBA supports the United Nations in its goals and aims to win support for those goals among the wider community. WNBA members are ambassadors for the UN, disseminating information through national and chapter publications and monthly programs, and participating in activities for NGOs at the UN, including regular briefings, workshops, and the annual DPI/NGO conference.

Member Involvement from the Beginning

During the terms of Dag Hammarskjöld (1953–1961) and U Thant (1961–1971), the WNBA was represented in various capacities by members

Helen Wessells, Beatrice James, Anne Richter, Iris Vinton, Lucille Ogle, and Rosa Eichelberger and was honored by an appointment to the U.S. Mission and to the Conference of UN Representatives, Council of Organizations, United Nations Association of the USA. During the terms of Kurt Waldheim (1972–1981), Javier Pérez de Cuéllar (1982–1991), and Boutros Boutros-Ghali (1992–1996), we were represented by Claire Friedland, Sandy Paul, and Sally Wecksler.

In the new century, during the terms of the Secretaries-General Kofi Annan (1996–2006), Ban Ki-moon (2007–2016), and António Guterres (2017–2021), the WNBA has been represented in various capacities by Sally Wecksler, Jill A. Tardiff, Nancy Stewart, Diane Ullius, Marilyn Berkman, and Kate Lyons, as well as youth liaisons Diana Cavallo, Jenna Vaccaro, Dena Mekawi, Caitlin Estelle Morrow, and Shimma Ibrahim Almabruk.

Notably, Jill A. Tardiff has performed the duties of NGO main representative to the United Nations Department of Public Information since 2002, while Dena Mekawi has performed the duties of NGO youth representative, including a stint as chair, DPI/NGO Youth Subcommittee of the UN DPI/NGO Committee since 2013.

Support for Human Development

Through a variety of activities, the WNBA has stood behind the UN's mission and helped to disseminate information about the UN's dedication to the well-being of people across the world. In 2000, specifically, the UN committed itself to the Millennium Development Goals (MDGs), which spurred global action on a range of fronts relating to the alleviation of poverty and suffering.

When the UN launched its MDG program, the WNBA affirmed its commitment to support the following UN Millennium Development Goals (http://www.un.org/millenniumgoals/):

#2 Achieve Universal Primary Education
#3 Promote Gender Equality and Empower Women
#7 Ensure Environmental Sustainability
#8 Global Partnership for Development

Our efforts in these areas have focused on the countries of Afghanistan and the United States. The organization recommitted itself to what is called the Post-2015 UN Development Agenda, which transformed the MDGs through a new focus on sustainable development. The new Sustainable Development Goals (SDGs; https://sustainabledevelopment. un.org/?menu=1300) that we focus on are:

#4 Quality Education
#5 Gender Equality
#10 Reduced Inequalities
#13 Climate Action
#16 Peace, Justice and Strong Institutions
#17 Partnerships for the Goals

This new strategy of incorporating sustainability into the UN's work was explored in the sixty-fifth Annual DPI/NGO Conference, "2015 and Beyond: Our Action Agenda," which WNBA members attended and reported on in *The Bookwoman*.

Other conferences that the WNBA has participated in include these annual DPI/NGO meetings:

- 1999: "Challenges of a Globalized World: Finding New Directions"
- 2000: "Global Solidarity: The Way to Peace and International Cooperation"
- 2001: "NGOs Today: Diversity of the Volunteer Experience"
- 2002: "Rebuilding Societies Emerging from Conflict: A Shared Responsibility"
- 2003: "Human Security and Dignity: Fulfilling the Promise of the United Nations"
- 2004: "Millennium Development Goals: Civil Society Takes Action"
- 2005: "Our Challenge: Voices for Peace, Partnerships and Renewal"
- 2006: "Unfinished Business: Effective Partnerships for Human Security and Sustainable Development"

- 2007: "Climate Change: How It Impacts Us All"
- 2008: "Reaffirming Human Rights for All: The Universal Declaration at 60"
- 2014: "2015 and Beyond: Our Action Agenda"

We also attended weekly briefings both in person and remotely. This sampling of briefings in 2015 reveals the range of issues that has engaged our UN DPI representatives:

- "A Future for All: The United Nations Through Women & Faith" (5 Feb 2015)
- "Partnerships for Success: NGOs, Youth, and the UN" (26 Feb 2015)
- "Youth-Led Briefing" (19 Mar 2015); "Women and Slavery: Its Impact on Women's Rights Today" (26 Mar 2015)
- "DPI/NGO Briefing in Observance of World Press Freedom Day: Let Journalism Thrive Towards Better Reporting, Gender Equality & Media Safety in the Digital Age" (1 May 2015)
- "Youth-lead Briefing: FANCV Participation at the Youth Reps" (7 May 2015)
- DPI/NGO Communications Workshop: "Acting Globally in the Digital Age" (11 June 2015)
- 2015 International Youth Day: "NGO Youth Representatives to DPI" (12 Aug 2015)
- General Assembly: "Post-2015 Development Agenda" (28 Sept 2015)
- DPI/NGO Briefing on Agenda 2030: "Agenda 2030 for Sustainable Development: Advocacy for Implementation and Global Partnership" (8 Oct 2015)
- "The UN at 70: Working Together to Make a Difference" (22 Oct 2015)
- "Youth-Led Briefing #4: Youth at the Forefront: Bridging the Gap Between Climate Change and Climate Action" (12 Nov 2015)
- "Combating Racism in the 21st Century (3 Dec 2015)"

Chapter Involvement in Our UN Commitments

WNBA-SF sponsors panel/presentation at the San Francisco Writers Conference, 2016: "Inspiring Voices of Hope: Afghan Women Writers" with guest speakers Lori Noack, Humaira Ghilzai, Parwana Fayyaz (SFWC Diversity Scholarship winner).

International Day of Peace 2016—Student Observance; theme: "The Sustainable Development Goals Building Blocks for Peace"; moderated by Messenger of Peace Michael Douglas et al., WNBA DPI/NGO Youth Representative Dena Mekawi.

WNBA-NYC chapter in partnership with VIDA: Women in Literary Arts presents "The Power of Poetry in a Complex World." VIDA is a nonprofit feminist organization committed to creating transparency around the lack of gender parity.

Youth Representatives Program

The Secretaries-General Kofi Annan, Ban Ki-moon, and António Guterres have been strong proponents of youth representatives in the United Nations system. Since 2012 the WNBA has had two graduate students as DPI/NGO representatives.

Past youth representatives included Diana Cavallo, Jenna Vaccaro, and Caitlin Estelle Morrow; current youth representatives include Dena Mekawi and Shimma Ibrahim Almabruk. During her tenure Dena Mekawi has served as chair of the DPI/NGO Youth Subcommittee of the UN DPI/NGO Committee and as a featured speaker at the International Day of Peace—Student Observance, September 2016.

The WNBA and UNICEF

The partnership between UNICEF, U.S. Fund for UNICEF (UNICEF USA), and the WNBA goes back to the late 1970s when all three organizations were preparing for the International Year of the Child. The WNBA promotes the UNICEF USA mission through chapter-wide advocacy and fund-raising held primarily in October in conjunction with the WNBA's National Reading Group Month and Trick-or-Treat for UNICEF. It also supports and promotes UNICEF USA initiatives such as the End Trafficking Project, Teach UNICEF, and the UNICEF Tap Project.

THE WNBA AWARD
Andrea Baron and NC Weil

In the official definition, the WNBA Award is given to "a living American woman who derives part or all of her income from books and allied arts, and who has done meritorious work in the world of books beyond the duties or responsibilities of her profession or occupation." It has been given since 1940 and has honored authors, librarians, booksellers, publishers, publicists, and editors.

Origins of the Award

In November 1939, the following announcement appeared in *The Bookwoman*: "For some time past, we have been considering the matter of a suitable method of keeping green the memory of our friend, Constance Lindsay Skinner. The decision has been made to make this in the form of an annual award to a woman who has done something outstanding in the book world. This award, to be presented for the first time at our Annual Dinner on February 16, 1940, will be of little intrinsic value, but will, we hope, serve as a pat on the back and a 'Well Done' to a woman who has earned it." The award was suggested by WNBA president Alice E. Klutas to honor Skinner, an active member of the New York chapter of the WNBA; one of the founders of the WNBA newsletter, *The Bookwoman;* and one of the first women to hold a major editorial position in American adult book publishing. The award has been presented continuously since 1940, at first annually, and since 1976 every other year in the even-numbered years. The year 2004 marked the fiftieth presentation of the WNBA Award.

Constance Lindsay Skinner

Constance Lindsay Skinner was born in 1877 and grew up on a trading post on the British Columbia frontier, and later in Vancouver. As a child, she loved the natural beauty of her surroundings: the rivers and forests and the culture of the fur traders and Squamish people. She also made good use of her parents' large library. From childhood, she knew she was destined for a life of writing and, indeed, she had a diverse and acclaimed literary career which encompassed newspaper reporting, and the writing of history, folklore, novels, plays, poetry, and children's books. She played an important role in the book industry as one of the first women to hold a major editorial position in American book publishing. As a member of the WNBA, she influenced the careers of many other bookwomen, for whom she was a critic, friend, and mentor.

Skinner began her writing career at newspapers in Los Angeles and Chicago, then left journalism to write her first play, *David*. She moved to New York City where she continued to write plays and also literary criticism. In 1919, she was asked to write several volumes for the Yale University *Chronicles of America* series. She was one of the few women authors in the series and also one of the few nonacademics. Among the topics she wrote about were the Kentucky-Tennessee frontier at the time of Daniel Boone and the fur trade in the Pacific Northwest. She was a researcher and co-author on several other books in the series as well. In 1934 she persuaded the young publishing firm of Farrar, Rinehart to hire her as the general editor of a new series, the *Rivers of America*. She envisioned it as a successor to the Yale *Chronicles* that would look at history through the lens of the great rivers of America. Skinner wrote, "Rivers, the perpetual motion in the quiet land…must ever have a powerful influence on the temperament and the imagination of mankind." She traveled across the country to promote it, explaining that the works were "to be a literary and not a historical series. The authors of these books will be novelists and poets." Many important artists and writers contributed in the ensuing years. Skinner worked on the first six volumes before her death; sixty-five volumes were eventually published over a thirty-seven-year period, with her name remaining as founding editor. She died at her desk, in 1939, while editing one of the volumes.

One of Skinner's most enduring contributions to literature was in the development of popular, high-quality children's books. She was a multifaceted writer who wrote exciting frontier action stories that were welcomed by librarians, critics, and children alike. Of the eleven children's books she wrote, several stood out for the role of young girls as heroines in the adventures.

Constance Lindsay Skinner joined the WNBA in 1936, and her colorful presence was an important influence in the growth of the

The 2015 WNBA Award was given to poet, professor, and activist Amy King, who serves on the executive board of VIDA: Women in Literary Arts. Pictured here, left to right, are Jane Kinney-Denning, then WNBA-NYC president; NC Weil, the chair of the WNBA Award; King; and Carin Siegfried, then president of the National WNBA.

organization. She was instrumental in launching *The Bookwoman*, the newsletter of the WNBA. She described its aim as taking books out of the luxury category and making them "a necessity in the lives of the literate." *The Bookwoman* would spread these ideas and strengthen the organization.

Her WNBA contemporaries commented on her spirit, vitality, colorful clothing, and fondness for costume jewelry as she promoted the organization and played an important role in supporting and mentoring young members. Her protégé, Helen Hoke Watts, explained that Skinner "gave me enormous courage.... She valued integrity, drive and ambition." Skinner never married; she lived from the income earned from her writing, pushing the boundaries of what women could do in the literary world.

In 1940, the year after her death, the WNBA established an annual award in her honor to recognize outstanding accomplishment in the book world. The Constance Lindsay Skinner Award has been given to

Amy Loveman Award, 1962–1969

One of the most unusual projects undertaken by the WNBA was creation of the Amy Loveman Award, given jointly with the Book-of-the-Month Club and the *Saturday Review* in the 1960s. The prize of $1,000 was given for "the best personal library collected by an undergraduate student attending a four-year college or university." At a distance of almost fifty years, when we now think of ourselves as consumers of digital content—much of which is ephemeral—the award sounds anachronistic, but who among us does not cherish even a small number of books?

Amy Loveman (1881–1955) was a founding editor of the *Saturday Review of Literature* and a member of the Book-of-the-Month Club staff. After her death, Norman Cousins described her work at the *Saturday Review*: "During the first fifteen years Amy Loveman assigned most of the books for review, wrote reviews of her own, handled a regular department in the magazine...edited copy, pinned up the dummy, read page proofs, and put the magazine to bed at the printer's." For the Book-of-the-Month Club, she was an early member of the preliminary reading committee; later she was named head of the editorial department; she also served on the Board of Judges. She read voraciously, widely, and with great discretion and insight. In her roles at the two organizations, she exerted a great influence on what Americans read in the 1920s and 1930s. Amy Loveman received the WNBA Award in 1946.

The excerpts below, from an article in the Fall 1974 *Bookwoman*, describe the history of the Amy Loveman Award and its demise.

"The award was a fitting memorial to the late Amy Loveman. As well as being active in all three sponsoring organizations, she was a discriminating book collector with a special interest in young people, and in the role of books as a means of broadening their outlook on the world...the Loveman award was intended to stimulate interest among students in reading and intelligent book collecting. The national entrants were required to have been the winners of their local contest. Entries were judged on the knowledge, scope, interest, value, and imagination shown in creating the collection, as expressed in the commentary and bibliography.

"The general remarks of the first winner, Walter S. Rosenstein of Dickinson College, show an avid love for his collection of English and American Literature. He confesses that he could have been a better student had it not been for the great amount of time devoted to personal reading!

"The remarkable aspect of the collection of Thomas M. White-head of Bucknell University (the 1963 winner) was its breadth within a selected area. Included under the topic of 'Ancient and Primitive Man' were books on archaeology, anthropology, ancient history, and mythology. The young man's determination to add to his library frequently caused him to spend his food allowance on books.

"1964's winning bibliophile was John R.T. Molholm of Ohio State University. A geology major and veteran of three Antarctic expeditions, he submitted his 131-book collection on polar exploration.

"The first young woman to be honored with the award was Jane R. Bogert of Wilson College, Chambersburg, Pennsylvania, in 1965... Miss Bogert's specialty was early American textbooks. It was a fascinating collection, gradually acquired as a result of 'many hours spent in old barns and in the attics and cellars of old houses, sorting through stacks of dusty, grimy old books which the owners have been glad to have someone take away.' Among her 'finds' were Dr. Samuel Johnson's Dictionary, a Noah Webster speller, and a copy of Guthrie's Grammar describing world history and geography according to eighteenth-century knowledge. The publicity from the Amy Loveman Award brought interest from others and Jane began to receive old textbooks from people all over the country. A letter from Jane in 1968 to the WNBA revealed that her collection had doubled in those three years, mostly as a result of publicity from the contest.

"The last winner of the Amy Loveman Award, in 1969, was Jerrold G. Stanoff of UCLA for his six-hundred volume collection on the subject of 'Lafcadio Hearn: The Man and His Literature.' An expert on Japanese and Chinese literature, history, mythology and folklore, Mr. Stanoff studied in Tokyo, where he did extensive research on Hearn.

"The New York Chapter...contributed a great deal of time and effort to the administrative aspects of the awards. Interest among students grew steadily, and with it the administrative work became more time-consuming and expensive. By 1963 there was too much work for the volunteer staff of the WNBA. The number of entries had doubled since the first year.... Unfortunately 1969 was the last year for the competition, which lost its financial support from the Book-of-the-Month Club and *Saturday Review*.

many women who made important contributions. The name was later changed to the WNBA Award, and continues today.

The list of winners of the WNBA Award can be found in the Appendix. And more information about the award can be found at the WNBA website at: http://www.wnba-books.org/wnba-award/.

THE WNBA PANNELL AWARD
Susan Knopf

In 1981, the WNBA established the WNBA Pannell Awards to recognize and applaud "the work of booksellers who stimulate, promote, and encourage children's and young people's interest in books." Lucile Micheels Pannell, a founding member of the WNBA-Chicago chapter, was born in the late 1800s in Menomonie, Wisconsin. A model bookwoman, Pannell began her career teaching in a one-room schoolhouse. Later, as a school librarian in Chicago, she was given the responsibility of organizing several hundred elementary school libraries. In 1943 she took a position at the landmark Chicago department store Carson Pirie Scott, as head of the Hobby Horse Bookshop until 1953. Pannell loved reading to children and introducing them to the world of books. Chicago schools would sponsor field trips to the Hobby Horse Bookshop because children and teachers loved visiting with her to listen to stories and learn about the world of books.

Before Pannell's death, she and her husband, who had no children, decided to leave their estate in trust to the WNBA "to honor Lucile Pannell because of her great love for children, young people, and books... the purpose is to stimulate, promote, and encourage children's and young people's interest in books." The first award went to the OxCart Bookshop in Rochester, New York.

In 1997, at the request of Lucile's younger brother, Bud Micheels, a special grant was made to the Menomonie Public Library from the Pannell Trust to help build a new children's wing. In 1998, during BookExpo (BEA) in Chicago, the WNBA was invited to present the Pannell Award during the Children's Book & Author Breakfast. This has

The Pannell Award honors two bookstores every year. Here, McLean & Eakin Booksellers in Petosky, MI shows off their pride for winning the award in 2000.

since become a tradition. Donna Paz, a past National WNBA president, wrote in the Fall 1998 *Bookwoman*, "the Pannell Award continues to be recognized as one of the major awards presented in the bookselling community, drawing coverage from *Publishers Weekly*, *Bookselling This Week*, and reported in the newsletters of the Association of Booksellers for Children and the regional bookseller associations. At a time when competition draws the work days out even further, and profits are more challenging to achieve, the Pannell Award is an important recognition that bookselling is a noble profession and fostering a love of reading is a lasting gift to children and society."

In an article about the Pannell Award that appeared in *Publishers Weekly* in 2004, Anne Irish, executive director of the Association of Booksellers for Children (ABC), told *PW*, "[Although] we recognize an ABC member every year for their energetic support of ABC, we look to the Pannell as the award for recognition as a bookseller. We feel that that's the pinnacle of awards, and everyone aspires to win it."

At the current time, the Pannell Award committee is chaired by Susan Knopf of Scout Books & Media. A panel of jurors selects the two winners: a general bookstore and a children's specialty bookstore. In addition to a monetary award, the winners receive original art donated by children's book illustrators. Penguin Young Readers Group has supported the Pannell Award program with a generous donation each year since 2007.

The list of winners appears in the Appendix; for more information, visit the WNBA website at http://www.wnba-books.org/pannell-award/.

THE EASTMAN GRANT

Given annually, the WNBA Eastman Grant is a $500 cash award given to a library association in a state where there is a WNBA chapter. The funds are given to support librarian professional development or training offered by an official library association. The purpose of the grant is to support the continuing education of librarians in their efforts to educate the public, keep up with technological change, and spread the word about the importance of learning and reading. The award was named in honor of Anne Heidbreder Eastman, a past National WNBA president, who held positions in several New York publishing companies in editorial, sales, and marketing. She was an active member of the American Library Association, where she chaired several committees, and at the Center of the Book at the Library of Congress.

For more information about this program, visit the WNBA website at http://www.wnba-books.org/wnba-eastman-grant.

NATIONAL READING GROUP MONTH AND GREAT GROUP READS—CELEBRATING THE JOY OF SHARED READING
Jill A. Tardiff

National Reading Group Month (NRGM) addresses the WNBA's mission to promote the value of books and reading. Through this initiative the WNBA aims to foster the values reading groups encourage: camaraderie, enjoyment of shared reading, appreciation of literature, and reading as a conduit for transmitting culture and advancing civic engagement.

The idea for National Reading Group Month originated with sisters Martha Burns and Alice Dillon, the authors of *Reading Group Journal: Notes in the Margin* (Abbeville Press, 1999).

Burns and Dillon contributed the following description of the origin of NRGM:

> *One night many years ago we sat talking about Wallace Stegner's masterpiece* Angle of Repose. *Maybe this is where we got the idea*

to create our journal, Reading Group Journal: Notes in the Margin. *But once the idea came to us we took off with it, designed it, and sold it to Abbeville Press. Our vision was to create a keepsake journal celebrating a personal history of shared reading. And then we had another vision, which was to create National Reading Group Month, which is, of course, October! We registered the designation with* Chase's Calendar of Events *and set out to promote the joy of shared reading with independent bookstores and libraries all across the county. And the idea caught on! A few years later it was our desire to find a vehicle for NRGM to spread and grow and so we reached out to WNBA. We were delighted with its enthusiasm and fresh vision. Our research for* Reading Group Journal *had shown us that reading groups are nothing new, but we are thankful that in our own way we helped to encourage the communities that shared reading creates. We hope that in one hundred years there will still be celebrations of shared reading each year in October.*

The sisters' plan was to launch October as National Reading Group Month in 2001. With marketing efforts halted by the tragic events of September 11, their ambition was put on hold until Burns, then a member of the WNBA-NYC chapter, approached National president Jill A. Tardiff in 2006 with the idea that the WNBA would assume National Reading Group Month's conceptual development. This proposal was overwhelmingly approved at the WNBA's annual meeting held that year in Boston. Jill A. Tardiff was designated National Reading Group Month chair and plans for 2007 were set into motion. The first National Reading Group Month program in October 2007 was the premier event of the WNBA's ninetieth anniversary celebration. The WNBA-NYC chapter hosted a panel program at the New York Center for Independent Publishing. Carol Fitzgerald of The Book Report Network moderated with guest authors Laura Dave, Wally Lamb, Matthew Sharpe, Beverly Swerling, and Adriana Trigiani.

Events are open to the public and reading group members are invited to take part in the festivities. Traditionally, a portion of the proceeds from the event is donated to the U.S. Fund for UNICEF. Susan Walker, National Reading Group Month events manager and former WNBA-Charlotte chapter president, has administered this highly acclaimed series since 2012.

Signature Events and Chapter Participation

All chapters hold authors events annually, but one event would become known as the Signature Event, hosted by an individual chapter each year.

Signature Event 2008: Hosted by WNBA-Seattle chapter at University Book Store and moderated by Nancy Pearl, with guest speakers Stesha Brandon (University Bookstore) and Mary Ann Gwinn (*The Seattle Times*), authors Diane Hammond and Nancy Horan, and bookstore owners Cheryl McKeon (Third Place Books) and Rebecca Willow (Parkplace Books).

Signature Event 2009: Hosted by the WNBA-Nashville chapter at the main Nashville Public Library in conjunction with the Southern Festival of Books "Breakfast with Authors," cosponsored with Davis-Kidd Nashville, and moderated by NPR Nashville *All Things Considered* host Nina Cardona, with guest authors Marie Brenner, Holly Goddard Jones, 2006 WNBA Award recipient Perri Klass, Inman Majors, and Kathryn Stockett.

Signature Event 2010: Hosted by the WNBA-Nashville chapter at the main Nashville Public Library in conjunction with the Southern Festival of Books "Breakfast with Authors," cosponsored with Davis-Kidd Nashville, and moderated by Nashville Public Radio WPLN *All Things Considered* host Nina Cardona, with guest authors Melanie Benjamin, Tom Franklin, Sena Jeter Naslund, Helen Simonson, and Lee Smith.

Signature Event 2011: Hosted by the WNBA-Nashville chapter at Nashville Public Library Downtown in conjunction with the Southern Festival of Books "Breakfast with Authors," cosponsored with Parnassus Books-Nashville, and moderated by Nashville Public Radio WPLN *All Things Considered* host Nina Cardona, with guest authors Tayari Jones, Ann Patchett, Tom Perrotta, as well as debut authors Erin Morgenstern and Justin Torres.

Signature Event 2012: Hosted by the WNBA-Nashville chapter at the main Nashville Public Library in conjunction with the Southern

"Coffee with Authors," hosted by the WNBA-Nashville chapter and Southern Festival of Books, has served as NRGM's signature event for several years. The program for the 2015 event and the featured books are shown here.

Festival of Books "Coffee with Authors," cosponsored with Parnassus Books-Nashville, and moderated by Nashville Public Radio WPLN *All Things Considered* host Nina Cardona, with guest authors Ben Fountain, Christopher Tilghman, Gail Tsukiyama, and Karen Thompson Walker.

Signature Event 2013: Hosted by the WNBA-Nashville chapter at main Nashville Public Library in conjunction with the Southern Festival of Books "Coffee with Authors," cosponsored with Parnassus Books-Nashville, and moderated by Nashville Public Radio WPLN *All Things Considered* host Nina Cardona, with guest authors Jill McCorkle, Cathie

Pelletier, and John Milliken Thompson, as well as debut authors Suzanne Rindell and Margaret Wrinkle.

Signature Event 2014: Hosted by the WNBA-Nashville chapter at the main Nashville Public Library in conjunction with the Southern Festival of Books "Coffee with Authors," cosponsored with Parnassus Books-Nashville, and moderated by Parnassus Books social media director and online literary journal editor-in-chief Mary Laura Philpott, with guest authors Nadia Hashimi, Lily King, Ann Weisgarber, and Gabrielle Zevin.

Signature Event 2015: Hosted by the WNBA-Charlotte chapter at Maggiano's Little Italy/South Park Mall, cosponsored by Park Road Books. The "bibliofeast" was emceed by WNBA National president and author Carin Siegfried with WNBA-Charlotte chapter president Kristen Knox and NRGM events manager Susan Walker, with guest authors Elise Blackwell, Nina de Gramont, Julia Elliott, Sarah Kennedy, Cindy Henry McMahon, Jonathan Odell, Brian Panowich, Hank Phillippi Ryan, Richard Wall (for Carol Wall), and J. Peder Zane.

Signature Event 2016: Hosted by the WNBA-San Francisco chapter at Books Inc. Opera Plaza, cosponsored by Litquake, and moderated by Edgar Award-winning mystery novelist Laurie R. King, with guest authors Cara Black, Jessica Chiarella, Patricia V. Davis, Mary Mackey, and Mary Volmer.

Other events held in chapter cities featured best-selling authors and book-club "faves" in partnership with local independent bookstores and libraries, such as **WNBA-Seattle** chapter's "Readings Round the Sound" that included authors Sherman Alexie, Amy Bloom, John Green, Debbie Macomber, Marilynne Robinson, Garth Stein, and Miriam Toews; **WNBA-Boston** chapter's "A Reader's Round-Robin" with authors Joan Anderson, Jennifer Haigh, Ann Harleman, Judith Nies, Deborah Noyes, and Gina Ogden; **WNBA-Dallas** with authors Dixie Cash, aka Pam Cumbie, and Jeffrey McClanahan; **WNBA-Detroit** with authors Marjorie Celona, Michael Harvey, Ray Robertson, and Larry Watson;

WNBA-Greater Philadelphia with Kim van Alkemade, Amy Jo Burns, and Annie Liontas; **WNBA-South Florida** with Lauren Groff and Hank Phillippi Ryan; **WNBA-New Orleans** with "Reading 'Round the Big Easy" with Anne Benoit, Amy Conner, Laura Lane McNeal, Michael D. Moffitt, Michael Pitre, Tom Piazza, Katy Simpson Smith, Rebecca Snedeker, and Jesmyn Ward; **WNBA-Washington, D.C.**, with Charles Belfoure, Dara Horn, Leslie Maitland, and Virginia Pye; **WNBA-Los Angeles**' "Let's Go [Book] Clubbing," with Cynthia Bond, Michelle Huneven, Gina B. Nahai, and Gabrielle Zevin.

Eager readers met authors, swapped writing tips, shared reading suggestions, and left with armloads of new books to read and plenty of memories.

National Reading Group Month Selects Great Group Reads

NRGM chairperson Jill A. Tardiff developed the Great Group Reads program in 2009 to highlight National Reading Group Month and provide a suggested list of titles that book groups would enjoy. Every year since, the Selection Committee—a group of twenty-five-plus readers comprised of WNBA members from chapters around the country—reads and picks the books for the list. These choices have become a highly anticipated resource for reading groups, bookstores, and libraries across the country. Titles are chosen on the basis of their appeal to reading group members for whom they are bound to open up lively conversations about a host of timely and provocative topics, from the intimate dynamics of family and personal relationships to major cultural and world issues. The Selection Committee also makes a conscious decision to focus its attention on underrepresented gems from small presses and lesser-known mid-list releases from larger houses.

Great Group Reads Selection Committee managers include Rosalind Reisner (2009–2013), Bebe (Sarah) Brechner (2014, 2015), and Kristen Knox (2016–). Selection Committee coordinators include Pamela Milam (2014–) and Linda Rosen (2014–). For more detail about Great Group Reads book selections, sponsors, and advisory board members, please see the Appendices.

For more information about these programs, visit the NRGM website at http://www.nationalreadinggroupmonth.com/.

THE WNBA NATIONAL WRITING CONTEST
Joan Gelfand

In 2010 the Executive Board voted unanimously to inaugurate a national writing contest. The initiative was proposed by Joan Gelfand, former San Francisco chapter president and immediate past president of the National WNBA Board.

After over ninety years of supporting extraordinary bookwomen through the WNBA Award, independent booksellers through the Pannell Award, and librarians through the endowed Eastman grant, the time was right for the WNBA to show support for emerging writers. The Board agreed that the initiative fit in with the organization's mission of "supporting women in all aspects of the world of the book."

The criteria specified that the contest would be open to all writers—members and nonmembers—and submissions would be accepted in two categories: fiction and poetry. Announcements were placed in national writers' magazines such as *Poets & Writers* and *Writer's Digest* and posted on listservs reaching hundreds of thousands of writers.

In the first year there was a modest response: about one hundred thirty-five submissions. The next year, response dropped to about one hundred twenty submissions. In the third year memoir and creative nonfiction were added as categories and submissions were over one hundred sixty. The fourth year, WNBA Communications Chair Penny Makras implemented a targeted social media campaign using Facebook posts and Twitter announcements. Those efforts resulted in an overwhelming response of two hundred fifty submissions.

From the beginning, the contest has secured high-profile judges. The judging is a critical component of the contest: The higher profile the judge, the greater the benefit to a writer's career. We have been fortunate to have as judges: Deirdre Bair (nonfiction); Mary Mackey, Ellen Bass, and Molly Peacock (poetry); Rosemary Daniel (memoir); and Meg Waite Clayton, Michelle Hoover, and Ann Harlemann (fiction).

Submissions are accepted for five months. When the contest closes, the submissions are disseminated among a committee of early readers. The top ten submissions in each category are read by the final judges. The winners are announced each year in May. Winning entries are published in a special June edition of *The Bookwoman* and publicized during National Reading Group Month and through a targeted ad campaign.

At this time, discussions are under way about adding a category for young adult literature and novels. An anthology of winning entries will be published by C&R Press in time for the Centennial Celebration in 2017.

For more information about this program, visit the WNBA website at http://www.wnba-books.org/contest. The list of winners can be found in the Appendix.

THE AFGHAN WOMEN'S WRITING PROJECT AND THE AFGHAN FRIENDS NETWORK AFFILIATION, WNBA SAN FRANCISCO CHAPTER
Kate Farrell, Lori Noack, and Humaira Ghilzai

The Afghan Women's Writing Project (AWWP) was founded in 2009 by WNBA-NYC chapter member and WNBA Award winner Masha Hamilton. It was dedicated to Zarmeena, a mother of seven who was executed by the Taliban in Kabul's Ghazi Stadium in 1999 for allegedly killing her husband. After seeing a video of the execution on the AP wire, Hamilton tried to uncover the details of Zarmeena's story with little success. Not only were Afghan women unseen beneath *burqas,* their stories were silenced as well. After several visits to Afghanistan visiting women in prisons, interviewing child brides, even speaking with the matriarch of a family of opium growers, Hamilton established the Afghan Women's Writing Project "to foster creative and intellectual exchange between Afghan women writers and American women authors and teachers." The website (http://awwproject.org) publishes the work of Afghan writers under the mentorship of AWWP participants, including authors, poets, essayists, memoirists, and others.

In 2012, a three-year grant through the U.S. Embassy in Kabul enabled the organization to expand its programs. Current initiatives include twelve online and seven local writing workshops in English, Dari, and Pashto; a women-only Internet café in Kabul; laptops and Internet service for writers in need; secure transportation to all local workshops; radio broadcasts; and print and online publishing for 409 enrolled writers who have produced nearly three thousand works. Each week, new writings are posted to the AWWP website and disseminated to over ten thousand active users per month through blogs and other social media channels. As a result of the workshops, writers have gained self-confidence and satisfaction, and critical thinking, literacy, English, and computer skills. This enhances educational and employment opportunities and potential for financial self-sufficiency.

San Francisco chapter members knew about the AWWP and about Lori Noack, executive director and Bay Area resident. AWWP's first formal contact with the WNBA was in 2010 when the WNBA Award was presented to AWWP founder Masha Hamilton. In 2014, WNBA-SF President Kate Farrell invited AWWP Executive Director Lori Noack to present a program on AWWP at a WNBA-SF chapter meeting. That fall meeting at the Temescal Public Library in Oakland, California, set into motion a series of relationships that have been helpful to AWWP in several ways, from gaining increased visibility to finding critical partners in core program areas.

AWWP's alliance with WNBA-SF has also increased the audience and visibility of AWWP's women writers in Afghanistan whose voices are continually repressed by the social and political conditions in which they live. The expansion of the women's readership increases awareness of their plight, gathers force in the global strength needed to enact changes, and strengthens the writers' spirits as they fight the daily battles as women in a deeply patriarchal and restrictive society.

YESTERDAY, TODAY, TOMORROW
Masooma

Yesterday my sister was afraid of going outside,
Today my sisters are going to school,
And tomorrow they will work outside of the home.

Yesterday my sister was stoned.
Today she is studying to be a doctor,
And tomorrow she will save a life.

Yesterday my sister's dream was to have a book.
Now she is in the library,
And tomorrow she will write the book.

Yesterday my sister looked at the world through a small window.
Today she sees the world through her camera,
And tomorrow the world will see everything through her
documentaries.

Yesterday my country's women had no rights.
Now they are fighting for their rights,
And tomorrow they will have the same rights as men.

Yesterday my country was a desert.
Now my brothers and sisters are planting trees,
And tomorrow, in this garden together, we will live in peace.

Afghan Friends Network

Afghan Friends Network (AFN; http://www.afghanfriends.net) is an all-volunteer, grassroots nonprofit organization delivering sustainable programs in education and cultural exchange that nurture potential, promote dignity, and support bold steps in Afghanistan. Afghan-American Humaira Ghilzai, cofounder and member of the WNBA-SF chapter, founded AFN in 2002, along with Carol Ruth Silver, a veteran 1960s Freedom Rider.

Since then, AFN has raised $450,000 for Afghanistan; educated forty-three hundred girls; provided literacy classes for two hundred fifty mothers; and taught English to boys. Twenty-two girls and six boys received scholarships for higher education, and four hundred fifty male and female teachers attended its teacher training workshops. AFN currently employs twenty-five Afghans and has a volunteer staff in the United States. In Afghanistan the AFN has two schools for girls, one school for boys, and two women's literacy programs.

AFN relies on its network of friends, volunteers, and donors to spread the word about the strength of Afghan women and the challenges facing them. In partnering with the WNBA and AWWP, the AFN has been able to share its message of education with a wider audience. In Afghanistan, AFN women students attend AWWP's writing workshops in Ghazni. Some have learned to use a computer so they can tell their stories in English to people around the world.

The San Francisco Chapter Helped Build a Network

Networking events facilitated by the WNBA-SF chapter provided many opportunities for support and growth of the two organizations, and helped to build a local Afghan network. In September 2015, the San Francisco chapter sponsored an event that brought the message of both groups to a larger audience. At the end of that presentation, Michael Larson, cofounder of the San Francisco Writers Conference, invited all three organizations to present at the West Coast's largest writers' conference. Writers from all over the United States who were attending the conference had a chance to hear about the work of the AWWP, the AFN, and the WNBA. Some of those women writers, now retired teachers of creative writing, offered their services as mentors and tutors in the AWWP online project. Also, out of the partnership with SFWC, AFN had the opportunity to recommend Parwana Fayyaz, an Afghan writer and graduate student at Stanford, for a scholarship to the conference and to speak at the SFWC joint session.

Though the chapter's original goal was to directly involve SF chapter members in the AWWP process, what members found was that they were helping to build a local Afghan network through their events. They advocated, educated, and connected. If the chapter had not sponsored these three events over a two-year span, some like-minded partners would not have met or worked together.

WNBA members were enriched by the resolve and spirit of the Afghan women and by continuing friendships with the local Afghan-American immigrants. The benefits of AWWP's collaborations with WNBA-SF and AFN, as with all healthy relationships of like-minded groups, will continue to grow in unpredictable ways. It is the visionary connections made by leaders in the WNBA-SF chapter that plant the seeds for growth, providing opportunities to make a difference in the world around us.

MARKING MILESTONES AND HONORING WOMEN'S VOICES

On the way to one hundred years, the WNBA has celebrated several significant anniversaries. Thanks to the forward-looking founders, activities were documented and saved, then stored in the Rare Book and Manuscript Library at Columbia University. In 1967, *Women in the World of Words*, an ambitious WNBA history, marked the first fifty years and an opportunity to look back and reflect on the accomplishments of the organization. *Women in the World of Words* can be viewed on the WNBA website at https://www.wnba-centennial. org/historical-highlights-1.

For the seventieth anniversary, in 1987, the WNBA chose to honor seventy women who have made a difference. As President Cathy Rentschler explained:

> *We invited the entire book world to nominate women who are dedicated, creative and catalytic. In response to our ads in the trade press, hundreds of names of outstanding women poured in, which were then reviewed by our judges...*

> *This list confirms the range of the roles and responsibilities of today's bookwomen. We are delighted to present the WNBA Book Women Award to these 70 women who have made a difference. They represent all that is special about the book world, an 'industry' which despite the changing world of business and technology still remains one of professionals dedicated to connecting the words and creativity of authors to the minds and lives of readers. There seems no better way to celebrate 70 years of WNBA in 1987 than to honor these women who are the reason WNBA was founded and remains so significant today, and will continue to do so into the next century.*

The honorees included women in all fields of the book world, from all eras and countries, reflecting the membership of the organization. Some of the honorees were: Florence Howe, founder of the Feminist Press; Patricia Miller King, director of the Schlesinger Library at Radcliffe; Esther Margolis, founder of Newmarket Press; Barbara Rollock, coordinator of children's services at New York Public Library; Louisa Solano, owner of the Grolier Bookshop in Boston; Helen Venn, director of the Radcliffe Publishing Procedures Course; Anita Silvey, editor of *The Horn Book Magazine*; and Nancy Larrick, author and founder of the International Reading Association.

The booklet, with the names and short biographies of all seventy women, can be viewed on the WNBA Centennial website's "Historical Highlights" page (https://www.wnba-centennial.org/historical-highlights-1).

The seventy-fifth anniversary called for a very different celebration, with a far-ranging booklist titled "75 Books by Women Whose Words Have Changed the World" and called the Diamond Anniversary Honor List. The intent, as noted in the pamphlet, was to celebrate the words of "seventy-five significant works by women. Their words have broken ground, changed our thinking, infuriated, soothed, or challenged us. Few things have endured as well over the years as the beauty and power of the written word." Authors included the Greek poet Sappho, Helen Keller, Margaret Mead, Maxine Hong Kingston, Elizabeth Kubler-Ross, and Doris Lessing. The entire list can be viewed on the WNBA Centennial website's "Historical Highlights" page (https://www.wnba-centennial.org/historical-highlights-1).

Another, very different booklist marked the eightieth anniversary: "80 Books for Twentieth Century Girls," filled with the classics of children's literature. The heading states: "As we also approach a new millennium, we thought it was a wonderful opportunity to reflect on the books we have enjoyed while growing up and share eighty favorite titles that provide smart, capable, and talented female role models for future generations of girls." The entire list can be viewed on the WNBA Centennial website's "Historical Highlights" page (https://www.wnba-centennial.org/historical-highlights-1).

Two booklists mark the Centennial: literary works (fiction, poetry, and memoir) and nonfiction, both covering works by American women writers. The project is called "Celebrating Women's Voices: 100 Books to Read and Talk About." The goal of the lists is to "start conversations, send people to their bookstores and libraries; motivate them to reread the copies on their bookshelves; talk to their families and friends about

The books sent to the new administration during Women's History Month in 2017, one of the centerpieces of WNBA's Centennial programming.

them; discuss them at their book groups; and inspire them to write their own stories to add to the complex and wonderful ongoing conversation about women's lives that the lists represent. The lists reflect the diversity of women's experiences in the U.S., including works by women of every race, creed, ethnicity, and sexual orientation, women whose words inspire us all to see our own lives in the stories of their joys, sorrows, struggles, and successes." The fiction/poetry/memoir list can be viewed on the Centennial website: https://www.wnba-centennial.org/100-books-fiction. The nonfiction list can be viewed at: https://www.wnba-centennial.org/100-books-nonfiction.

These two hundred titles sparked another project. In 1955, for an entire month, the WNBA sent a book a day to President Dwight D. Eisenhower as he was recuperating from a heart attack at his home in Gettysburg, Pennsylvania. The WNBA chose to create another Book-a-Day program, with books chosen from the 100 Books lists, to send to the newly elected president during Women's History Month in March 2017. The list of books chosen, with annotations, can be accessed at this link: https://www.wnba-centennial.org/book-a-day.

The WNBA Second Century Prize Honoring Little Free Library
Jane Kinney-Denning

One of the signature initiatives of the WNBA's Centennial was the awarding of the WNBA Second Century Prize, a $5,000 grant to an organization that supports the power of reading, past, present, and future. The one-time cash award was given to the Little Free Library (https://littlefreelibrary.org), a nonprofit organization that promotes reading for all ages, but especially children, by building free book exchanges. Upon learning of the award, founder and executive director Todd Bol said, "This means so much. Little Free Library participants are about 90 percent women, so it really is a women's movement, supporting friends and family and community."

Under the guidance of the Second Century Prize cochairs, Mary Grey James and Susan Larson, nominations for the prize were considered from WNBA chapters throughout the country. An executive committee voted and chose Little Free Library (LFL) based on the nature of its grassroots organization, which has affected thousands of readers of all ages and backgrounds. LFL embodies the goals of the Women's National Book Association: promoting literacy and the love of reading.

A Little Free Library is a neighborhood book exchange where anyone passing by can take a book to read or leave a book for someone else to read. Little Free Library was founded in 2009 in Hudson, Wisconsin, by Todd Bol, to honor his mother, a schoolteacher. He made a small box designed to look like a one-room schoolhouse, filled it with books and placed it in his front yard. Only eight years later Little Free Library has become an international movement of mini-libraries sharing the message of "give one, take one." In May 2012, as a result of its international success, LFL was officially incorporated and became a 501(c)(3) nonprofit organization. The original goal of LFL was to create 2,150 Little Free Libraries, a number that surpasses the number of libraries funded by Andrew Carnegie. This goal was easily met. As of this writing, LFL had over fifty thousand registered Little Free Libraries in more than seventy countries around the world with millions of books exchanged annually.

LFL owners are known as "stewards." The libraries can be purchased on the LFL website or stewards can make their own. The styles are varied and creative, from the one-room schoolhouse model offered by LFL to the wonderful handmade LFLs in all shapes, sizes, and designs. Stewards of registered LFLs receive a sign for their library that reads "Little Free Library" and an official charter membership number. Registered LFLs are also featured on a world map that uses GPS coordinates.

Little Free Library continuously develops new initiatives beyond its charming small libraries placed in front yards and public spaces. The WNBA particularly applauds the LFL's new Kids, Community, and Cops program, which helps police departments set up book exchanges in their precincts (https://littlefreelibrary.org/community), and Action Book Club™ (https://littlefreelibrary.org/actionbookclub), which encourages social engagement through shared reading—a commitment that resonates with the WNBA's own National Reading Group Month program. Another program, the LFL Impact Fund, puts Little Free Libraries in communities where they can truly make a difference. Recipients have included homeless shelters, schools, and other sites in need of greater access to books. The Impact Fund is made possible by individual donors, partner organizations who share a vision for spreading the word about the power of sharing books, as well as LFL's retail sales and library registration fees.

CHAPTER 5

WNBA CHAPTER HISTORIES

In 1936, at a WNBA board meeting, Constance Lindsay Skinner remarked that "no one was as responsible for the development of new ideas, stimulating thought and general culture in a community as the local bookseller and librarian, and yet they were too often cut off from people of similar experience who could share their problems and bring them encouragement." At this time, nineteen years after the WNBA was founded, there were no chapters outside of New York City. The president, Rosamund Beebe, wrote to members that "Miss Skinner's remark came to us as a sort of challenge, for the Women's National Book Association, made up of representative women in every field of the book trade, is established in the heart of the book publishing world. At our monthly meetings distinguished authors familiarize us with their books, and outstanding booksellers tell us how they solve their problems. This suggestion set us to thinking how we could share the advantages of our Association with other women actively engaged in the book trade outside of New York City."

The plan that emerged from Skinner's comments was twofold: to establish Corresponding Memberships for women who lived outside New York, and to publish a quarterly newsletter "giving news of the book world, reports of the talks which we all enjoy so much at our regular meetings, and containing an open forum in which you will be able to discuss your own problems and report your activities. In this way we believe a real service can be given both you and the Association and a new and vital force brought into the book trade, a force which would be a stimulus to the community as a whole. The dues for the Corresponding Members will be only $1.00 a year which will cover the cost of the Bulletin." It was hoped that these out-of-town members would schedule trips to New York to attend WNBA programs. Whether spreading the news about the WNBA would lead to chapters in other cities was not noted in the minutes of that meeting, but that happy consequence could have been an underlying motivation.

With funding by Constance Lindsay Skinner, our newsletter, *The Bookwoman*, was born in 1937 and women all over the U.S. could become part of the WNBA. It was from this modest start, spreading the news, that WNBA chapters arose. *The Bookwoman* continues as our newsletter, received by every member, now in digital form.

Until 1954, the president of the New York chapter was the National WNBA president and the New York City chapter functioned as the National chapter. That year, an expansion committee was formed to explore the potential for creating individual chapters around the U.S. By that time, groups of Corresponding Members around the country needed their own chapters. The first five to be established were Boston, Chicago, Cleveland, Nashville, and New York. Chapters in Binghamton, New York; Birmingham, Alabama; Dallas; Detroit; Grand Rapids; Little Rock, Arkansas; Los Angeles; Pittsburgh; San Francisco; and Washington, D.C., came on board before the millennium and were joined in the new century by Charlotte, North Carolina; New Orleans; Seattle; Philadelphia; South Florida; and Greater Lansing, Michigan. As of 2017 there were eleven active chapters. As of this writing, additional chapters are in the process of organizing: Atlanta, Minneapolis, and St. Louis may join the WNBA in the centennial year.

From the beginning, chapters have had distinct personalities, memberships, and interests. Some chapters are comprised mostly of authors or librarians or publishing professionals; their ambitious and diverse programming and enthusiasm has sustained and energized the organization and contributed to the literary life in their communities. A common link among the chapters is members' love of books and a mission to promote literacy. Capsule histories of all the currently active chapters follows, followed by information about chapters now, sadly, disbanded.

BOSTON, MA
Nancy Rubin Stuart

In 1954, a group of women publishers, booksellers, writers, reviewers, and librarians founded the Boston chapter of WNBA. Within the first five years the chapter had successfully campaigned for the inclusion of children's literature courses at a local college, and, under the aegis of Alice Dixon Bond, book editor for the *Boston Herald*, launched a Book and Author Luncheon series. For the next twenty-five years, book lovers attended the very popular event; attendance at one point reached one thousand. Funds raised from the series enabled the WNBA-Boston to support local museums, public broadcasting, and the Boston Public Library for its retrospective children's book collection.

Over the years, the series became so popular that it regularly attracted distinguished speakers, including film star Lillian Gish, who in 1967 spoke about her memoir, *Autobiography*. That same year the chapter presented a gift of $1,000 to the Boston Public Library on behalf of the new Alice M. Jordan Collection of children's books. To enhance that collection, WNBA-Boston members donated books from their personal libraries. In 1968, the chapter drew national attention when children's literature specialists joined with the National Board and other chapters to honor *Horn Book Magazine* editor Ruth Hill Viguers at the Constance Lindsay Skinner Award Banquet. In 1970, the fund-raiser was cosponsored with the *Boston Herald-Traveler*, and speakers included Erich Segal, author of that year's mega-best seller *Love Story*.

By the 1990s the chapter's ongoing interest in children's literature sparked a series of annual holiday teas resulting in sales of a thousand books for youth and a sum in excess of $30,000. Thanks to those funds, WNBA-Boston was able to help support the Boston Public Library's summer reading readiness programs for disadvantaged preschool children.

In 1996, several members of the Boston chapter joined members in sister chapters in Dallas, Detroit, Nashville, New York, and Washington, D.C., for a WNBA National Literary Tour of London. Members visited Canterbury Cathedral, the destination of pilgrims in Chaucer's *Canterbury Tales*; the tower where Virginia Woolf's friend and lover Vita Sackville-West wrote; the favorite inn of Charles Dickens; and the home and grave of Jane Austen.

Tapping the rich resources of Boston's literary scene over the years, the WNBA-Boston chapter has included programs ranging from brunches with best-selling authors to roundtable discussions with publishing professionals and writers. During its long association with the National WNBA, the Boston chapter has continued to maintain strong ties to the national organization and its sister chapters. Boston members have served on the National Board, and in 1997 the chapter hosted the National meeting. Members have served on WNBA award committees and volunteered on the Eastman Award and United Nations committees. In 1999, the chapter initiated a Teen Literacy Outreach Project to supply books and writing materials to an often-overlooked population: incarcerated adolescents. Thanks to members' generosity, the chapter provided books, journals, and a mobile library cart to its primary partner, the Metro Detention Center.

Through the late 1990s and into the early 2000s, the chapter sponsored monthly programs from September through June. Visits to specialty bookstores, libraries, and literary landmarks added a new dimension to these activities. Among these were visits to Jack Kerouac's Lowell, Emerson's Concord, a private tour of the Massachusetts Historical Society, and a visit to the "literary dead" in Mount Auburn Cemetery.

The Sunday Salon Series of three literary brunches, launched in 2001, became an instant hit with members. It was coupled with WNBA-Boston's publication of a pamphlet celebrating "New England Book Women Who Have Made a Difference." Robert Taylor, book columnist for the *Boston Globe*, described the chapters' members as "movers and shakers" in the world of books. The chapter continues to work to merit that distinction. In 2004, the fiftieth year of the Boston chapter, under the leadership of National president Laurie Beckelman (a former president of the local chapter), the Boston Public Library began a permanent collection of

WNBA members' books for its research division. This program is open to all members of the National WNBA organization who wish to have their books become part of the library's permanent collection.

In 2007, the WNBA-Boston chapter again hosted the annual National board meeting. Growing attention to women's history in the "cradle of liberty" prompted the Boston chapter to cosponsor the launch of the third edition of *Boston Women's Heritage Trail* guidebook. Also that year, the chapter honored women of color through participation in a tour and reception for the new African Meeting House.

In recent years, the chapter has sponsored holiday events, such as the tea in 2014 at the Copley Fairmont Plaza keynoted by Kimberly Elkins, author of *What Is Visible,* and cosponsored a panel with the National Writers Union at the Boston Public Library with several literary agents, including Amaryah Orenstein, copresident of WNBA-Boston. On October 24, 2015, the chapter participated in the Boston Book Festival with a booth in Copley Square; WNBA-Boston copresident and author Nancy Rubin Stuart moderated the festival's panel "Portrait of an Artist" with authors B.A. Shapiro, Courtney Maum, Peter Davis, and Elena Delbanco. In honor of National Reading Group Month, the chapter hosted an author panel moderated by Lisa Borders, author of *The Fifty-First State.* The final event of 2015 was a Sunday brunch at the College Club.

As WNBA-Boston looks to the future, the chapter's role in helping women achieve equity in the arts remains critical.

CHARLOTTE, NC
Carin Siegfried

The Charlotte chapter came into being because Carin Siegfried, who had been a member of WNBA-Nashville and WNBA-New York City, moved to Charlotte in 2004 to work at Baker & Taylor. Although she stayed a network member of the New York chapter for five years, that just wasn't enough. In the spring of 2009, she met with Tracey Adams of Adams Literary Agency, and Betsy Thorpe, an independent editor, to discuss starting a chapter.

They invited other friends to join them at an organizational meeting a few weeks later and found they had a core group of twelve to fifteen women from across the industry who were excited about this new venture. Mary Grey James, then National WNBA president, flew out from Nashville to meet the group and provide additional details about the WNBA. The group then hammered out bylaws and elected officers, and in May 2009 held its first official event at Park Road Books. At the event, bookstore owner (and new WNBA-Charlotte treasurer) Sally Brewster presented the books she was recommending for reading by the pool that summer. In June, newly elected president Carin Siegfried attended the National annual meeting in Nashville, and the chapter was officially recognized.

The chapter has many annual events, including a fall mixer, a book swap, a panel on publishing cosponsored with the Charlotte Writing Club, and a novels. An anthology of winning entries will be published by C&R Press in time for the Centennial Celebration in 2017. event. For National Reading Group Month, the chapter hosts the annual "Bibliofeast," a literary dinner in celebration of National Reading Group Month. In the course of the evening, authors rotate to each table for conversations with guests. Each year culminates with bookseller Sally Brewster's annual recommendations for summer reading. Nearly seventy members strong, the Charlotte chapter of the WNBA represents a broad swath of the book world, from publishing professionals to writers and authors to teachers and librarians to readers. With a monthly book club reading Great Group Reads books and occasional happy hours, there's something to please everyone.

GREATER LANSING, MI
Denise M. Acevedo

The Greater Lansing chapter was started by Denise Acevedo, a writing professor at Michigan State University, who was interested in joining a literacy-based, professional development, and networking organization. The WNBA looked like the right fit. After Acevedo contacted interested colleagues and friends, the group met for the first time in May 2016 and elected board members. The board spent the next few months writing bylaws, planning events, and strategizing regarding membership recruitment and involvement. By the fall of 2016 the group was meeting monthly and planning its first event as a chapter. In January 2017, the chapter hosted an inaugural program attended by Bebe Brechner, vice president of the WNBA National Board. Since then, in an effort to offer the Greater Lansing community monthly events that meet its interests in all things books, the chapter has invited local authors to speak; celebrated Women's History Month and Poetry Month; and begun a drive to collect books for the YMCA Mystic Lake Camp's Treehouse Library. Planning for the next two years of events and membership recruitment is underway.

GREATER PHILADELPHIA
Elizabeth Mosteller and Carli Ducko

The Greater Philadelphia chapter of the Women's National Book Association was established in 2015 by Elizabeth Mosteller, as a result of her desire to surround herself with strong women who aspire to promote literacy and the world of books in their daily lives. Liz Dowiak, Dee Kindt, Angie Venezia, Kate Sandora, Cindy Mannon, and Maria Thomson served as the initial board for the organization and worked very closely with Mosteller in the chapter's infancy. In addition to the executive members, Brittany Berry served as the social media chair, Shelly Douglas as the outreach chair, and Carli Ducko as the Centennial chair.

The chapter celebrated its first membership event in honor of National Reading Group Month by hosting an author panel at Towne Book Center and Cafe in Collegeville, Pennsylvania, in October 2015. Membership meetings are held monthly and rotate in agenda, but consistently support the mission of the National chapter to support reading, literacy, and the role of women in the community of the book.

During its charter year, chapter membership reached twenty-seven members. The executive board and members continue to establish their presence in the Greater Philadelphia suburbs and look forward to increasing membership as they participate in various events throughout the community. There are plans to reach out to area writers' conferences, universities, and publishers.

Many of the executive board, committee chairs, and members have backgrounds in the field of education and strive to spread literacy and reading in their day-to-day lives. The Greater Philadelphia chapter also strives to be a local resource to encourage the empowerment and education of future generations, and to encourage young people to value books and literature as they continue to grow in both their personal and professional lives.

LOS ANGELES, CA

Rachelle Yousuf

The Los Angeles chapter of the Women's National Book Association was founded in 1975 by Lee K. Levy, a member of the New York chapter who had moved to Los Angeles. Levy became the first president, and under her aegis the chapter developed into a true support group for women, and eventually men, in the book world. Sylvia Cross, the second president, later became National WNBA president. Since then the chapter has had many talented leaders, including Sue MacLaurin, who also went on to become National president. In 2005, the chapter was recognized by the Los Angeles mayor for thirty years of involvement in the community.

From the beginning, WNBA-LA's membership has reflected the city's diverse literary community: writers in all genres (including screenwriters), editors and other publishing professionals, agents, publicists, librarians, booksellers, teachers, and readers who live part of their lives in the world of books whatever their day jobs may be.

The chapter's activities have been very eclectic over the years. Some of the most memorable programs in the past include: the Dream Project (2007), a program inspiring children to solve global issues described in the United Nations Millennium Development Goals; "Birthing a Book: The Shero's Journey" panel at the West Hollywood Bookfair (2008); and the risqué "Breaking Down the Bedroom Door: Erotica and Pornography in Today's Literature" panel (1986).

For many years now, the chapter has presented an annual daylong conference, the LA Writers Conference (formerly known as Book Savvy), covering all aspects of publishing. In recent years the conference has grown to host two hundred attendees and dozens of experts presenting on writing, publishing, editing, publicity, and more.

Since 2012, the chapter has hosted biannual literary teas, one of the most popular chapter events, where local authors are invited to read from their work and to participate in discussions with members on their novels and the writing craft. Other current chapter offerings include a Writing Critique Group; a holiday potluck with live entertainment; member readings at a local bookstore; an author panel in October for National Reading Group Month; booths at local book fairs and conferences; social gatherings where members can enjoy local literary events; and author meetups.

In 2013, the chapter partnered with Curacao, a retail store chain that serves the Hispanic community, to host a summer-long literacy program. Volunteers from the chapter read and do crafts with children under the age of twelve every Saturday from June to August.

Since 1985, the chapter has cosponsored the Judy Lopez Memorial Foundation Award for Excellence in Children's Literature. The awards, which have grown in prestige over the years, were established to honor the memory of one of the chapter's founding members. They are given annually by the Judy Lopez Memorial Foundation to recognize works of literary excellence for nine- to twelve-year-olds.

Reflecting the history of the national organization, the Los Angeles chapter celebrates and maintains the sense of community and support that served as the inspiration for the national founders in 1917.

NASHVILLE, TN
Carolyn Wilson

The Nashville chapter had its beginning with an organizational meeting on May 20, 1955, with twenty-seven people attending. Earlier, a larger group had heard Anne Richter, from the New York chapter, speak about the organization. At the May meeting, officers were elected. Mary Kate Ellen Gruver, juvenile editor at Broadman Press, was the first president. Nashville was the fourth WNBA chapter established.

In the early years chapter members were educators (primary and secondary schools, colleges, and universities), librarians, authors, members of the local publishing community, and book lovers. In the ensuing years, members came from many other areas of the book community.

In 1987 the chapter participated in the Tennessee Literary Homecoming Celebration in 1986, an event that eventually became the Southern Festival of Books. From the early years of the festival, chapter members formed a core group of volunteers; participation has grown into major support in all areas of this notable October event. In recent years, the chapter has hosted one of the signature events at the festival, "Breakfast with Authors;" its panel of high-profile authors always attracts a large audience.

In 1990, the chapter formed the Tennessee Writers Alliance, assuming oversight of the group until it became a more self-sufficient body in 1994. Many WNBA members served as members of the TWA Board of Directors through the years.

In an effort to provide children's materials on Tennessee history, the chapter published *Tennessee Trailblazers,* written by Nashville natives Patricia and Frederick McKissack and published by March Media, owned by board member Etta Wilson. It has become a staple across Tennessee in libraries and through book sales. In another publishing venture, the chapter produced the *Literary Allusions Cookbook* in 1982.

Another chapter activity of long standing is the Summer Reading and Book Discussion Series, held for twenty-six years at Lipscomb University. It features six weeks of book discussions facilitated by scholars from local schools and colleges. The series initially highlighted books from the WNBA's "75th Anniversary List of Books by Women Authors," and its popularity led to a recurring summer event directed by member Carolyn Wilson. Popular themes for the series have included Southern literature, humor, writing about food, international writers, and books into movies. The program was renamed the Willodene Scott Summer Reading and Discussion Series, honoring Willodene Scott, a charter member of the chapter. Building on the success of the summer reading and discussion series, a smaller book group began meeting at a branch library, which initially focused on the Great Group Reads selections.

In 1995 the chapter joined with the Tennessee Bicentennial Committee and the Tennessee Council of Teachers of English to produce a literary map of Tennessee. This map hangs in the Center for the Book in the Library of Congress along with other state literary maps. For many years the chapter has participated in the ATHENA Awards, considered the highest recognition of women of achievement in Nashville. Chapter members Donna Paz and Sue Bredensteiner were WNBA representatives to the awards committee. Each year the chapter nominates an outstanding member for the award.

Many programs have been developed to promote the value of books and reading to youth audiences. "Books Change the World" was a Saturday discussion at public libraries featuring successful Nashville women sharing the importance of reading in their lives. In the spring of 2005, a day focusing on writing, "Connecting: A Day for Readers and Writers," was held at the Hume Fogg Academic Magnet School: Fourteen writers joined in this effort with keynote addresses presented by authors John Egerton, Tony Earley, and storyteller Estelle Condra. This was directed by member Alice Sanford, with proceeds from the event providing scholarships for the Tennessee Young Writers Workshops. This program has continued and expanded in subsequent years. For many years, the chapter has supported Book'EM, a local incentive directed by WNBA member Lee Fairbend that provides disadvantaged children with books of their own. Each year volunteers go into the public schools in metropolitan Nashville to read to children. Honoring a commitment to education, scholarships are offered to young students pursuing careers in books, libraries, and writing. Currently scholarships are given to attendees of the Young Writers Workshops, held each summer by Humanities Tennessee.

When the new downtown Nashville Public Library opened in 1998 an event was held to raise money for the library featuring Tennessee writers Ron Kidd, Cherie Bennett, and Patricia McKissack. In 2002, to further support the new Nashville Public Library, the chapter donated two original watercolors by Caldecott Award winner Jerry Pinkney from Patricia McKissack's book about the old Nashville Public Library, *Goin' Someplace Special*. In 2005, chapter member Kathy Gore led the fiftieth anniversary celebration of the chapter, which included an exhibit of chapter history at the new public library, an anniversary dinner with guest author Jeanne Ray, and a commemorative poster created by Nashville artist Gary Gore.

The Nashville chapter remains a vital force in Nashville and the surrounding areas with diverse programs, cooperative ventures with other book-related groups to promote the value of books and reading, educational activities through schools and libraries, and efforts to raise the recognition of outstanding women who have been part of the book community. We consist of a widely diverse membership bringing much expertise and enthusiasm to our planning, programs, and mission.

NEW ORLEANS, LA
Susan Larson

The Women's National Book Association of New Orleans grew out of a chance conversation after the Tennessee Williams/New Orleans Literary Festival in March 2011. Mary Grey James, then WNBA National president, appeared on a panel at the festival; afterward, Susan Larson, host of WWNO-FM's "The Reading Life," asked her friend what was giving her the most satisfaction in retirement. "Easy," James said. "My work with the WNBA." After listening to her extol the value of the organization, Larson was hooked. "We need that in New Orleans."

In June 2011, a group of more than twenty women—librarians, book lovers, writers, publishers—met at the historic Latter Library on St. Charles Avenue to discuss forming a chapter. Mary Grey James came down for a meeting in July, and the chapter was on its way.

The first officers were Susan Larson, president; Amy Loewy of Garden District Book Shop, vice president; writer Christine Wiltz, secretary; and Peg Kohlepp of the Tulane University Bookstore, treasurer. Over the course of the first four years, Judith Lafitte of Octavia Books became vice president, Abi Pollokoff of Pelican Publishing became secretary, and writer/designer Karen Kersting became treasurer.

The chapter's mission has evolved over time. We support local writers and booksellers and literacy efforts. Most of all, we support one another.

Little Free Libraries have been a priority of the chapter from the very beginning, and Linda Prout, the leading advocate for the libraries in the New Orleans area, is a board member. Prout was the first person in our area to have a Little Free Library, and she has guided the movement in New Orleans, where there are now approximately eighty of the little book boxes in all areas of the city.

Literacy activists Kelly Harris DeBerry of STAIR (Start the Adventure in Reading) and Shannan Cvitanovic of the YMCA's Adult Literacy program have spoken about their ongoing efforts to the membership.

After the death of founding member Diana Pinckley, the Pinckley Prizes for Crime Fiction were established by the chapter. These are two annual prizes of $2,500 each. One recognizes a distinguished body of work; the other, a fine debut novel. The first honorees, in 2014, were Laura Lippman for her body of work and Gwen Florio for her debut novel, *Montana*. The second honorees were Nevada Barr for her body of work and Adrianne Harun for *A Man Came Out of a Door in the Mountain*. In 2016, WNBA-New Orleans recognized Sara Paretsky for her distinguished body of work and Christine Carbo for her debut novel, *The Wild Inside*. The judges for the Pinckley Prizes are Constance Adler, Mary McCay, and Christine Wiltz; Susan Larson is the administrator.

A fund-raising event that has become identified with the chapter is the annual Art-of-the-Book contest and auction, which invites artists to submit their interpretations of book arts using recycled materials—everything from jewelry to woven vests to extraordinary altered books.

The chapter has also adopted the Metropolitan Women and Children's Center and conducts an annual book drive in December to donate much-needed reading material to the Center. In 2015, WNBA-New Orleans hosted the National board meeting, which included the presentation of the WNBA Award to VIDA founder and poet Amy King.

Programs over the last years have been many and varied. Among the more popular have been visits to libraries and archives. Charles Brown, executive director of the New Orleans Public Library, has kept the chapter up-to-date on local progress in the challenging post-Katrina years. Susan Tucker, curator of books and records for the Newcomb Archives and Vorhoff Library at Tulane University, gave a presentation on how to maintain personal archives and papers; Hortensia Calvo of the Latin American Library at Tulane University presented fascinating items in that book collection; Liz Williams of the Southern Food and Beverage Museum showed members the treasures of that culinary library.

Member Sheila Cork introduced us to artists' books in the New Orleans Museum of Art Collection.

Other meetings have focused on writing. Member Steve Beisner provided an informative introduction to new software available for writers; Dianne de las Casas presented a program on social media for book marketing; Candice Huber of Tubby and Coo's Book Shop offered a PowerPoint primer on the use of social media in establishing an online presence. Attorney Marie Breaux gave a fascinating lecture on the evolution of copyright law.

Programs have also focused on bookselling, including a look at the role of college booksellers and college bookstores with Peg Kohlepp of Tulane University. Elizabeth Barry Ahlquist of Blue Cypress Books, and Maggie McKeown of McKeown's Books and Difficult Music (now closed, sadly) presented an amazing evening of tales from the antiquarian trade, right down to unusual items they've found inside books.

National Reading Group Month events have included a Sunday morning coffee panel of mystery writers at Newcomb College Institute; two Book Club Conferences at the New Orleans Museum of Art; and Readings Round the Bayou in conjunction with local independent bookstores.

Membership grew to sixty-six in our fifth year. Included in that number are published authors, librarians, publishers, book lovers, editors—and even a couple of men! We do everything with a New Orleans flair. We don't hold meetings in August in case of hurricanes. Wine flows generously at our meetings. We serve extraordinary food at our parties and have hosted some legendary potlucks to celebrate chapter anniversaries. Best of all, our chapter grew out of one enduring friendship between two women. And now there are countless friendships among the sixty-six of us!

NEW YORK CITY, NY
Sheila Lewis

The history of the New York City chapter is closely entwined with the history of the National WNBA, because for thirty years, from its founding in 1917, the WNBA was based solely in New York City. With the arrival of chapters in Chicago, Cleveland, Boston, and Nashville in the 1950s, the organization needed a new structure. In 1958, a National Board was established, New York City became a chapter, and its president no longer served as National president. This history focuses on the New York City chapter from the 1950s to the present and its place at the heart of the U.S. publishing and literary worlds. Early WNBA history is covered elsewhere.

From its early days, one focus for the New York City chapter has been cooperation with other professional organizations and community groups. In 1953 and again in 1956, the chapter presented programs during the annual Festival of Books sponsored by WNYC, at that time New York's municipal radio station. In 1966 over three thousand books were donated and distributed to settlement houses, childcare centers, and hospitals throughout the city in a joint program with the Publishers Ad Club and the Publishers Publicity Association. In that same year, the New York Board of Education asked the New York City chapter to conduct a full-semester in-service workshop for school librarians on young adult literature, the first in a multiyear project.

In the 1970s, the chapter addressed disparities in the hiring, promotion, and salaries of women in the publishing industry. An ad hoc Status of Women in Publishing committee was formed and developed a questionnaire "to elicit anonymous information from all women in publishing in all job classifications." The report—with its dispiriting results—was released in 1974; the lesson learned was that much work needed to be done to bring women up to parity. The chapter started a second newsletter, called "Did You Know?" It was dedicated to "imparting news about the status of women (and men) in publishing."

Professional education and career development programs for chapter members have been a major focus and have included workshops on major publishing topics. In 1975, an overflow crowd attended three afternoon programs titled "The Economics of Book Publishing." In the 1980s, fiction editors of *Cosmopolitan* and *Glamour* magazines spoke about serial rights for authors; Doubleday and Penguin editors spoke on the upsurge in paperbacks; and editors at *Publishers Weekly* and the *New York Times Book Review* predicted publishing trends. In addition, *Village Voice* columnist Nat Hentoff spoke on censorship issues faced by libraries, and

Harriet Pilpel, lawyer and editor at *Publishers Weekly*, spoke on the legal ramifications of blending fact and fiction. Anticipating developments in the publishing field, the chapter began to offer programs on electronic publishing in the 1980s. As technology changed, hands-on workshops for writers on using social media platforms and panel discussions on the latest digital publishing developments have also been offered.

Perhaps the most inspiring nod to progress took place in 1987, the year of the WNBA's seventieth anniversary. The NYC chapter coordinated a celebration of "70 Women Who Have Made a Difference" with a reception at Barnard College and a booklet detailing the accomplishments of seventy women publishers, editors, writers, librarians, and others who are "committed, dedicated, creative, and catalytic." The list is a roster of luminaries, including Frances Steloff, Nan Talese, Nancy Larrick, Doris Grumbach, and Margaret Chase Smith.

Through the decades the chapter has consistently maintained its unparalleled access to publishing professionals so that members have been able to keep up with trends on such topics as memoirs, food writing, historical fiction, young adult fiction, mysteries, graphic narratives, the author/agent connection, and more. Because our New York City location is in the heart of publishing country, for over ten years we have hosted the popular Query Roulette, a program where writers meet with agents in speed-dating-style sessions to get feedback on their query letters. In an effort to give writer members exposure, an Open Mic program has been offered at various locations around New York City for members to share their work-in-progress. In October, for the annual National Reading Group Month program we have offered panels of well-known writers talking about their own works and the state of the literary community. A relatively new program has been an In Conversation interview with such prominent writers as Ruth Ozeki, Carole DeSanti, Lynne Sharon Schwartz, and Hilma Wolitzer.

The chapter continues to develop partnerships that bring benefits to members. In 2012 we were asked by the U.S. State Department to host three women writers from Kazakhstan who were touring this country; we held a reception for them at Books of Wonder, the children's bookstore in the Chelsea neighborhood, and learned about the literary world in their country. We have partnered with Pace University to present in-depth panels on such topics as women writing about the environment and the challenges of writing political fiction. Since 2013, we have joined with New York University's Creative Writing Program to host an annual author panel; the panel recently brought together authors and agents to address the difference between literary and commercial fiction; another panel focused on women writing about sex. We collaborated with Random House on a program that followed Helen Simonson's novel *Major Pettigrew's Last Stand* on its successful path from the writer, agent, editor, and publicist to reviewers and readers. In addition, we have offered literary programs with the Women Writing Women's Lives seminar at the City University of New York, and with Wix.com to help our members understand e-book publishing and marketing in the digital age. In 2014 the chapter presented a program on "Trends in Young Adult Publishing" at BookExpo featuring noted editor Arthur Levine (of *Harry Potter* fame). An ongoing community connection in recent years has been the chapter's relationship with the Kids Research Center, a children's literacy nonprofit organization founded by one of our members. KRC works with the New York City Housing Authority to place children's libraries in community centers. Our members have donated books, funds, and time to help set up these wonderful libraries.

In recent years, we have offered an annual program on career development in partnership with the Young to Publishing Group, part of the Association of American Publishers. The chapter's prominent social media presence (blog, Facebook, Twitter) has been managed by recent graduates of Pace University's Master's in Publishing programs. Their expertise has been invaluable for the chapter and for their résumés.

In our continuing efforts to meet the needs of members—writers, publishers, editors, agents, librarians, publicists, and booksellers, to name a few—a diverse array of programs and networking events is planned throughout the year where members can relax and get acquainted. Traditionally, the September meeting is an informal open house welcoming members back from a summer break and providing new and prospective members with a chance to meet and learn more about WNBA-NYC and the National organization. The December meeting is a holiday party where in years past well-known authors such as Mary Gordon, Erica Jong, Fran

Lebowitz, and Toni Morrison have read from their works-in-progress. For additional networking opportunities, neighborhood lunches are held throughout the year and an annual potluck spring brunch is held at a member's home. Writing groups, book discussion groups, and even job opportunities have developed from these ostensibly social gatherings.

Recent chapter presidents—Jill Tardiff, Valerie Tomaselli, and Jane Kinney-Denning—have all moved from the presidency of the NYC chapter to that of the National WNBA, attesting to the important position the chapter holds in shaping and leading the organization. Moving forward into the next century, there is no doubt that WNBA-NYC will continue in its unique role of bringing diverse literary and publishing communities together, while anticipating trends and meeting the needs of its members.

SAN FRANCISCO, CA
Mary E. Knippel

Founded in 1968 by Effie Lee Morris, then coordinator of children and youth services for the San Francisco Public Library, the San Francisco chapter's membership has ranged from sixty to over one hundred. Our chapter connects members of diverse backgrounds and expertise in the literary world in order to exchange ideas and resources. Our members often include writers, booksellers, agents, editors, publishers, publicists, librarians, graphic designers, web designers, social media experts, career coaches, literacy specialists, marketing specialists, conference planners, aspiring authors, and avid readers. Our mission is to pave the way for women's voices, promote literacy, and collaborate effectively within the literary community of the San Francisco Bay Area to reach those goals.

The continual demand for professional development programs, along with networking and marketing opportunities, drives our programming choices. For many years, we met monthly at Fort Mason in San Francisco, with a dinner format along with programs, speakers, and workshops. As our membership grew and changed, we adjusted programming to reflect the need for more flexible scheduling. Panels, readings, member mixers, and collaborative events now take place throughout the greater

Bay Area. Members and nonmember participants have the opportunity to learn more about their craft, hone new skills, and network.

A landmark event for the San Francisco chapter was hosting the 2008 WNBA Awards ceremony, with best-selling author Amy Tan as our featured speaker, honoring recipient Kathi Kamen Goldmark. As part of our fortieth anniversary celebration in 2008, we held a festive banquet and silent auction. Members and guests bid on everything from editing expertise to website development, restaurant certificates, artwork, and handmade jewelry and books, reflecting the range of expertise among our members.

With the new century, our chapter became tech forward: An upgraded website now serves as a platform for information sharing in weekly blog articles written by members, digital newsletters, and frequent social media posts on Facebook and Twitter. Our coordinated tech outreach to members, the literary community, and other WNBA chapters will only increase.

Though there have been changes in our programming over the decades, some events have endured due to their collaborative nature and repeated success. Our annual Effie Lee Morris Children's Lecture Series, held each spring, was created by WNBA-SF to salute Morris for her outstanding contributions to the San Francisco Public Library and the children of San Francisco. The series began in 1996 and remains a collaborative effort with the San Francisco Main Library's Children's Center and the Friends of San Francisco Public Library. These free annual family-friendly lectures have featured many distinguished authors and artists as guest speakers: Patricia McKissack, Javaka Steptoe, Tomie dePaola, Pamela Munoz Ryan, Nikki Grimes, Daniel & Robert San Souci, Milly Lee, Thacher Hurd, Alma Flor Ada, Ashley Bryan, Laurence Yep, Linda Geistlinger, Karey Wehner, Jerry Pinkney, Yuyi Morales, and Christian Robinson. In 2016, we celebrated the twentieth anniversary of this informative and inspirational series that seeks to showcase diversity in children's books.

Our most popular community offering continues to be our annual fund-raiser, Pitch-O-Rama: Meet the Agents & Acquisitions Editors, typically held in March. We bring together some of the best publishing professionals in the Bay Area to listen to a writer's pitch. With pre-pitch coaching and limited enrollment, we provide a safe environment for aspiring writers to have an opportunity to present their work to a professional who can make a decision to represent or publish.

Our chapter has increased its partnerships in the literary community in Northern California, at times partnering with branches of the California Writers Club to produce writing workshops and programs. We have exhibited at the Sonoma County Book Festival, the California Capital Book Festival, and the Bay Area Book Festival. We are sponsors of the Northern California Book Awards ceremony that acknowledges Northern California authors in a variety of genres each May.

The San Francisco chapter is now an established partner with Litquake and Books, Inc., cosponsors of the annual National Reading Group Month event each October. We are exhibitors at the San Francisco Writers Conference held in mid-February and cosponsor of the SFWC free children's community event that features an outstanding children's author on Saturday morning. Individual chapter members are also invaluable in providing expertise and support for the San Francisco Writers Conference and have been since its founding in 2004 by former longtime WNBA board members Elizabeth Pomada and Michael Larsen, now WNBA-SF chapter lifetime honorary members.

As advocates of literacy, especially for children, WNBA-SF literacy partnerships have included:

- The Teddy Bear Room. With the encouragement and supervision of our founding president and San Francisco Public Library children's librarian Effie Lee Morris, WNBA-SF collected books to donate to the Teddy Bear Room at the San Francisco district attorney's office for children of incarcerated parents or those on trial.

- Project Read. Volunteers tutor children and adult learners to enhance reading skills and instill a love of reading. This San Francisco nonprofit organization is located within the San Francisco Main Library.

- Reach Out and Read trains doctors and nurses to advise parents about the importance of reading aloud and to give books to children at pediatric checkups from six months to five years.

- Bring Me a Book provides easy access to the best children's books and inspires reading aloud to children.

- The Living Room. At the day center for homeless mothers and children in Santa Rosa, early childhood books are the cornerstone of the early literacy read-aloud program.
- Afghan Women's Writing Project and Afghan Friends Network. These programs, especially AWWP, seek to educate women and girls, and to provide voices for women, their stories and poems.

The San Francisco chapter continues to work hard to become integrated into the Bay Area literary community and to connect with its members. Our long-range plans call for continuing to learn the needs of the membership while addressing the needs of the community at large. We look forward to celebrating our fiftieth anniversary in 2018.

SOUTH FLORIDA
Michelle J. Putnik

Escaping New York's winters of snow and ice for warm, sunny Florida was an easy decision for WNBA-NYC members Linda Rosen and Andrea Baron. But giving up WNBA programs and networking was not. So, in 2015, the two set out to start a chapter in South Florida. From their winter homes in Boynton Beach and Delray Beach, respectively, they contacted and met with librarians, writers, bookstore owners, and creative writing teachers. Joann Sinchuk, manager of Murder on the Beach Mystery Bookstore in Delray Beach, graciously offered her shop for their introductory meeting.

On a warm December evening Rosen and Baron introduced the organization to a room full of writers with the added incentive of wine and cheese. The women attending were all very excited about the idea of having a chapter in South Florida, but no one volunteered to be on the board. Without a president, secretary, and treasurer, there would not be a new chapter. Feeling a little letdown but unwilling to give up, Rosen and Baron told the women to think about it and call them with their questions and concerns. The next morning, while having breakfast, Rosen was considering their next move. How were they going to get WNBA to South Florida? Her cell phone rang and on the other end was a very excited voice. "I couldn't sleep last night," Michelle J. Putnik said. "We need the WNBA down here. I've talked to my friends and we're ready. I'll be president and I've got a board ready to start: VP Carol White, Secretary Susan Cox, Treasurer Barbara Bixon, and Publicity Chair Mary Yuhas." During its first year as a chapter, WNBA-South Florida has had a program every month, kicking off with a party in April 2016 at Murder on the Beach Bookstore. That June, Carla Norton spoke about her book *What Doesn't Kill Her*, and in July editor Susan Bryant spoke on "How to Work with an Editor." Workshops were held in August and October on "Romance Between the Pages" and "How to Self-Publish." For its first National Reading Group Month the new chapter welcomed authors Lauren Groff and Hank Phillipa Ryan, and in November its own board member Susan Cox talked about her road to publishing her debut mystery, *Man on the Washing Machine*. A holiday party was held in December, and January found Prudence Taylor Board speaking on "Setting as Character." Talia Carner, guest author, addressed members that February, and a membership recruiting party and elections for a new board rounded out the chapter's first year. The mission of the South Florida chapter is to encourage women to read, write, and network and to support literacy among young people in their communities. To that end, the chapter is donating books to school libraries and classrooms. Clearly, the new chapter is off to a great start.

WASHINGTON, D.C.

Tabitha Whissemore and Mary Berghaus Levering

On May 24, 1978, WNBA National president Ann Heidbreder Eastman met with a group of women and men interested in organizing a WNBA chapter in the D.C. area. Eastman, Mary Gaver (also a past National president), and others had been interested in this project for a number of years, observing that Washington was a natural location for WNBA's special professional contributions. With encouragement from Sandy Paul of the New York chapter and others, Carol Nemeyer, then Assistant Librarian of Congress for National Programs, agreed to chair meetings of an organizing committee. As a result of these meetings, the chapter was born amid great enthusiasm and interest, with Carol Nemeyer as its first chapter president. Organizing members, including Susan Bistline, the chapter's first vice president and cofounder, agreed that the Washington/Baltimore area was ripe for WNBA's special ability to develop a strong network within the book and publishing communities in these two neighboring cities.

The chapter's official birthday is September 14, 1978, when more than one hundred people came to a meeting at George Washington University to officially establish the WNBA-Washington/Baltimore chapter and discuss the topic "The Importance of a Network." At the second meeting on November 21, 1978, at the National Press Club, panelists explored another Washington, D.C.–oriented topic, "What is This Thing Called Government Publishing?"

By January 1979, membership had risen to eighty-two paid members and represented all stripes of book- and publishing-related professionals. The concept of cosponsoring programs with other related groups in the metropolitan area was initiated early in the chapter's history. On January 24, 1979, Doris Grumbach, noted author and critic, gave an insightful talk on reviews and the review process to a joint gathering of the WNBA-Washington/Baltimore chapter and the Washington Publishers at the headquarters of the Carnegie Endowment, prominently located on the Embassy Row section of Massachusetts Avenue in D.C.

The personality of the D.C. chapter is probably unique among the various chapters, with so much representation of government and association publishing in addition to trade and university presses, as well as professionals connected to the world of books and publications from such great institutions as the Library of Congress, the Smithsonian Institution, the National Geographic Society, the U.S. Government Printing Office, and the Brookings Institution, to name only a few. In addition, the chapter has members from such professional and trade organizations as the American Library Association, the Association of American Publishers, and the American Historical Association, among others, as well as a number of freelance writers, editors, authors, picture researchers, reviewers, literary agents, librarians, technical writers, booksellers, and other professionals involved in the world of books and publishing in its many diverse facets. Bringing together such a varied group challenged the new chapter to search for common interests for the chapter's monthly professional development programs, defining "book" in its broadest sense.

In 2000 the chapter produced a four-color, poster-size literary map of metropolitan Washington, D.C., developed by Martha Hopkins, an exhibit director of the Interpretive Programs Office at the Library of Congress, and produced in partnership with the Center for the Book at the Library of Congress. The map celebrates locations associated with forty-four authors who have lived or worked in Washington and the surrounding areas, including Rachel Carson, Frederick Douglass, Langston Hughes, Sinclair Lewis, Clare Booth Luce, Mark Twain, and Walt Whitman, along with other information.

The chapter has regular monthly programs from September through June, many in conjunction with other organizations in the two metropolitan areas. Two of the chapter's monthly gatherings are traditionally chapter brunches—professional/social events that give members and their guests a chance to mingle with other congenial professionals in a relaxed setting, usually at the home of one of the chapter members. Other monthly programs cover a broad spectrum of topics, including children's book writing, local publishing efforts, career-development topics, author panels, trends in the publishing world, and tours of local facilities such as the book conservation labs at the Folger Shakespeare Library.

The first issue of the chapter newsletter, *The WNBA Signature,* was published in 1980. During the mid-1980s it grew to fifteen to twenty pages per issue and was mailed to over four hundred addresses. The newsletter has been one of the chapter's most popular communication tools. It is now produced and distributed online, with e-mail updates and chapter announcements distributed online as well.

The chapter experienced some organizational difficulties, with resulting decline in membership, during the early 1980s as officers and board members struggled to cope with the problems inherent in maintaining board representation and program offerings in two cities more than thirty miles apart, along with their other professional commitments. This challenge was finally resolved in 1984, when the chapter board agreed informally to concentrate the chapter's efforts, including board membership and monthly programs, in the greater Washington metropolitan area. A formal name change to the WNBA-Washington, D.C., chapter was approved by the chapter membership in January 1987.

One of the chapter's strengths continues to be its close association with other related professional associations in the Washington metropolitan area. In addition to exchanging newsletters and other timely information, most of the chapter's programs are cosponsored with other appropriate local professional groups, including the Washington Book Publishers, the Washington Edpress Association, the Washington Independent Writers, the D.C. Library Association, the Society of Children's Book Writers, Women in Communications, American Society of Picture Professionals, the Baltimore Area Conservation Guild, and the Baltimore Publishers Association, to name just a few. Cooperation with other related professionals has been a real strength for the WNBA in this city where networking and connections are so important. During the mid-1980s the chapter's membership grew steadily to reach almost three hundred by 1988. In 1988, the Washington chapter celebrated its tenth anniversary with a special reception and program at the Embassy of Australia.

Several *Washington Chapter Membership Directories* have been produced over the years, listing names and contact information for all chapter members, as well as providing an organizational listing of members' professional affiliations and a Resource/Networking Index of members by their professional specialties.

With special recognition and thanks to its devoted and hardworking members, the Washington chapter continues to connect like-minded professionals not only through its directory but with periodic professional programs, twice-yearly networking brunches, monthly small-group social gatherings, online newsletter and email updates, an annual holiday party, and many volunteer opportunities.

Former Chapters

Chapters are founded with high hopes, but not all chapters survive. The very first chapter, in Chicago, with a birth date of 1947, had a vibrant history for many years but disbanded in 1974. The 1967 WNBA fiftieth anniversary history publication records how the chapter sponsored several popular lecture series with the University of Chicago about writing, publishing, bookselling, and book design, with well-known editors and publishers as speakers. The chapter also became a cosponsor of the *Chicago Tribune* Miracle of Books Fair and members donated books to schools and libraries.

In 1954, a chapter was formed in Binghamton, New York, with a core group of librarians, booksellers, and editors from Syracuse University Press and the State University at Binghamton. Its entry in the WNBA fiftieth anniversary publication reports that "Our most outstanding and successful project has been our First Annual Book and Author Dinner, held April 17, 1967, with the *Sunday and Evening Press* as cosponsor. Three authors attended and spoke. It was well received by the community and we plan to continue this project each year." Other programs mentioned: "The Lively Art of Picture Books" (with accompanying brochure and exhibit); "The Three Stratfords" (England, Canada, and Connecticut), slides and commentary on the four hundredth anniversary of Shakespeare's birth; "Collecting of Rare Books and Maps"; "Local History and Local Authors—Treasured Collections" presented by the director of the Binghamton Public Library; and several meetings with local authors. This very active chapter disbanded in 2007.

In 1952, a Cleveland chapter was founded and within several years there were well over one hundred members. The chapter hosted lectures and cosponsored events such as a Children's Book Fair and a National Library Week Luncheon. A careers committee provided vocational guidance for those in the publishing industry. The chapter disbanded in 1984.

The Detroit chapter of the WNBA was formed in 1966 and during its fifty-year existence was active in literary and literacy activities. It was an active sponsor of the Metropolitan Detroit Children's Book Fair from 1969 until the fair's demise in 1986, as well as the Metropolitan Detroit

Book and Author Society. Book donation drives, dinner meetings with authors and publishing industry professionals, a book club, and other literacy initiatives kept members active. In 2016, Detroit celebrated fifty years as a chapter, but closed soon thereafter.

A Grand Rapids, Michigan, chapter was formed in 1968. Members came from many aspects of the book world: authors, illustrators, editors, journalists, booksellers, book buyers, and librarians. The chapter disbanded in 1980.

In 1967, Hiroe Komine, president of the newly formed Japanese Women's Book Association, wrote to WNBA president Victoria Johnson, seeking to become the organization's first chapter outside the U.S. Its first meeting, a tea party, was attended by thirty-six people. In March 1968, Komine wrote to say that "our membership is forty-seven at present and is increasing steadily month after month. It consists of authors, writers, illustrators, librarians, publishers, and those working as editors and for publishing companies." The chapter report for that period describes programs given by members who traveled to other countries and reported on the literary communities in Europe and the U.S.S.R. Sadly, no further communication was found in the archives.

Founded in 2008, the focus of the Seattle chapter reflected the mission of the national organization, to support reading and to champion the role of women in the world of books. The history of the chapter, written in 2017, tells how the National Reading Group Month author event was a highlight of the year, with prominent Pacific Northwest authors. Another literary event, "Readings Round the Sound" was a month-long lineup of author appearances cosponsored with local bookstores and libraries. Literacy activities included working with Page Ahead, which provides new books and develops reading activities that empower at-risk children; and Powerful Schools, which supports high-quality educational enrichment for elementary students. The chapter disbanded in 2017.

Other chapters existed in Dallas; Little Rock, Arkansas; Pittsburgh; and Atlanta, each successful for a while; we look forward to new chapters in those cities in the future.

APPENDICES

WNBA PRESIDENTS

Until 1947 the WNBA existed only in New York City. In 1947, the Chicago chapter was founded, followed by other chapters in other cities. By the mid-1950s, with the addition of several more chapters, it was clear that the WNBA needed a national structure. The constitution was changed and in 1958 Anne J. Richter became the first president to represent the entire organization.

Presidents During the Time New York Served as the National Chapter

Pauline Sherwood
Madge Jenison
Belle Walker
Marian Cutter
Effie C. Hubley
Muriel Simpson Fitzsimmons
Lilian Gurney
Marjorie Seiler
Alice E. Klutas
Rosamund Beebe
Lillian Bragdon

Mary Slavin
Helen S. Lowitt
Margaret Mitcham
Anne J. Richter
Elizabeth Morton
Martha Huddleston
Helen Parker
Mary J. Shipley
Helen Jo Jasper Turner
Virginia Mathews
Edith Busby
Dorothy West
Mary Turner
Eleanor Smith
Eleanor Nichols
Kathryn M. Nick
Dorothy M. McKittrick

National WNBA Presidents

1958–1960	Anne J. Richter, New York City chapter
1960–1962	Lilian Gurney, New York City chapter
1962–1964	Betty Russell, New York City chapter
1964–1968	Victoria S. Johnson, New York City chapter
1968–1970	Anne J. Richter, New York City chapter
1970–1972	Virginia H. Masters, New York City chapter
1972–1974	Lillian L. Schapiro, New York City chapter
1974–1976	Mary V. Gaver, New York City chapter
1976–1978	Ann Heidbreder Eastman, New York City chapter
1978–1980	Ann Heidbreder Eastman, New York City chapter
1980–1982	Mary Glenn Hearne, Nashville chapter
1982–1984	Sylvia H. Cross, Los Angeles chapter
1984–1986	Sandra K. Paul, New York City chapter
1986–1988	Cathy Rentschler, New York City chapter
1988–1990	Marie Cantlon, Boston chapter

1990–1992	Patti Breitman, San Francisco chapter
1992–1994	Carolyn T. Wilson, Nashville chapter
1994–1996	Sue MacLaurin, Los Angeles chapter
1996–1998	Donna Paz, Nashville chapter
1998–2000	Diane Ullius, Washington, D.C., chapter
2000–2002	Nancy Stewart, Nashville chapter
2002–2004	Margaret E. Auer, Detroit chapter
2004–2006	Jill A. Tardiff, New York City chapter
2006–2008	Laurie Beckelman, Boston chapter
2008–2010	Joan Gelfand, San Francisco chapter
2010–2012	Mary Grey James, Nashville chapter
2012–2014	Valerie Tomaselli, New York City chapter
2014–2016	Carin Siegfried, Charlotte chapter
2016–2018	Jane Kinney-Denning, New York City chapter

WNBA AWARD WINNERS

The WNBA Award is presented by the members of the Women's National Book Association to "a living American woman who derives part or all of her income from books and allied arts, and who has done meritorious work in the world of books beyond the duties or responsibilities of her profession or occupation." The award was formerly known as the Constance Lindsay Skinner Award. Its namesake was a playwright, critic, editor, and author active in the book world from early in the twentieth century until her death in 1939.

The award has been presented continuously since 1940, at first annually, and then every other year since 1976.

List of Winners

1940	Anne Carroll Moore, librarian
1941	Blair Niles, novelist, travel writer
1942	Irita Van Doren, book review editor
1943	Mary Graham Bonner, author
1944	Mildred C. Smith, editor
1945	Lillian Smith, author
1946	Amy Loveman, editor
1947	Emily P. Street, book sales and advertising executive

1948   May Lamberton Becker, reviewer, lecturer, editor, author
1949   Lucile Micheels Pannell, bookseller
1950   May Massee, children's book editor
1951   Dorothy Canfield Fisher, novelist, translator, educator, critic
1952   Margaret C. Scoggin, children's and young adult librarian
1953   Lillian C. Gurney, bookseller
1954   Elizabeth Gray Vining, author, teacher
1955   Bertha Mahony Miller, bookseller, editor
       Fanny Butcher, book reviewer
1956   Mary Ellen Chase, author
1957   Anne J. Richter, editor
1958   Edith Hamilton, author, scholar, educator
1959   May Hill Arbuthnot, editor, critic, teacher
       Marchette Chute, author
1960   Pearl S. Buck, author, activist for women's rights,
       Nobel Prize winner
1961   Eleanor Roosevelt, first lady, author, activist
1962   Catherine Drinker Bowen, author
1963   Rachel Carson, author, scientist
1964   Polly Goodwin, children's book reviewer
1965   Virginia Mathews, school library consultant
1966   Blanche W. Knopf, publisher
1967   Mildred L. Batchelder, children's librarian, teacher
1968   Ruth Hill Viguers, children's librarian, author
1969   Victoria S. Johnson, public relations professional
1970   Charlemae Hill Rollins, librarian, author, storyteller
1971   Augusta Baker, librarian, storyteller
1972   Ursula Nordstrom, children's book editor
1973   Mary Virginia Gaver, librarian, educator
1974   No award given
1975   Margaret K. McElderry, children's book editor
1976   Frances Neal Cheney, educator, author
       Helen Honig Meyer, publisher
       Barbara Ringer, lawyer, register of Copyrights
1978   Mary Stahlman Douglas, book reviewer
1980   Anne Pellowski, librarian, author, storyteller

1982	Barbara Tuchman, historian, journalist
1984	Effie Lee Morris, children's librarian
1986	Ann Heidbreder Eastman, editor
1988	Claire Friedland, book production specialist
1990	Barbara Bush, first lady, literacy advocate
1992	Jessie Carney Smith, author, librarian, educator
1994	Janet Palmer Mullaney, literary journal founder
1996	Carolyn Heilbrun, author, feminist scholar
1998	Doris Kearns Goodwin, historian, author
2000	Hon. Patricia Schroeder, Congresswoman; publishing executive
2002	Patricia McKissack, author
2004	Nancy Pearl, author, librarian, book reviewer
2006	Perri Klass, MD, author, pediatrician, literacy advocate
2008	Kathi Kamen Goldmark, author, musician, literacy advocate
2010	Masha Hamilton, international journalist, author, women's activist
2012	Ann Patchett, author, bookstore owner
2014	Amy King, poet, feminist scholar, literary activist, Executive Board member of VIDA: Women in Literary Arts
2017	Louise Erdrich, novelist, Native American rights activist, bookseller
	Carla Hayden, librarian of Congress

WNBA PANNELL AWARD WINNERS

This award recognizes the work of booksellers who stimulate, promote, and encourage children's and young people's interest in books. The award honors Lucile Micheels Pannell, an exemplary librarian and bookseller, and a founding member of the WNBA-Chicago chapter. Since 1989, two awards have been give: one to a children's-only bookstore, mentioned first in the list below, and the other to a general bookstore with a children's department.

1983
OxCart Bookshop, Rochester, New York

1984
R.M. Mills Bookstore, Nashville, Tennessee

1985
Toad Hall Children's Bookstore, Austin, Texas

1986
The Children's Hour, Salt Lake City, Utah

1987
The Children's Bookstore, Chicago, Illinois

1988

A Likely Story Children's Bookstore, Alexandria, Virginia

1989

Children's Book & Gift Market, Atlanta, Georgia
Judi's Bookstore, Twin Falls, Idaho

1990

Rabbit Hill Children's Bookstore, Hewlett, New York
The Kids' Place, Marshall, Michigan

1991

Rosemary and Michael Stimola, A Child's Story, Teaneck, New Jersey
Janet E. Grojean, Little Professor Book Center, LaVista, Nebraska

1992

Skippack Children's Books, Skippack, Pennsylvania
Red & Black Books, Seattle, Washington

1993

Kathy L. Patrick of Barron's Books, Inc., Longview, Texas

1994

Adventures for Kids, Ventura, California
Compass Rose Bookshop, Orleans, Massachusetts

1995

Award not given

1996

Edward T. Rabbit & Co., Richmond, Virginia
Barron's Books, Longview, Texas

1997

Enchanted Forest Books for Children, Dallas, Texas
R.J. Julia Booksellers, Madison, Connecticut

1998

Toad Hall Children's Bookstore, Austin, Texas
Eagle Harbor Book Company, Bainbridge Island, Washington

1999

All for Kids Books, Seattle, Washington

2000

Children's Bookshop, Brookline, Massachusetts
McLean & Eakin Booksellers, Petosky, Michigan

2001

Whale of a Tale, Irvine, California
Quail Ridge Books, Raleigh, North Carolina

2002

Eight Cousins Children's Books, Falmouth, Massachusetts
Anderson's Bookshops, Naperville, Illinois

2003

Halfway Down the Stairs Children's Book Shop, Rochester, Michigan
Dutton's Brentwood Bookstore, Los Angeles, California

2004

Hicklebee's Children's Books, San Jose, California
UConn Co-op, Storrs, Connecticut

2005

Reading Reptile Books and Toys for Young Mammals,
  Kansas City, Missouri
BookPeople, Austin, Texas

2006

A Likely Story Children's Bookstore, Alexandria, Virginia
Northshire Bookstore, Manchester Center, Vermont

2007

Wonderland Books, Rockford, Illinois
Books & Books, Coral Gables, Florida

2008

The Flying Pig Bookstore, Shelburne, Vermont
Kepler's Books and Magazines, Menlo Park, California

2009

Mrs. Nelson's Toy and Book Shop, LaVerne, California
Joseph-Beth Booksellers, Cincinnati, Ohio

2010

Little Shop of Stories, Decatur, Georgia
Green Toad Bookstore, Oneonta, New York

2011

Fairytales Bookstore, Nashville, Tennessee
Queen Anne Books, Seattle, Washington

2012

Monkey See, Monkey Do, Clarence, New York
The Book Beat, in Oak Park, Michigan

2013

The Bookbug, Kalamazoo, Michigan
Nicola's Books, Ann Arbor, Michigan

2014

4 Kids Books and Toys, Zionsville, Indiana
Devaney, Doak and Garrett Booksellers, Farmington, Maine

2015

Once Upon a Time Bookstore, Montrose, California
Anderson's Bookshop, Naperville, Illinois

2016

Wild Rumpus Books, Minneapolis, Minnesota
Brookline Booksmith, Brookline, Massachusetts

2017

Children's Book World, Los Angeles, California
Bookworm of Edwards, Edwards, Colorado

WNBA WRITING CONTEST WINNERS

2013

Poetry

1st place: Ellaraine Lockie, "Abandoned Garden"
2nd place: Harriet Shenkman, "Mirror, Mirror"
3rd place: Ruth Hill, "Light Bends Around Shadows"
Honorable Mention: Amy Wright, "Airport Proposal"

Fiction

1st place: Jessica Wallin Mace, "A Prize in Every Box"
2nd place: Anne Pound, "Beauty"
3rd place: Deborah Batterman, "All Mine"
Honorable Mention: Christine Eskilson, "Dorie"

2014

Poetry

1st place: Rebecca Olander, "Late October Light"
2nd place: Kate Hovey, "Demeter's Lament"
3rd place: Amy Schmitz, "The Night a Woman Died on My Street"
Honorable Mention: J.H. Yun, "Milk"

Fiction

1st place: Gayle Towell, "Uncertainty"

2nd place: Susan Doherty, "Place Settings"
3rd place: Tracy Sottosanti, "Katie Earnhardt's Theory of
Eggs-Over-Easy"
Honorable Mention: Julia Tracey, "Five O'Clock Somewhere"

2015
Poetry
1st place: Diana Whitney, "Curiosity"
2nd place: Sarah Wolbach, "Words [in transit]"
3rd place: Michelle Regalado Deatrick, "The Light-Lust of Trees"
Honorable Mention: "Tanya Hyonhye Ko, "Comfort Woman"

Fiction
1st place: Allison Har-zvi, "If You're Ready"
2nd place: Vicki DeArmon, "Hydroplaning"
3rd place: Kathleen Spivack, "Moths"
Honorable Mention: Kristen MacKenzie, "Cold Comfort"

Creative Nonfiction/Memoir
1st place: Diane Kraynak, "Science Project"
2nd place: Renate Stendhal, "Kiss Me Again. She Did."
3rd place: Jayne Martin, "The Only Child"
Honorable Mention: Laura Ruth Loomis, "Ghost House"

2016
Poetry
1st Place: Gail Entrekin, "Before Making Love"
2nd Place: Grace Grafton, "Gold, Labor and Exotic Materials"
3rd place: Nicole Eden, "Mortgage"
Honorable Mention: Judy Bebelaar, "Gliding"

Fiction
1st Place: Nina Smith, "Chef"
2nd Place: Juliet Wittman, "The Ballerina and the Butcher"
3rd Place: Molly Giles, "Wife with Knife"
Honorable Mention: Rochelle Distelheim, "Home Movies"

Creative Nonfiction/Memoir

1st Place: Wendy Brown Báez, "Pilgrimage"
2nd Place: Nadina LaSpina, "Falsomagro"
3rd Place: Marie Chambers, "On the Challenges of Not Reading in Planes or Decisions Born in the Dark"
Honorable Mention: Rita Juster, "Vera Sheets"

2017
Poetry

1st Place: Stacey Balkun, "When I Am Red and the Moon Full"
2nd Place: Alice Osborn, "Southern Ice Storm"
3rd Place: Andrea Young, "Aleppo"
Honorable Mention: Anna Hernandez-French, "At Sea"

Fiction

1st Place: Robyn Corum, "Coffin-Maker"
2nd Place: Karin Fuller, "Dancing on a Stump"
3rd Place: Christine Eskilson, "Taking Care of Harry"
Honorable Mention: Patty Somlo, "Since Letitia Williams Saw Jesus"

Creative Nonfiction/Memoir

1st Place: Jean Choy Tate, "White Woman Passes"
2nd Place: Nicole Ayers, "Pink Hats"
3rd Place: Sarah Birnbach, "Climbing Back Up"
Honorable Mention: Joanne Godley, "Doubling Back"

CONTRIBUTORS AND CREDITS

Denise M. Acevedo is a full-time assistant professor at Michigan State University, where she teaches freshman composition, and an adjunct professor at Spring Arbor University, where she teaches graduate literacy courses to K–12 teachers and classes that focus on working with discouraged/troubled youth. She edited *Discovering Michigan County by County* and will lead a yearlong (2017–2018) project based on a faculty professional development program she designed, "Transforming Teaching Through Learning," and the 2002 publication *To Teach With Soft Eyes.* She founded the Greater Lansing chapter of the WNBA in May 2016.

Leslie Adams is an active community volunteer, supporting women and children through her work with Assistance League of the Eastside, Junior League of Seattle, and the WNBA. Her favorite ways to spend her spare time are reading and participating in book groups.

Andrea Baron has worked in the book and magazine publishing industry for over twenty years. She has been an adjunct professor in the MS in Publishing Program at Pace University since 2002, giving students a grounding in the industry through networking with industry leaders. She participates in Pace University's Sino–American Publishing Research Center, planning and facilitating seminars for visiting Chinese executives. She is a member of the executive board of the WNBA-NYC chapter, and has served as vice president and treasurer of the chapter. She currently works as a freelance book indexer.

Blanche Wiesen Cook is Distinguished Professor of history and women's studies at John Jay College of Criminal Justice and the Graduate Center of the City University of New York. She is the author of the critically acclaimed, best-selling three-volume biography of Eleanor Roosevelt; *The Declassified Eisenhower: A Divided Legacy of Peace & Political Warfare*; *Crystal Eastman on Women and Revolution*, among other books. The New York State Council on the Humanities honored her as Scholar of the Year in 1996. She is a frequent author of reviews and columns, and has received numerous awards for her writings.

Carli Ducko is a student at West Chester University of Pennsylvania where she is currently pursuing a degree in English literature and teaching. She is an avid reader, aspiring author, and a reader on the Great Group Reads Selection Committee.

Kate Farrell, librarian, storyteller, author, and educator, taught language arts in schools, colleges, and universities, and has published numerous educational materials. More recently, she coedited two award-winning anthologies: *Times They Were A-Changing: Women Remember the '60s & '70s* and *Cry of the Nightbird: Writers Against Domestic Violence*. She is currently working on a collection of her own stories, *Woman Wonder Tales*. Visit her at: www.katefarrell.net.

Joan Gelfand's reviews, stories, and poetry have appeared in over one hundred national and international literary journals, including *Rattle*, *Prairie Schooner*, *Kalliope*, and *California Quarterly*. She has been a featured reader at numerous venues in the U.S. and Mexico, including the New York Public Library, Litquake, and the Southern Festival of Books. She is a member of the National Book Critics Circle and a juror for the Northern California Book Awards.

Céline Keating's short fiction and nonfiction have been widely published, and she is the author of the novels *Layla* and *Play for Me* and the editor of

On Montauk: A Literary Celebration. She is the secretary of the National board of the WNBA. Her website is www.celinekeating.com.

Jane Kinney-Denning is the current National president of the WNBA (June 2016 to June 2018). She served two terms as the WNBA-NYC chapter president. She is a professor and the executive director of Internships and Corporate Outreach for the MS in Publishing Program at Pace University.

Mary E. Knippel is a journalist, author, speaker, writing coach, and publisher, a past president of the WNBA-San Francisco chapter, and a member of the San Francisco Writers Conference team since its inception in 2004. Her website is www.yourwritingmentor.com.

Susan Knopf founded Scout Books & Media Inc in 2011; it specializes in children's books and adult nonfiction; creates original projects; brings publishers' concepts to life; develops series and brands; and provides consulting services. Previously, she was senior vice president at Parachute Publishing, vice president and publisher of MouseWorks and Seafarer at Penguin, and vice president and publisher of HarperAudio and Caedmon. She is also the author of numerous books and serves as the chair of the WNBA Pannell Award.

Susan Larson is the host of "The Reading Life" on WWNO-FM, New Orleans' NPR affiliate; from 1988 to 2009, she was the book review editor of *The New Orleans Times-Picayune.* She is the author of *The Booklover's Guide to New Orleans,* which has appeared in two editions from LSU Press.

Mary Berghaus Levering worked at the Library of Congress for forty-five years, rising from an entry-level junior professional in 1966 to the senior government executive level, retiring in 2011. During her long career, she worked in every major department of the Library in a variety of positions of increasing responsibility and significance. She is a member of the District of Columbia Bar and the Supreme Court Bar, an active member of many professional associations, and the recipient of many awards and honors. She was a founding member of the WNBA-Washington, D.C., chapter and served as president from 1984 to 1988.

Sheila Lewis is an instructor at New York City's JCC Makom Center for Mindfulness and The Jewish Journey Project, a children's writer, tutor, and writing coach. "My Calm Place: Yoga, Mindfulness & Meditation Strategies for Children," her fifty-card deck for all ages, was published in July 2016 (PESI Publishing & Media). She has written for WNBA-NYC newsletters and blogs since 2009.

Joyce Meskis owned the Tattered Cover Book Store for forty-three years until her retirement in 2017. When she purchased the three-year-old store in 1974, it was a small shop in the Cherry Creek area of Denver that evolved into one of the country's nationally recognized independent bookstore operations, which included four stores located in Metro Denver plus three licensed stores at Denver International Airport. She has been active in the support of First Amendment rights and is a recipient of many intellectual freedom awards; the recipient of an honorary doctorate of humane letters from the University of Denver; the Distinguished Service Award for Outstanding Achievement and Exceptional Service to the Denver Metropolitan Area from the University of Colorado; and the Lifetime Achievement Award from the American Booksellers Association. In 1987 she was designated by the WNBA as one of seventy women who have made a difference in the book industry.

Elizabeth Mosteller is the founder and president of the Greater Philadelphia chapter of the WNBA. By day she is an educator, teaching both English language learners and gifted support students. She also teaches college courses to future educators.

Michelle J. Putnik is the founder and first president of the South Florida chapter. When she isn't busy slaying evil dragons, she's busy being a playwright, screenwriter, poet, teacher, and public speaker.

Rosalind Reisner is a librarian and author of the award-winning *Jewish American Literature: A Guide to Reading Interests* (Libraries

Unlimited, 2004) and *Read On...Life Stories: Reading Lists for Every Taste* (Libraries Unlimited, 2009). She chaired the WNBA's Great Group Reads selection committee from 2009 to 2013. She speaks and writes about reading and Jewish literature. Her website/blog is www.areadersplace.net.

Linda Rosen is a writer and fitness professional. Her stories have appeared in *Foliate Oak, Crack the Spine,* and other print and online literary journals; she is a member of the Women's Fiction Writers Association and the WNBA, where she is selections coordinator of the Great Group Reads committee, which chooses books for National Reading Group Month. Her website www.linda-rosen.com links to her blog, The Literary Leotard.

Carin Siegfried has worked as a bookseller at Bookstar, a buyer at Ingram Book Group in Nashville, an editor at St. Martin's Press in New York, a sales rep at Baker & Taylor, a freelance editor in Charlotte, and sales manager for Soho Press in New York. She is currently the Mid-Atlantic field sales rep for Macmillan. Her book *An Insider's Guide to a Career in Book Publishing* came out in 2014. She founded the WNBA-Charlotte chapter and is past president of both the Charlotte chapter and of the WNBA national board; she is currently a member of the New York City chapter.

Nancy Rubin Stuart is an award-winning author of seven nonfiction books about women, including *Defiant Brides: The Untold Story of Two Revolutionary-Era Women and the Radical Men They Married,* and *Muse of the Revolution: The Secret Pen of Mercy Otis Warren and the Founding of a Nation.* She also serves as the executive director of the Cape Cod Writers Center. Her website is www.nancyrubinstuart.com.

Jill A. Tardiff is the WNBA's National Reading Group Month chair and its United Nations Department of Information Nongovernmental main representative. She has been affiliated with the association since 1996, serving as the New York City chapter's newsletter editor, vice president, and president, then as National vice president and national president. She has held senior management positions at such companies as Hallmark Cards Inc., Doubleday Book Shops, and Tiffany & Co. She was the sole proprietor of Bamboo River Associates, a publishing and bookselling consultancy that served Japanese publishers and bookselling groups; and a contributing editor at *Publishers Weekly* for fifteen years. Most recently, she has been working in the food world with a focus on artisanal cheese and sustainable development.

Valerie Tomaselli is founder and president of MTM Publishing, an award-winning editorial-services and book-producing company, where she has led the team responsible for creating a long list of acclaimed books for such clients as CQ Press, Charlesbridge, DK Publishing, Macmillan Reference, Oxford University Press, Princeton University Press, Routledge, Sage, and the Sculpture Foundation. She currently serves as the series editor for *Foundations in Global Studies* for Routledge/ Taylor & Francis. She is active in the world of publishing, having served as treasurer of the American Book Producers Association and on the board of the Women's National Book Association—including as National president and currently as chair of the Centennial committee. She is also a member of the advisory council of the Women's Media Center.

Doris Weatherford has been publishing books on women's history for over thirty years. Her first was *Foreign and Female: Immigrant Women in America, 1840–1930* (1986, revised and expanded in 1995). Later books include *American Women's History: An A–Z* (Prentice Hall, 1994) and *Milestones: A Chronology of American Women's History* (Facts on File, 1997). Weatherford has also managed political campaigns and chaired the Florida Women's Hall of Fame. Governor Lawton Chiles appointed her as a trustee of Hillsborough Community College, and she is an adjunct professor at the University of South Florida. She is also a member of the advisory board of the Center for Florida History at Florida Southern College. Weatherford has received grants from the Florida Humanities Council and other organizations, served on numerous advisory boards, and received many honors for her writing and her public service.

NC Weil writes novels and short stories, sonnets, song lyrics and free-form poetry, and reviews of books and films. Her short stories have appeared in the anthology *Electric Grace*, edited by Richard Peabody (Paycock Press, 2007); the online journal ArLiJo. She was a winner in the 2017 Westmoreland Arts and Heritage Festival Fiction Contest. Her novel *Karmafornia* was published in 2011, and its sequel *Superball* in 2016. She serves as WNBA Award chair, National website co-chair, and newsletter editor for the Washington, D.C. chapter. Her website is: http://ncweil.com and her blog is: www.aestheticpoint.blogspot.com.

Tabitha Whissemore is an editor at the American Association of Community Colleges in Washington, D.C., and president of the D.C. chapter of the Women's National Book Association. She wrote the story "Suffragist City"" for the online ReDistricted Comics, and "Vinnie & Abe" for District Comics.

Carolyn Wilson has been actively involved in the WNBA since 1975, including service as president of the Nashville chapter and National president; she continues to serve on the Nashville chapter board. She retired recently as director of library services for the Beaman Library at Lipscomb University in Nashville.

Rachelle Yousuf is the current co–vice president of the Women's National Book Association and a freelance editor. She is also the membership assistant at PEN Center USA and a member of the web team for VIDA: Women in Literary Arts.

Photo and Document Credits

Cover Photo
Roomsmoody1924/Wikimedia Commons

Chapter 1
Page 22: Portraits of American Women; author unknown/ Wikimedia Commons
Page 26: Lydia Maria Child/Wikimedia Commons

Page 30: Godey's Lady's Book, March, 1864; engraver unknown/ Wikimedia Commons

Page 40: author unknown/Wikimedia Commons

Page 44: Gertrude Käsebier/Wikimedia Commons

Page 52: George Grantham Bain Collection/Library of Congress

Page 57: Carl Van Vechten/Library of Congress

Page 62: U.S. National Archives and Records Administration/ Wikimedia Commons

Page 71: "WPA Packhorse Librarians in Kentucky," Goodman-Paxton Photographic Collection, Special Collections, University of Kentucky Libraries

Page 86: Alfred T. Palmer/ Farm Security Administration - Office of War Information Photograph Collection (Library of Congress)

Page 95: Alex Wong/Newsmakers

Page 99: Mel Finkelstein/Library of Congress

Page 100: Mike Allred; Ms. Spring 1972, Liberty Media for Women, LLC/Wikimedia Commons

Page 112: Permission granted by Tina Perricone, for the estate of Celeste West

Page 115: "Women in the World of Words," WNBA

Page 119: Laura Patterson, Library of Congress/Wikimedia Commons

Page 123: William J. Clinton Presidential Library/Wikimedia Commons

Page 128: Steve Kagan/Publishers Weekly

Page 133: Parnassus Books

Page 137: Geraldshields11/Wikimedia Commons

Page 139: Sally Wiener Grotta

Chapter 2

Page 158: Bernhard Wall/Sunwise Turn: A Human Comedy of Bookselling

Page 159: Article reproduced by ProQuest LLC as part of Gerritsen Online; www.proquest.com

Page 169: Kimon Berlin/Wikimedia Commons

Chapter 3
Page 178: WNBA Archives
Page 190: WNBA Archives

Chapter 4
Page 205: Photo by Ann Benoit LLC Photography © 2015
Page 209: McLean & Eakin Booksellers/WNBA Pannell Award
Archives
Page 213: WNBA-Nashville Archives
Page 223: WNBA Centennial Archives

ACKNOWLEDGMENTS
AND SUPPORTERS

The idea for this centennial publication came from Valerie Tomaselli, WNBA Centennial chair and head of MTM Publishing. Valerie had the vision to make this book more than just a history of the WNBA, to take the organization's history and extend it outward to encompass the industries and professions that make up our membership: publishing, bookselling, librarianship, and writing. Valerie asked me to be the editor, and in early 2016, we assured ourselves that there was plenty of time before the Centennial celebration in the fall of 2017 to put the book together. As we gathered information and contacted contributors, we realized that we had a unique opportunity to provide an overview of a portion of our literary and cultural history in a way that hadn't been done before. Suddenly, the time seemed barely sufficient. So it is with heartfelt thanks that we acknowledge all the people who helped to make this book the remarkable document that it is in time for the Centennial celebration of the Women's National Book Association.

We are grateful to our founders for their foresight in saving every scrap of paper from the early years of the WNBA; it's an irreplaceable trove of information and insight into the late 1910s and 1920s. Columbia University's Rare Book and Manuscript Library has been a great home for our archives; the archivists there have not only been extremely helpful, but friendly and welcoming, even as we repeatedly requested the same archival boxes.

Huge thanks to Doris Weatherford, whose expertise in U.S. women's history, especially in the critical periods of late nineteenth and early twentieth centuries, informs the first chapter. She's a writer with skill and verve, able to make narrative history compelling. Nancy Rubin Stuart, WNBA Boston chapter member and author of many books and articles on women's history, worked with excerpts from the WNBA archives and brought to life several significant WNBA events and programs. Andrea Baron, Linda Rosen, and Kate Farrell researched and wrote several sidebars. And heartfelt thanks to Blanche Wiesen Cook, whose foreword so wonderfully captures the enthusiasm with which we worked on this project.

One of the most wonderful moments in this research and writing process was the rediscovery of Madge Jenison, part of the group of founding booksellers and the second president of the WNBA. Jenison was full of idealistic energy and activism on behalf of the WNBA, and when we found her article "Bookselling as a Profession for Women," we knew that we had to share it with the world. Joyce Meskis, owner of the Tattered Cover Book Store in Denver for many years, and well known in bookselling circles for her innovative approach to bookselling and advocacy of free speech, was kind enough to read Jenison's article and write a response from the contemporary bookseller's point of view. Joyce graciously wrote her article on faith, before we had a publisher.

So many WNBA members contributed their writing and ideas to this book that it would be hard to list them all. Their names appear on the articles they wrote about WNBA programs and the chapter histories. Jane Kinney-Denning, New York City chapter president and then WNBA National president during the writing of this book, was an enthusiastic cheerleader and sounding board for the project, always full of ideas and suggestions. Thanks to Hannah Bennett, WNBA-NYC chapter president and first reader, for her insightful comments and enthusiasm. Thanks also to Céline Keating, who cheerfully took on the project of obtaining and editing the chapter histories, and to Elaine Ruth Boe and Leigh Eron, who spent hours fact-checking. Leigh also handled many of the tedious details of file management, an invisible but vital task in a book with so many different pieces. To Miranda Schwartz we owe a huge thank-you for her speedy and excellent copyediting. Miranda did more than correct wobbly sentence structure and word choices; she also took a step back from the detail level and offered astute comments and suggestions. Heartfelt thanks to Nolde Alexius, who enthusiastically took on the task of proofreading the first page proofs, and Céline Keating for her proofing of the second and final page proofs. A big thanks goes to Andrea Baron for our excellent index, produced under a tight deadline—the finishing touch to our many hours of research and writing. A call-out is also due to Isolde Maher of 4 Eyes Design for the beautiful cover and interior layouts, and to Andrew Sullivan and John Goslee of C&R Press for their unfailing support of this endeavor.

And, of course, thanks to all the friends, family members, and partners who put up with us when we were preoccupied with thoughts about the book or occupied with hours of meetings, phone calls, and emails.

—Rosalind Reisner

SUSTAINER SPONSORSHIPS

Silver Level
Baker & Taylor

Friends of the WNBA
Hachette Book Group
Ingram Content Group
MTM Publishing
Women's National Book Association, New York City chapter

WNBA PANNELL AWARD SPONSOR

Penguin Young Readers Group—*Gold Level*

NATIONAL READING GROUP MONTH SPONSORS

Silver Premier Level
Sourcebooks—An Independent Vision

Friends of National Reading Group Month
American Booksellers Association (ABA)
Andrew Carnegie Medal for Excellence in Fiction
Baker & Taylor—the future delivered
The Booklist Reader (Booklist, American Library Association)
Conscious Images LLC
Edelweiss—Above the Treeline
Fishergate Inc.
Ingram Content Group
NetGalley—We Help Books Succeed
Reading Group Choices—Selections for Lively Book Discussions
Reading Group Guides—The Online Community for Reading Groups
Southern Independent Booksellers Alliance (SIBA)

INDIVIDUAL CONTRIBUTORS

Premier
Nancy Newman

Platinum
Barbie Chadwick
Joan and Simone Gelfand

Gold
Sarah Brechner
Mary Grey James
WNBA-LA Chapter Members

Silver

Leslie Adams
Deirdre Bair
Martha Conway
Elizabeth Harris
Mary Hildebrand
Jane Kinney-Denning
Kristen Knox
Roxana Robinson
Nina Smith
Valerie Tomaselli
Julie Trelstad
Victoria Weiland

INDEX

Italicized page numbers refer to illustrations

WNBA Centennial poster; designed by Kerstin Vogdes Diehn, KV Design.